# The Shak

*The Shaken Path* is a detailed account of the Revd. Paul Cudby's research into modern Pagan pathways. Stemming from a period of study leave, Paul immersed himself in many different Pagan worlds, meeting, befriending and experiencing Pagan beliefs and practices in a spirit of openness and friendly Christian engagement. The result, a description of and reflection on, the worlds of Wiccans, Witches, Druids, Heathens, Animists and Shamans, is an in-depth description and critical reflection on what he found and, because of the trust he built up within his Pagan encounters is a unique piece of research.

Paul's research includes personal story and powerful reflection through an unwavering Christian lens. He offers the reader an account of how he has been challenged and changed by spending time alongside people whom many Christians regard with suspicion and sometimes fear. He records the kindness, hospitality and profound love of Pagans for the natural world, but also does not shy away from things he cannot explain or finds deeply problematic in Pagan practice.

In my role as National Adviser for New Religious Movements and Alternative Spiritualities I am approached by many people who are concerned about Pagans or who simply believe that Pagans are in league with the devil in some way. Some of these find the idea of Pagan rituals, spells and magick both frightening and threatening. Paul's research will provide such people with an accessible account of Pagan life which should go a long way to dispersing hostility and creating a better understanding on which Christians can get to know their Pagan neighbours.

Paul, like other diocesan new religious movements advisers, is aware that Christians who pioneer this kind of work, may themselves attract suspicion or hostility from other Christians. He is therefore to be applauded for the thoroughness of his investigation and the care with which he has taken to represent himself as nothing other than a Christian priest willing to learn from and through others.

I recommend this research to you and hope it will be successfully published as a major contribution to the understanding of modern Pagan religion in the UK.

**Anne Richards**, Church of England's National Adviser for New Religious Movements

Paul Cudby's book, *The Shaken Path*, clearly demonstrates his openness to hearing about Pagan spirituality from Pagans themselves whist retaining his Christian faith. In doing so, he has been able to shine a more accurate light on how modern Pagans view their beliefs and practices, and to present them in a context that should help to remove much of the fear of Pagan traditions often experienced by Christians.

*The Shaken Path* guides the reader through a variety of the main Pagan traditions, reflecting on similarities and differences found in Christian denominations and, in doing so, provides Christians with an opportunity for deeper reflections upon their own faith traditions and practices. My own experiences of dialogue with those from other faiths as a Pagan have led me to deeper reflections upon my own Pagan path and practices, providing insights that I might not have otherwise gained whilst also leading to a greater understanding of 'the other'. *The Shaken Path* has the potential to do the same for the Christian reader. I look forward to meeting and engaging in dialogue with Christians who have been accurately informed about Pagan traditions as a result of reading Paul's book.

**Mike Stygal**, Chair of the Pagan Federation

This is a must-read book for anyone interested in interfaith work.

Pagans seeking ways to more productively talk about themselves to Christians will find it really helpful, and the aspects of comparative religion will reward anyone interested in religion as subject.

**Mark Townsend**, author and Former Anglican Priest, now Druid and Independent Celebrant

# The Shaken Path

## A Christian Priest's Exploration of Modern Pagan Belief and Practice

To Colin and Diane.

With love.

Paul

x

# The Shaken Path

A Christian Priest's Exploration of
Modern Pagan Belief and Practice

Paul Cudby

CHRISTIAN
ALTERNATIVE

Winchester, UK
Washington, USA

First published by Christian Alternative Books, 2017
Christian Alternative Books is an imprint of John Hunt Publishing Ltd.,
Laurel House, Station Approach,
Alresford, Hants, SO24 9JH, UK
office1@jhpbooks.net
www.johnhuntpublishing.com
www.christian-alternative.com

For distributor details and how to order please visit the 'Ordering' section on our website.

Text copyright: Paul Cudby 2016

ISBN: 978 1 78535 520 2
978 1 78535 521 9 (ebook)
Library of Congress Control Number: 2016944527

All rights reserved. Except for brief quotations in critical articles or reviews, no part of this book may be reproduced in any manner without prior written permission from the publishers.

The rights of Paul Cudby as author have been asserted in accordance with the Copyright, Designs and Patents Act 1988.

A CIP catalogue record for this book is available from the British Library.

Design: Stuart Davies

Printed and bound by CPI Group (UK) Ltd, Croydon, CR0 4YY, UK

We operate a distinctive and ethical publishing philosophy in all areas of our business, from our global network of authors to production and worldwide distribution.

# CONTENTS

This book is dedicated to two groups of people:

To the people of St. Mary Magdalene Church, Tanworth in Arden, who have accompanied me on a journey none of us would have predicted when I arrived in 2006, and have given me huge amounts of encouragement and strength, whilst being willing to ask the difficult questions and being open to the honest answers.

And to the Pagans who have welcomed me into their homes, circles and moots, telling me their stories and their beliefs, reading the drafts, correcting my mistakes, joining in the discussion, and simply for trusting me.

Thank you.

*Ὁ θέος αγαπη έστιν, και ὁ μενων εν τη αγαπη εν τω θεω μευει και ὁ θεος εν αυτω μενει.*

# Acknowledgements

A book like this cannot come out of nowhere, and I am extremely indebted to a large number of people.

First to my wife, Alison Eve, whose support has encouraged me and whose insight astounds me. Her spiritual courage is greater than mine and often it feels that I tread a path that she has already sung into being. (Not every author gets his own bard!)

Also to the Bishop of Birmingham, Rt. Revd. David Urquhart, who allowed me the research time for my sabbatical which began this journey, has encouraged me in my research and who has written the foreword to this book.

I am deeply indebted to the good people of Ecclesiastical Insurance for their Ministry Bursary Award which made a big difference in meeting the costs of the sabbatical study leave on which this research was based.

Tim Scarborough and Keith Claringbull accompanied me closely at the start of the writing of this book and gave me precisely the kick up the backside I needed at the appropriate time.

My sister, Ruth Garrett, put in lengthy time proofreading and making much needed editorial suggestions to make this ready for submission. Ta muchly sis. Maybe now Nick will buy you a puppy... Thanks also to Mum and Dad for their excitement and searching questions.

To Nimue and Tom Brown for guidance, encouragement and patience with my incessant questions, and to Trevor Greenfield and all at John Hunt for taking a risk on me. I promise to work hard at selling this!

Anne Richards the National New Religious Movements Advisor at Church House who has read pretty much every word I've written on this subject, provided endless guidance and thought-provoking questions, and written some lovely things about the book to help me get others to look at it seriously.

And also on that note to Nimue (again), Mark Townsend and Mike Stygal for reading the completed drafts and giving me some great copy to offer to publishers.

Ancient Arden Forest Church, thank you all for sharing this with me, and especially to Simon and Sarah Marshall and Hazel Hewlett for regular love, support and moon prayers.

And then to a huge number of Pagan, Forest Church and Christian people who have become friends. This bit I'd better do in (roughly) alphabetical order...

Vicki and Harry Aiano for welcoming us, laughing with us and trusting us; Ruth Aitken and Sir Leslie Kellie for hospitality, laughs and generous sharing, and indeed to everyone in the Boscastle and Tintagel Pagan circle – you have been amazing and welcoming people; Dennis and Rita Andrew for such a lovely welcome and for the gift of my trusty staff; Matt and Jo Arnold for friendship and love; Geoff and Sky Boswell, and especially Geoff thank you for trusting me to contribute at a Druid ceremony; Corwen Broch and Kate Fletcher for your hospitality, songs, and a willingness to challenge me about what I thought, and to continue the conversations online; Philip Carr-Gomm for taking us seriously and believing in Forest Church; Hilary Coombes for smiley owls and encouraging words; Richard and Margaret Deimel for leading the way; Divine Moon Moot – all of you for such wonderful welcoming openness, especially to Annie, Naomi, Em, Barry, Julie and David; Suzanne and Catherine Fraser-Martin for being so open about Heathenry and welcoming me into your home and camp; Graham Harvey for a lunchtime full of questions and for telling me that actually I'm a Pagan(!); Fiona Hoad for finding me on Facebook and inviting me along to your Lughnasadh ritual; Steve Hollinghurst for pointing me in the right direction; Simon Howell for organising Ammerdown and introducing us to so many new faces; Caz Istead for making some great introductions; Trevor Jones for a welcome, an inspiring shop and an amusing insight into life in Glasto! Talis Kimberley-Fairbourn for incredible trust in letting this djembe player gig with you when we only just met; Gypsy and Nathan Leaver – Gypsy you opened up the whole sabbatical sojourn in Cornwall with your warmth, vision and trust – so much of this wouldn't have happened without you; Valerie and Stuart Legg for your friendship and the privilege of sharing in the wedding blessing; Vicky Lowles for listening and sharing so warmly; Loz Knight for opening that door and welcoming me in to drum with you; Em and Gary Seren-Franklin for wonderful Irish tales of hauntings, Bansidhes and knocking; Gordon MacLellan for answering all my questions, raising a whole heap of new ones and helping me with Shamanism; Annika Mongan for an inspiring and challenging blog; Charlie the Monkey for being the stuff of nightmares; Paul Mitchell for truly inspiring songs and for making me wonder if I ever dare turn up at a camp in my caravan; Ashley Mortimer for encouragement, friendship and keeping Charlie (almost) under control; James Nichol, J.J Middleway and all the Auroch Grove for showing me a quieter way; Emma and David Restall-Orr for warm hospitality and great cooking, and Emma especially for your deep and searching questions that opened up so many horizons I'd been unaware of; Philip Shallcrass for wolfish inspiration; Bruce, Sara and Gracie Stanley for being co-sojourners in the Forest; Beverley Thorne and all at the New Forest for your welcome, deep questions and help with Heathenism (and for not thinking I looked like a vicar!); Cat Treadwell for inspiring priestly questions; Mark Townsend for Hedgechurch, advice, leading the way and encouraging me; Tess Ward for prayers for the journey and going there ahead; Morgana West for your time and for answering such a stream of questions; Liz Williams for answering tons of my questions and inspiring new lines of thought; Helen and Mark Woodsford-Dean for more things than I can even begin to write about, but especially for offering such deep friendship and sharing your beliefs so deeply with us, and for your insights and corrections.

Inevitably there are others and my apologies if I haven't named everyone, but I've tried to mention all those who made an important contribution to how this has all turned out. Any mistakes and misunderstandings of what you told me are, of course, my own.

I'm very grateful to Brenda Henderson who supplied the cover picture which is copyright © Brenda Henderson 2016. For more of her amazing photos and artwork she can be contacted on sildil@sildil.net

You can find me online at www.the-vics-blog.blogspot.com and at www.facebook.com/altar.ego.7
I am very open to online discussions, especially on Facebook.

And finally, to the One who called me into the Green and who resides at the heart of it all. The path may be narrow, but the scenery's amazing. Thank you.

# Foreword

Paul Cudby's fascinating introduction to Paganism, written for Christians and others, is a welcome contribution to a field which until now has been largely neglected by the Church of England. His accessible style of writing belies the wealth of knowledge and insight contained in its pages, and he writes with sensitivity and understanding of Pagan praxis and practitioners, whilst remaining rooted within the Christian tradition. He weaves together story, reflection, and analysis as he examines different strands within Paganism, and introduces the reader to the diversity of Pagan practice and belief. His is an unusual journey.

As the author acknowledges, some readers within the Christian tradition will struggle with aspects of this study and reach different conclusions to Paul Cudby himself about the extent to which it is appropriate to enter into aspects of Pagan ritual in the quest to engage and learn. Yet, as he notes in reference to his study of Animism in chapter 5, he tries to follow the Church of England model of using 'scripture, reason and tradition to understand experience,' although he cautions that 'there is very little tradition here beyond a tradition of suspicion which has a tendency to limit our beliefs rather than giving us the freedom in Christ to explore'. The fruits of his study are well worthy of the attention of a church which is new to the process of interfaith dialogue with Pagan partners; as he observes, the Druid Network was only admitted to the Interfaith Network as recently as 2014, and other Pagan streams are yet to be welcomed to the table. The desire in the church to engage well with such partners remains at an embryonic stage, as do broader questions about how best the church may enter into such dialogue. I expect this volume will help to shape a discourse which will mature in years to come.

This work also hints at broader questions concerned, for

1

example, with the determination of truth; our imagery of God and use of language; and about some of the gaps within Christian theology which would themselves merit further study. Paul Cudby's research also offers a timely critique of the church's engagement with creation and ecology, and in the final chapter he offers an introduction to Forest Church through the lens of his own experience as part of a group which leads Ancient Arden Forest Church. As a result, this volume offers the necessary focus of an introduction to the subject of Paganism, whilst also inviting the reader to ask searching questions of his or her own faith and faith tradition.

I am pleased to commend it to you.

+David Urquhart
Bishop of Birmingham
Ascension Day 2016

# Introduction

How did a Church of England parish priest who had once been a scientist come to write about Paganism?

*It's been a wonderful evening spent in the pleasant company of a group of Pagans living in Cornwall, many of whom choose the label 'Witch' to describe their spiritual path. They invited my wife, Alison, and me to share a meal with them in the Tintagel Arms in the seaside town of Tintagel where so many of them live, to cement the friendships we have grown and to show how much they have appreciated a Christian priest and his wife asking to find out more about their beliefs. Much of the evening has been full of frivolity, with the ale flowing and the food being just what we needed on the last night of our three and a half month trek around Britain before returning to the parish. Occasional quiet and more serious conversations have taken place with those sat around me, but as we wind towards the end, Laurence, or Loz as we all know him, approaches me. Loz is usually very jovial, but he also has a serious side which I have glimpsed once or twice. He has his serious face on now as he tells me an apocryphal story of a Roman Catholic Priest who came upon the nature deity Pan in a forest. Thinking him to be the devil, the Priest throws holy water over him and commands him to leave in the name of Jesus. Pan, perhaps rather nonchalantly, explains that he is not the devil and so will not leave. Patiently, he explains to the Priest who he really is. Eventually the Priest begins to listen, and, being satisfied in his own mind that the horned being in front of him really is who he says he is, he takes no further action. However, when the Priest returns home **he tells no one of what he has seen**. At the conclusion of his story, Loz, who is normally so affable and laid-back, looks straight at me from under his black leather hat and says, 'Paul, don't be like that Priest. Tell them the truth about us. Don't keep what you've learned to yourself.' I assure*

*Loz that I have no intention of keeping what I have learnt to myself.*
*Satisfied, he smiles, and the ale richly flows again.*

That's really one of the main reasons why this book came into existence, (although I'll explain in more detail in a moment as to what I am aiming to achieve by writing this); because of a promise that I made at the end of my sabbatical study leave, but it's not where this all started. This book's journey, like mine, began some years earlier...

I'm an Anglican priest now, having been ordained in 2002, but my background is in science and I worked in that field for eleven years before retraining as a priest. Scientific training is something that stays with you because it develops a particular way of questioning everything. Consequently, my mind has tended to work away at problems quite rationally and, although some people might imagine that moving from science into religion is a less than rational move, the reality is that much of what we regard as core Christian theology, especially the branch called 'Systematic Theology', is, indeed, quite rational. An example of what I mean is the belief in the Trinity. Consider it like this: many early Christians came from a monotheistic viewpoint. As Jews they believed God was one God, yet their experience was of three distinct personalities: Father, Son and Holy Spirit. The experience and the theology were unified by the belief that the one God did, in fact, have three distinct persons, but they were still all part of one God. It may seem confusing, but it is logically and experientially consistent and that is how much theology is worked out. The disagreements arise because, unlike science, the beliefs cannot be tested experimentally, but those concepts which are not internally consistent with core doctrines tend to be rejected.

For the rationally minded there is a lot to be satisfied with in the way Christians approach what they believe and that was certainly true for me. I enjoyed theology because, to me, it was often about problem solving, much as my previous employment in science had been. Yet, in common with many people who have been Christian believers for years, somewhere along the line something began to shift for me. At some point I began to be aware that the concept of mystery was becoming more important. Although for me, being a Christian has always revolved around being invited into a relationship with God through Christ, it began to feel that trying to do theology when you are also trying to relate to God personally was like trying to squeeze a wet piece of soap in a bath. You never quite get hold of God before he slips out of your hands and disappears into the foam. It's probably different if you try and study him from a distance, but close-up?

Unfortunately, 'close up' was what happened when tragedy hit my family. Following a seven-year struggle with a brain tumour, my eldest sister finally lost her battle and died in 2007. I had all my theology of free will and the freedom of the universe to grow and develop worked out, beliefs that I still hold to today, but all the theology in the world doesn't help in the midst of a deep personal grief, and I am convinced that her death was a part of the trigger. My interest in Celtic Christianity and its emphasis on God in everyday things deepened and the greatest mystery, that a loving God could have let this happen and that I still loved this God despite what had taken place, has gnawed away at me ever since.

Gradually, I began to listen to the still-small voice inside me explaining that my understanding of God was too small and too rational. I now believe that to be the voice of the Holy Spirit and have learned to trust that voice, however unsettling it is, and so it feels in many ways as if God approached me in a way that seemed more motherly than the Father I had previously known and found me weeping in the gravel, took my hands and said, 'Come with me into the trees and walk on the grass. I won't promise you answers, but the scenery is much better for your soul.' And so it began...

Every few years, Anglican priests are granted a sabbatical, a space of about three months to study outside the parish in order to recharge and gain new spiritual perspectives. My wife, Alison, and I didn't have to think very long about how we would use this time as by now it was seeming pretty clear to us that we ought to try and find out more about Paganism, especially given that the modern understanding of Celtic Christianity seems to share similar imaginative and romantic roots with the modern under-standing of Paganism and, as many of our friends were influenced by both, the planning began. It's surprising just how long it takes to put together a period of study leave if you're going to use the time properly and we were relieved when my Bishop gave his blessing to the project, going so far as to ask me to become his advisor on such matters. We then had a choice: were we going to make this an academic exercise, or were we going to go and actually visit as many Pagans as would be willing to see us? The answer, of course, was both and so over the next few months we set about researching and buying the best reviewed books on Wicca, Witchcraft, Druidry and so on. Alongside that, I made good use of email, Facebook and various webpages to contact Pagans up and down the country asking if they would be willing to spend some time with an Anglican priest and his wife who simply wanted to know more about what they believed. The response to these enquiries was in itself enlightening and encour-aging and has really rather set the tone for how the project has progressed. A few people checked me out online, or via mutual friends, to make sure I really was who I said I was and not some undercover reporter looking for a story style exposé. One or two said I would be very welcome just as long as I didn't try and convert them! Only one person went on to ignore me after having made an initial positive response.

So it was that in the pouring rain on the day of the Queen's Diamond Jubilee celebrations in 2012 we finally bundled into our caravan with more than sixty books, bikes, walking gear and just about anything else you can imagine you need for a three and a half months' trip, and headed north. Our journey took us through the Lake District, up the West Coast of Scotland to Orkney in time for the summer solstice where we were invited to participate in an open ritual and to be a witness at a handfasting (a Pagan wedding – legal in Scotland), and then back down to the Stirling area. Then, on the wettest day of the summer, we drove from Stirling down to Somerset, before moving on to Cornwall, back to the New Forest in time for Lughnasadh (the festival of the first fruits of the harvest, known as Lammas or 'loaf-mass' in the Church), up to Cheltenham for the Greenbelt festival and finally back to Cornwall. The time was spent reading (and we probably bought another twenty or so books while we were away), writing and visiting Pagans, either in their homes, at informal gatherings (Moots), at Circles and at Ritual, in shops they owned or simply in the pub. Over and over again we discovered friendly faces who were eager to explain what they *really* believed and who were very ready to engage in debate about the differences and some of the surprising similarities between aspects of Christian and Pagan beliefs. The level of honesty was sometimes breathtaking as we heard stories of spiritual experiences that were mainly (but not entirely) full of love and light and not at all what I had imagined.

Somewhere in the midst of it all I began to realise that a part of my reason for being called into this work was because of the need for a better dialogue, which is where we come up against a difficulty: the Church of England has historically held a position of having no official interfaith dialogue with any of the Pagan organisations. Its official interfaith partners have been the historically recognised world religions such as the Jews, Muslims, Hindus, etc. Late in September 2014 the British interfaith landscape seemed to have altered as, amongst others, the Druid Network were admitted to the Interfaith Network. At the time of writing we are awaiting developments with interest. So right from the outset I need to state my own beliefs that we should be entering official dialogue with some of the Pagan organisations in this country. This book is my contribution towards giving reasons why we should be engaging and trying to make that happen and when it does, to facilitate better understanding. I am fully aware that even though they may claim ancient roots, many of the Pagan religions are modern re-imaginings, but that does not, to me, seem like a good enough reason to ignore them. After all, exactly the same charge can be levelled at Celtic Christianity, but we take that seriously. Unlike new religious movements such as Scientology, Pagans generally struggle with any idea of earning money from what they believe, so I can affirm that Paganism is not some kind of money-making scam, but an expression of a deep earth-centred spirituality which is life-affirming and, for many, life-changing.

This, therefore, brings us to the aim of this book which is twofold: simply to inform Christians and other interested parties about what Pagans in this country really believe, and to show both Christians and Pagans alike that we have much to debate and some unexpected commonalities that some on either side might be uncomfortable with. Many of the books you can buy in Christian bookshops that relate in some way to Paganism will refer to it in the same breath as Satanism, effectively closing down the debate. This is unhelpful in the extreme, so I want to add something rather more informed to the debate. The way I intend to do this is by using a number of different formats in each chapter. Sometimes, as at the beginning of this chapter, I will include an experience or conversation in italics. Some of the names will be actual names and sometimes I will use a pseudonym to protect someone's identity, given that there remains much anti-Pagan feeling in the popular press and I don't want to 'out' someone who would prefer to keep their beliefs private. For Pagans and Christians alike a significant amount of what we believe is formed around story and so I will tell some of the stories of my experiences.

Much of the rest of the book will be simply trying to explain, in fairly straightforward terms, what it is that I have learned about a particular subject. In addition to this, there will be parts of the book where I want to be rather more in-depth about a subject, so when you encounter those sections be aware that what I'm saying at that point is treated rather more academically for those who wish to go a little deeper.

I do, however, think I need to offer a word of warning: if you choose to try and learn about and come alongside people who follow a Pagan path, you need to recognise that many Christians will misunderstand you and perhaps condemn you. I and some of my colleagues in this field have experienced this and it can be deeply distressing. It is not just some Christians who seem to have some kind of revulsion about Paganism, but also vast swathes of the British public, often fuelled by ignorance within the press. My belief is that, surely amongst committed Christians, there should be love, since our religion teaches that perfect love drives out fear. I began this journey recognising in myself a sense of fear of the unknown, but found instead that I was drawn to love the people I was meeting. They were open and honest with me. They didn't expect me to believe what they believed and trusted me not to try and argue them into believing what I believed. Instead, by engaging in dialogue, we learned mutual respect and a deeper understanding and appreciation of our own paths. But still there were things about which it was right to be worried:

*It was one of the first times I had sat down with a Pagan. She is a Hedgewitch, meaning she is a lone practitioner of her arts. She has a deep respect for Christianity and she is scared for me. We've been sat in a café at a garden centre near where she lives for a couple of hours and she has been gracefully answering all my questions, whilst gently nudging me when I have completely misunderstood something. The elderly couples and mothers with playful children who surround us are oblivious to the depths and seriousness of our discussion. Our time is coming to a close and, as I have experienced many times subsequently with other Pagans, she gives me a warm hug goodbye and then tells me of her fears. She warns me that it is not Pagans that I should be afraid of, but other Christians, Christians who will misunderstand me and pillory me for what I am trying to do. Over the coming months I recognise the Holy Spirit saying to me, 'Whatever you do, stay within the Church of England. That's where I have placed you. That's where I want you to be.' I will try hard to obey that gently given command, but it gets difficult when, on two separate occasions, I try to engage with the same Christian leader about this subject, only for him to, perhaps unconsciously, warn me off by getting the word 'syncretism' into his conversation before I have really even begun to explore my experiences with him. The Hedgewitch's words echo long after she spoke them and I back off, changing the subject...*

Syncretism is a difficult subject, but if you try to develop friendships with Pagans it is likely that some learned Christian will accuse you of it at some point, so it is worth at least knowing what it is so that you can respond. It is essentially the idea of blending two religions to come up with something new, but which is no longer completely true to a previous path. Syncretism is particularly strongly condemned amongst the so-called 'revealed religions' of which Christianity is one. Within these religions they are counted by most of their followers as bearers of exclusive truth, that is to say that they are based on the revelation to, or of, an individual, and so that 'truth' excludes all other 'truths'. Instrumental in this way of thinking in Christianity's case is the saying of Jesus, 'I am the way, the truth and the life. No one comes to the Father except by me.' (John 14:6) Personally, I believe that this is more to do with a particular intimacy of a parent-child relationship within Christianity rather than a condemnation of other paths, and we will revisit this later in the book. I think the point I would want to raise here is that all religions, be they revealed or otherwise, have syncretistic elements to them. Early Christianity has a significant amount of Greek philosophy built into it. One need look no further than the first chapter of John's Gospel and his application of the Greek title, 'The Word', referring to Jesus to see this. A Jewish scholar might argue, in particular, that Christianity is a syncretistic blending of the Jewish faith with the sayings of a wise man whose followers claimed he was the messiah. Likewise Judaism is also not completely 'pure' but has echoes of Canaanite Pagan religion such as one of the names of God being El, (also often found as a suffix to angelic names such as Gabriel and Michael), where El was the chief god in the Canaanite pantheon. The list goes on and can include the amount of Jewish Kabbalah and Christian prayers which find their way into some forms of traditional Witchcraft, as well as the possible use of some Pagan symbols such as the Christmas tree and bringing in of greenery at Christmas, both of which may be Pagan-derived practices, but the point is made. No religion, however 'revealed', is pure and, consequently, the fear of syncretism is an inadequate reason to avoid religious dialogue. To put it another way, whilst I believe Jesus Christ to be the incarnational revelation of God and to have provided an understanding of God's nature that is unique, I also believe him when he says, 'Seek and you shall find.' By that I mean that the joy of being found by a searching heart is a part of God's nature, and so those who have been inoculated against institutional Christianity by the behaviour of some of its followers will still find that God is waiting to spend time with them. Christian-Pagan dialogue, to me, sometimes feels like a way of finding some of the other songs that God sings to those who are searching and who have been put off by more traditional religious practices.

So, I invite you to turn the page and walk with me 'into the Green'. I've called this book, 'The Shaken Path' for two reasons: firstly, the name came in a dream – hopefully a good sign – and secondly because it describes what the last few years have been like. By that I mean that if you are on one spiritual path and you investigate another thoroughly then expect to have your own path and beliefs shaken. You may find some of this unsettling, or you may find you resonate with it. You may discover, as I have, that when you walk this path you will be shaken too. Contrary to what some expected, I have not felt the need to abandon my Christian faith because it felt to me that when I walked 'into the Green' I was led by the hand of the Holy Spirit. Not all of my Christian friends understand what I mean by that and some are disquieted by my beliefs. But for me, I would echo what St. Peter said to Jesus, "You have the words of eternal life" (John 6:68). That is and remains my experience.

## Chapter One

# What is Belief and What do Pagans Believe?

## Introduction

Before we start getting into specifics about the different types of Paganism, we need to take a step backwards and think about belief and what it actually is. Pagan belief and Christian belief have a rather different feel about them, which can mean there are grounds for misunderstanding each other before we have even started. It's a little like the man who pulls up to someone in a car in the middle of nowhere to ask for directions only to be met with the phrase, 'Arrr, you don't want to be starting from here.' The reality is that, in practice, we are starting from two different places, so we need to go on a small excursion to understand what we mean by belief to begin with. Christians will often feel that they have a stronger foundation for their beliefs because they have a holy text, the Bible, whereas Pagans have no single source that they all depend on. The intriguing thing is that both parties look at the other's stance as being a weakness.

## What is belief?

To illustrate what I mean about starting from different places:

*It had been a delightful evening of rich and wide-ranging conver-sation, debate and sharing of stories. After meeting a Pagan couple, both of whom were also musicians, at a Moot they had invited Alison and me to share a meal in their caravan later that week. We had spent a lively evening talking about the different things we believed, listening to each others' stories and playing some songs together. The conversation finally turned to the differences in the ways we believe. 'You need to understand', he explained to me, 'that the focus in Christianity is on orthodoxy, whereas in Paganism it is orthopraxy.' I must have looked puzzled and so he explained what he meant: 'For Christians, you all worship in different ways in different denominations, but you all believe more or less the same thing – that's orthodoxy. But for us as Pagans, we may all perform the same ritual within the same circle, yet we can each believe something quite different within the same shared experience – that's orthopraxy.'*

Christians tend to test what they believe against a sacred text. Pagans simply don't, and many of the most acute differences stem from this. The result is that, despite our many differences and denominations, Christianity tends to have far less diversity of belief because of the desire to be sure that what is being experienced spiritually has an explanation that has been tried, tested and certified as being genuine. In other words, with the exception of some of the more extreme Pentecostal movements, Christians tend towards being fearful of a new spiritual experience until they are sure it's not counterfeit. Pagans, on the other hand, relish new spiritual experiences and accept them at face value. I've lost count of the number of times that I've heard the phrase, 'It is what it is', from a Pagan. That is not to say that they have no fear, because many of the Pagans I've met have had troubling spiritual experiences too, and the older, wiser ones recognise that not all spiritual experiences are inherently helpful or good. But the clear distinction is that for a Pagan they decide *for themselves* what they think is happening whereas Christians tend to look to a higher authority, either a minister, something they've been taught in the past, or the Bible. Immediately, you can see that there is a tendency towards a hierarchical belief system within Christianity as opposed to a more free, maybe even anarchic, spirituality within Paganism. Each has their own drawbacks. Christians can tend towards a lack of maturity (and even a sense of fear) because they let someone else tell them what is right or wrong, whereas Pagans can move more swiftly to an outlook based on making up their own minds. The flip side of this is that the caution exercised by Christians should tend to keep them out of spiritual dangers, whereas an inexperienced Pagan could inadvertently find themself becoming a plaything of a malevolent spiritual entity, or simply having a naive belief that something entirely explicable in natural terms was some kind of spiritual experience. Given that experience is so important to Pagans, let us go a little further with this and see how much both experience and context shapes what we believe.

## Belief and experience

The Oxford Dictionary defines belief as:

> '...an acceptance that something exists or is true, especially one without proof.'

For example, there are plenty of people who believe that our planet has been visited by aliens. There is no substantiated proof, but for them such visitation makes sense of the scant unproven evidence which exists. If we were to turn purely to religious beliefs then I would prefer to describe belief with my own definition:

> Belief is the constructs that we develop with time in order to make sense of an experienced spiritual reality.

Let me give you an example from my own experience. The following took place when I was a new Christian, perhaps fifteen or sixteen years old. I had been on the receiving end of a conversion experience that had radically changed the direction I was taking in life, and had started attending a Church-based youth group that was able to provide me with some solid age-appropriate grounding in my new faith. I was also an altar server at a very middle of the road Church of England church. This episode took place a week after I had a sharp disagreement with the vicar who was absolutely convinced that angels, as supernatural beings, did not exist. It's important that you understand that context in terms of what happened next:

*We are in the middle of the communion part of the service. The vicar is in the sanctuary area in the church, standing behind the altar. My position as a server during this part of the service is kneeling at a stall outside the sanctuary, off to one side. The vicar has just completed the Eucharistic prayer and we are all about to say the Lord's Prayer. Suddenly, and with no prompting, I feel wrapped in an incredibly intense love that feels like human love feels, but goes so much further than I can begin to describe. I am aware that I am loved absolutely and completely by God. The experience doesn't last for very long, about which, in one sense, I am glad because the intensity of feeling is so unbelievably powerful that I'm not sure for how long I could stand it. But then, with my eyes closed, I have a vision: two angels are coming down through the roof of the church to the altar, one following the other. The details have blurred with time, but it is absolutely clear to me what they are since they are large and a very pure white. Intriguingly, I can't see their faces – which just seem blank. Then, in an instant, the entire experience is over, but now I know for sure that the vicar was wrong – angels **do** exist.*

I still believe this. That was the only true visionary experience of my life and although it was a long time ago, it left a lasting effect. However, the main reason for my telling this story is because it illustrates my definition of belief. What I felt was love and what I saw were two large bright white beings coming through the ceiling. What I believed about it was based on the context and the teachings of Christianity. The love that I felt, I believe, came from God. The beings, I believe, were angels. I have no evidence to support this, but it is consistent with the scriptures that I hold dear. However, it could be interpreted quite differently. In his book *Pagans and Christians*, Gus diZerega[1] describes his own conversion experience to a Pagan path. In this context he has an encounter with 'the Lady', whom he interprets as the Goddess who comes to him with an absolutely overwhelming love. He experienced something similar to what I had felt, but his world view, and the context within which it all took place, led him to a different set of beliefs. We both had incredible and life-changing spiritual experiences, but we interpreted them quite differently because of the contexts within which they happened. It therefore follows that what we believe about a spiritual experience depends a lot on the context in which we live and the religious constructs that we have developed for ourselves or adopted from others with whom we have decided to share a religion. Where we differ, though, is that within Christianity, because it has a sacred text and a huge number of traditions that remain anchored to that text, the interpretation of a spiritual experience tends towards having an internal consistency. My interpretation of my vision as being of angels and of experiencing the love of God is internally consistent with the beliefs and experiences of Christians for two thousand years. For the modern Pagan, though, with the exception of Heathenism, there are few sacred texts and none held with the same regard as how Christians view the Bible, although there are plenty of traditions and stories. This means that a spiritual experience has far less to which it can be anchored and it is therefore likely to be interpreted within a much wider framework and, because no Pagan paths make a claim to exclusivity, each one is counted as valid.

The outcome of all this is that I suspect that diZeriga and I would look at each other's experiences and interpret them differently. I look at diZeriga's encounter with the Goddess and think to myself that, since I believe there is only one God who is Father, Son and Holy Spirit, and that God has both masculine and feminine characteristics, diZeriga has experienced exactly the same God as I have, but he's interpreted it differently. I therefore interpret his Goddess encounter as being with the same God that I worship. I would imagine, though, that diZeriga would be unlikely to do the same reinterpretation exercise with my experience. If he follows the model that most Pagans I have met do, then he will quite happily accept that I encountered angels and that I was loved by God, but with the understanding that I was loved by one God, but not the same God as his Goddess.

I hope that these stories have illustrated the reason for this excursion into understanding the link between belief and experience. It is not a simple matter to say what Pagans believe because the foundations for their beliefs are totally different from that of Christianity since they are not anchored to a sacred text. What Pagans believe is far more dependent, therefore, on which Pagan you ask, what tradition they follow and their own individual context within which they have interpreted their spiritual experiences. Indeed, animated conversations sometimes arise amongst Pagans about what is actually 'Pagan' and whether a person or group truly qualifies. Furthermore, in this country you will usually find that Pagans have an eclectic gathering of traditions within their own personal path, especially near the beginning of their journey. With these things in mind then, let us ask the question:

## What do Pagans believe?

Answering this is more difficult than you might imagine and, to be honest, the rest of this book is about engaging with this question. What I want to do here is simply provide a foundation on which to build and perhaps one of the first things we need to establish is that Paganism should not be classed as a New Age religion, even though in a few places we can see some crossovers. There is a degree of antipathy amongst many Pagans towards New Age belief, with the latter often derided as 'Fluffy New Agers'. New Age beliefs tend to be an amalgam of various eastern religions and philosophies tied to various popular psychologies all to do with personal growth, (although they might appropriate Pagan titles if it makes a particular therapy more marketable). Pagan beliefs are far more earthy, being tied to the gods and spirits of this land and its plant and animal inhabitants, (with the exception of Heathenism where the balance is shifted more towards the Nordic deities), and the seasons of the year. Paganism is, by and large, an earth-based group of religions which recognise both the beauty and the cruelty of the planet and lives as close to the land as personal circumstances will allow. Indeed the word 'Pagan' comes from the Latin *paganus* meaning 'Country Person', coming to be used as a term of abuse applied by Romans to the simple country folk as opposed to the more refined city-dweller. It's also worth noting that I make no distinction here between Pagan and Neo-Pagan. I think this is an artificial label since, even if a good deal of what is being ritually practised now is new, the philosophies on which they draw and the stories which are foundational are old. (I have also used a capital letter throughout for Paganism since this is a mark of respect, just as I would with Hinduism, Buddhism, Judaism and Islam. Pagan authors refer to Christianity not christianity and I wish simply to afford them the same courtesy.)

Here, then, is my definition:

> A Pagan is someone whose experiences in the natural world have led them to believe that the world is spiritually alive and diverse, and that through ritual or meditation, both solo and in a group, that world and its inhabitants can be accessed in order to grow personally and spiritually, and to offer help to others in need.

So far so good, except that this definition barely scratches the surface (hence the need for a book!)

The first thing you notice about it is that I don't mention gods in it, but refer simply to the idea of spiritual diversity. This is because if you ask any group of Pagans what gods they believe in you will get a multitude of different answers:

*We stood in his shop chatting away jovially. He had told me the story of the healing that he had received through a Pagan ritual. So I asked him who he believed in. He laughed and said, 'I'm a polyatheist. I've believed in all the gods at one time or another, but now I don't believe in any of them!' Yet when I pushed him a little more in this he said, rather more sombrely, that he believed there was one supreme and unapproachable power behind all the expressions of deity.*

So at one end of the spectrum you may find Pagans who are atheist, believing that all the gods are simply Jungian archetypes of the self, or, in other words, that each deity is simply a part of yourself that the ritual you are using is allowing you to access and interact with. Some, such as the gentleman above, will go further than this and imagine that there is some kind of inaccessible supreme spiritual power behind this. Progressing from that position, there are others who believe that there is indeed one power which on its own is inaccessible, or only barely accessible, but that the deities which these Pagans honour are the accessible faces of the one Great Spirit. This kind of pseudo-monotheism seems broadly consistent with some aspects of modern Hinduism.

Other Pagans believe that there is no single power but all the gods are exactly that – individual gods with whom one can interact. Some will recognise a hierarchy within their gods, for example amongst Heathens, but for others this is not the case. Regarding the United Kingdom and Ireland, however, and putting Heathenism to one side for reasons that will become clear in Chapter 7, the position that seems to be the most commonly held is a duotheistic one which is that there is a Goddess and a God whose relationship is expressed through the changing seasons of the year. This position is shared by most Wiccans and also, though perhaps to a lesser extent, by many Druids (who are just as likely to be poly-, or monotheists) and I will explore it in far more detail in the chapter concerning Wicca.

One final belief worth considering about deity, is pantheism, because it seems to weave in and out of all of the above, although, as with all Pagan beliefs, it is by no means universal. Pantheism literally translates as 'Everything is God'. For the pantheist, they view themselves, and indeed the whole universal order, as part of God. There are many variations on this definition, but it seems to be a particular characteristic that informs a lot of modern Paganism.

This diversity can be observed at any Pagan informal gathering (called a 'Moot') that usually seem to take place in pubs. This is entirely acceptable to those present. No one is told that what they believe is incorrect. This is in contrast, and perhaps in reaction, to what most Christians find within their own church where there may be a diversity of experiences, but they will all be centred on a belief in the one God who is Father, Son and Holy Spirit. This may lead to a discussion of the different Christian experiences in an attempt to understand who has the correct interpretation of what took place. For most Pagans, though, it is rare to ask if something is correct. They are far more likely to question whether the experience was a helpful one to the individual. This difference is a vital one for Christians seeking to understand Pagans. Christians generally want to be sure that they are believing all the right things and are correct in their belief. Pagans are rarely remotely concerned about this. For them, if the experience was helpful in personal and/or corporate growth, then it was worth having, regardless of the different ways in which it could be interpreted.

## The impact of nature on Pagan deities

One further aspect of Pagan belief and how it differs from Christian belief is that Christians believe that God is separate from creation although fully present within it. That is not to say that God is emotionally unmoved by what takes place here, just that it cannot impact on who God actually is. God is not changed in who God is by our suffering, even though Christians believe that the sending of Jesus was in loving reaction to humanity's need. Nor does the wanton destruction of many of earth's natural habitats alter who God is, even though it may make him angry. This, however, is not how Pagans view deity. York[2] puts it like this:

> 'The dynamic of paganism is such that... the world or nature is altered by humanity and the gods as they are both by it and one another. In paganism, the essential realms of reality, however conceived, are essentially codependent.'

This is a fundamental difference between Christianity and Paganism. Even the name given by God to himself in Jewish tradition, YHWH, means 'I am what I am,' which carries the weight of there being no possibility that God can be anything other than what God is, and that God has no need of humans but interacts with us out of a choice driven by love. For the Pagan there will be many gods and spirits who will also interact with us out of love and a desire to help us grow, as there will also be gods and spirits who couldn't care less about anyone human. However, the Pagan gods are not separate from the universe but are a part of it. If a deity or a spirit is a part of a place and that place is changed by human activity, then the deity will also be affected:

> *'Adrienne' told me that she had found the dryad* (tree spirit) *by a fallen tree. It was devastated because the tree was its home, but the*

*tree had been felled and the dryad had nowhere to go. She went on to explain to me that there is a ritual whereby a dryad can be taken to a new tree and 'rehoused' and so she did this for the dryad, taking it with her to a new place where it would be safe.*

Although perhaps a minor example, since a dryad is thought of as a local spirit rather than a deity, and regardless of how you might interpret this story, it serves to illustrate the point that in Pagan beliefs it is widely held that the gods are tied to the land, and so what affects the land affects them and vice versa. (We will return to this story in more detail and in a different context in Chapter 5 with regards to Animism.) I have also heard Pagans tell of the dangers of trying to strip ancient woodlands because of what dwells there, and who will, therefore, be extremely 'upset' at having their environment altered by human action, an upset that might lead to a negative spiritual reaction against trespassers.

## What do Pagans believe about evil?

Hopefully by this point you will already have recognised that there is a huge diversity of belief within Paganism, and the same applies with respect to evil. At one end of the spectrum you will find Pagans who quite simply do not believe in evil. To Christians, and indeed perhaps to the majority in the western world, this seems like a simple denial of reality, but many Pagans see the world quite differently. Many believe that there is a natural place for everything and that the causing of harm does not necessarily mean that the harm comes from evil intent. At one level Christians can see the point of this argument. For example, an earthquake can cause great harm to life that is in its vicinity, but the earthquake has made no decision of will. Some theologians may refer to it as a natural evil, but an earthquake is clearly morally neutral. In fact, from a scientific perspective, an earthquake is a necessary part of our planet being able to sustain life; without tectonic activity there would be no recycling of carbon dioxide, which, in turn, would ultimately lead to it all being removed from the atmosphere as plants die and lock their carbon dioxide into carboniferous rock, which, in turn, would lead to planet earth turning into 'Snowball Earth'. Earthquakes, volcanoes and the like are a necessary part of life.

What, then, about causing deliberate harm to another? Could this not be construed as evil? Again, to most westerners the answer would be 'yes', but not all Pagans would agree. Some Pagans would say that all things are permissible provided you are willing to accept the consequences of your action. If you take the life of someone else, you had better be willing to go to prison for it and you had better have a very good reason for having committed the crime. It is also important to add that Pagans oppose harming anyone or anything; yet, having said that, many Pagans still do not believe in the existence of evil. For my part, I suspect that this comes as a reaction against Christianity, given that many western Pagans have Christian backgrounds. Christianity is not actually a dualistic religion, but it often presents itself as if it is (particularly in fundamentalist circles), with the created order being the battleground between God and the devil. Since many Pagans have rejected Christianity and view it as responsible for great suffering in the world, it is completely understandable that they should choose to reject some of its central beliefs, such as evil. It almost goes without saying that most Pagans also do not believe in the existence of the devil, with the exception of some traditional witches. (This will be covered in more detail in Chapter 3 on Wicca and Witchcraft). To sum up, a large proportion of Pagans do not believe in evil, but, of course, this belief is not universal:

*The couple told us the story of how they were aware of a place being used for black magic, for dark practices, and it was known locally as such. They explained how they had naively gone there in the belief that they could spiritually cleanse the place to make it instead a centre for love and light. Yet these were not Christians speaking to me, but initiated Wiccans. When they arrived and began their ritual they said it was as if they had set off some kind of psychic bomb, planted there to ward off anyone who attempted exactly what they were trying to do. As they retreated, they became aware of some kind of spiritual entity following them home. It stayed on the edge of their consciousness, disturbing them and their sleep for some time until, finally losing his temper, the husband used all his power to dismiss it, at which point calm returned.*

Here were two people who knew that they had encountered something nasty, and indeed I found, particularly on the part of some of the older and more experienced Pagans that I met, that evil was acknowledged as a reality. One older couple actually told me that they thought some younger Pagans were simply naive if they didn't believe in evil. Some had been on the receiving end of it, and some recognised humbly that they had been responsible for it at times. Once again, as with all things Pagan, there is a huge diversity of belief and understanding.

## A valid diversity

There is much more to be said about Pagan belief which will emerge in each individual chapter as we go. However, the aim of this chapter has been to show just some of the diversity of belief that you will find expressed throughout this book. For someone to say that they are a Pagan is similar to another saying that they are a monotheist in that both are labels for an extremely broad range of beliefs. The difference between Pagans and monotheists, though, is that extremist Jews, Christians or Muslims might go to war against each other over their differences, whereas Pagans will normally just accept that they believe different things as a part of the valid diversity of their chosen path.

# Notes for Chapter 1

1   diZerega G., *Pagans and Christians*, Llewellyn, U.S.A., 2004, 55.
2   York M., *Pagan Theology*, London: New York University Press, 2003, 158.

## Chapter Two

# Why Are People Drawn to Paganism?

## Paganism as an experiential spirituality

One of the criticisms often levelled at Christianity is that it is dry and cold. Whilst this is not my experience, many Pagans have told me that they stopped going to church some time ago because it simply wasn't very spiritual. Yet in Paganism, there seems to be this sense in which people go looking for spiritual experiences and then they have them. It's not quite a sense of spiritual experiences 'on tap', but there is clearly something going on, and I've felt it myself:

*I've been invited to a weekend gathering of a local moot, more or less a Pagan camp. The couple who have invited me are gentle and caring people who spend most of their day with me, showing me around the stalls and explaining it all to me. At one end of the camp is a Goddess icon who I believe they called 'The Cosmic Goddess'. It's an amazing piece of artwork considering the weather conditions in which it's been erected. Essentially they have used a tailor's female dummy to provide the curves, a horned goat skull and some sort of silvered paper to wrap her in. The effect is impressive and, since I am quite new to this, slightly scary. This is one of my first exposures to Paganism and I am having to fight with my 'inner fundamentalist'! We have lunch together at an adjoining pub and then my host gives a lecture on her own Pagan belief. Given that this is a general gathering there are Pagans of all different kinds here, each eager to understand the other. I attend as much as I feel able to and then observe a ritual, standing just outside the circle, with the permission of those gathered.*

*Throughout the whole time I become steadily more aware of a spiritual sense of 'wildness'. There is very definitely a spiritual temperature which is quite unlike anything I have ever experienced before. It is not wholly uncomfortable, and I certainly would not describe it as evil, but it has a potency to it which I have never experienced before. I believe now that I am more able to understand a little of what draws people to this. Several months later I sit down with my Hedgewitch friend again to talk about this 'wild spirituality' and she coins a phrase which stays with me. She calls it 'Feral', and as she says that I realise she knows exactly what I mean because the word captures it. It is not a feeling of evil, but is, instead, wild, untamed and feral, whilst very definitely spiritual, with a sense of danger, perhaps because it is uncontrolled. Immersing oneself in it is not dissimilar to taking a body-board into a rough sea; you treat it with respect, knowing that if you get caught up in it you could be hurt, but that's the risk you take for getting an amazing ride.*

I tell this story with a caution attached: this is just one experience of many and no one should get the impression that all Pagan gatherings feel like this; certainly other Pagan rituals that I have subsequently been to have felt very different from this, whilst some have felt similar. However, since this was my first time it left a deep impression and I believe I can at least begin to understand why some people are drawn to this kind of spirituality. It is very earthy and sensual, and in a culture which is becoming more steadily technological and controlled, there will inevitably be those, myself included, who want an alternative approach to life. This kind of spirituality feels very connected to nature and it allows people to explore the parts of themselves that feel closer to the wild, allowing people to integrate their passions into one whole rather than subsuming them into a form of control that can turn sour with time. It is deeply experiential and to that end many of the Pagans I have spoken to have told me that they have never actually converted to Paganism, but, instead, either whilst in conversation with a Pagan, going to some kind of Pagan day or whilst reading a book about it, have discovered that this is what they were all along, it's just that they never had a label for it. Many go on to say that it simply feels like coming home. As someone who feels deeply drawn to panentheism, (the belief that God is present in all things – divine immanence – as well as being separate and uncreated – divine transcendence), and the experience of God through nature, I believe I can understand what they mean, and it is not difficult to comprehend why people are drawn in this direction. For me, though, God's presence has broken into my conscious experience in such a variety of places that I find my 'treasure' is more widely dispersed.

## Christian and Pagan approaches to spiritual experiences

The questions raised by the spiritual experiences I have had alongside my Pagan friends have underlined a criticism that is often directed at Christianity by them. As mentioned in the previous chapter, in Pagan spirituality a spiritual experience is taken at face value: 'It is what it is.' This is in quite a strong contrast to Christianity where in many cases it is felt that the experience should be tested against scripture to ascertain its validity. Gus diZerega[1] is just one of many Pagans who have voiced this concern that Christians take every experience back to the Bible to determine whether it is real or counterfeit; of God or the devil. I can certainly speak from experience in saying that many of my Pagan friends have said as much to me too. For many Christians, it seems, when it comes to matters of spirituality there are only two definitions: good or evil. It seems likely that this stems from what St. John refers to as, '...Testing the spirits'. The following comes from 1 John 4:1-3:

'Beloved, do not believe every spirit, but test the spirits to see whether they are from God; for many false prophets have gone out into the world. By this you know the Spirit of God: every spirit that confesses that Jesus Christ has come in the flesh is from God, and every spirit that does not confess Jesus is not from God. And this is the spirit of the antichrist, of which you have heard that it is coming; and now it is already in the world.'

The first question this raises for many is what did John, and what do we, mean by 'spirits'? The answer to this could be quite complex, but a brief answer might be that a spirit is simply a non-corporeal person. In the Christian tradition that could refer to an angel, for example, or some might think it could also mean a fallen angel, one that has been expelled from heaven and is now a demon. We might also consider the possibility of the spirits of the dead, those who once had bodies but have died. Amongst Pagans we should also include those whose nature means that they have never been corporeal such as faeries, elementals, deities and so on. All of these and others will be explored to one extent or another during the course of this book.

Pagans with any degree of experience know for themselves that not every spirit that they encounter is either harmless or wishes them goodwill. It has been said to me that some spirits do not apparently care and others appear to be malevolent. However, I have begun to wonder whether the dichotomy is as clear as Christians have formerly suggested when they interpret the above passage. Perhaps this is a good space in which to introduce an example of my own experiences to illustrate how I did *exactly* what Christians are often accused of by Pagans. I will go into this story in much greater detail in Chapter 5, but it serves here to underline the point:

*Alison and I are prayerfully walking in some woodland near our home, seeking to honour the feminine within God in a natural setting. We find ourselves disturbed by a noise ahead, coming closer. As we wait in silence we witness numerous squirrels (they're not easy to count) rushing around each other excitedly. Already we know we're on the verge of something quite special and, as if on cue, they just melt away into the trees. We quietly stand up, wondering silently at what we've seen when out of nowhere an owl flies down in front of us, close enough to touch, and as she disappears up into the trees there is suddenly a sense of what I can only call a divine, feminine love. It is so very gentle and welcoming, and just simply feminine...*

I found this experience to be both beautiful and, at the same time, troubling and I did exactly what any Pagan would have expected me, a Christian, to do: I began to reason through what had happened in the light of scripture. Some Pagans would have given thanks to the Goddess for showing herself like that. Others would have blessed the spirit of the forest for coming to say, 'Hello', and still others would have done both with a belief that all goddesses are faces of the One Goddess. But for me this was something totally new. I have experienced the presence of God in many ways and many times over the years. As a male I don't think I've ever questioned the gender of the experience, but it has been by turns joyful, powerful, awe-inspiringly terrifying and loving beyond anything I can begin to put into words. But, nevertheless, when I reflect on it I would have to say that if there was any sense of a gendered experience it was male. But not this time.

Now when one starts reflecting on scripture in this context it quickly becomes plain that the idea that God is exclusively a male deity can be challenged by using the Bible. In the Old Testament the word for Spirit/Wind/Breath is a feminine word, so one might argue for a sense of feminine within the Spirit of God. For me, this is further reinforced by Genesis 1:2 which refers to the Spirit of God brooding over the unformed waters of creation, which seems to me to be very much a poetic description of a mother-to-be with her hand on her swelling belly pondering what her unborn child will be like. The universe is the child about to be born and God the Mother is wondering what will become of her child, much like any mother.

One can see something more explicitly stated in Genesis 1 where God declares that humankind is to be made in God's image, both male and female, indicating that God is genderful not genderless. Or, one can recall that an oft-used name for God in the Old Testament is Elohim, a feminine plural word always used with a masculine singular verb. Even in some of God's names we find possible evidence for this femininity. The Hebrew name El Shaddai is often translated as meaning 'God Almighty', but a viable alternative translation of the Hebrew would say it means 'God the-many-breasted-one'. All of this suggests that we should not be so surprised when God reveals God's self in the feminine, but you can see that I did exactly what any Pagan would have predicted of me and went back to scripture to find an interpretation. Yet still I was concerned. Was this God's feminine side that I had encountered, or was this a 'spirit of place', (an entity whose existence we don't really understand yet which seems bound to one location), that we had run into? I am beginning to recognise the possibility that such things may exist, so was that what had happened? To continue the tale, a second encounter ensued shortly afterwards:

*Not long after, we are walking together in the Wyre Forest. Once again we are walking in near silence, gazing at nature, prepared, as a Christian friend of ours has suggested, for nature to stare back. As we stand quietly in a glade, an unforgettable presence reasserts herself. 'She's back', I say to Alison as I recognise that clearly identical feminine sense of welcome that we had both felt in our local woodlands.*

With that, my mind was made up. Leaning on the Anglican model of 'scripture, reason and tradition', I decided that my experience could be analysed as a genuine experience of God's femininity and not a spirit of place because I had experienced the same presence in two different places. Yet I recognise that many of my Pagan friends would be exasperated in knowing that I had felt the need to interpret an experience rather than simply accepting what had happened at face value. I hasten to add that I also work like this because of my scientific background wherein the analysis of the results leads to a conclusion which is consistent with the theory. For me the theory is that God expressed God's feminine side to us, feeling exactly the same in two places and that result is consistent with my theology that God is trinitarian in nature and genderful rather than genderless. But, likewise, I admit that a Pagan could look at the same experiences and declare them also to be consistent with encountering the Goddess. We discussed this in the previous chapter as we looked at my angelic encounter and experiences of God's love in comparison to diZeriga's conversion to Paganism when he encountered what he described as the love of the Goddess. Once one recognises that what appears to be the same experience can be interpreted in two different ways, one then has to question a number of conclusions, maybe even going so far as acknowledging the possibility that in some encounters the Goddess of the Pagans might be the Holy Spirit of the Christians.

## Being called to Paganism by the gods

Not all Pagans discover the path by some form of accident or intent. Some Pagans feel that they were called by the gods they honour:

> *This wonderfully hospitable Heathen woman has not just allowed me to visit her in her own home, but has cooked a meal for me and made me very welcome. When I thank her for this she smiles as she*

*more-or-less brushes the compliment off, explaining that hospitality is a part of her religion's tradition. Heathenism is something with which I am, at this point, most unfamiliar and so I ask her to tell me the story of how she came to believe as she does. She explains that she didn't go searching for the gods, but that they came looking for her. And it wasn't so much a gentle call in the night, but more a case of a feeling as if she had been hit with Thor's hammer to get her attention. Following the Heathen gods was less of a choice and more of a case of obedience to higher powers.*

This is just one example that was explained to me and I include it because of the way it mirrors what some Christians would say are their experiences of being called to belief by a direct encounter with Christ. One need not go further than to read St. Paul's Damascus Road experience of the risen Christ in Acts 8 to see an example of how the divine can break into our conscious reality. For Christians, however, the challenge here is that the religious experience of being called happened in the context of the Heathen path rather than the Christian one. In fact, I would go so far as to say that this young woman's experience is not so far removed from my own conversion to Christianity:

*As a fifteen-year-old I have long had a family association with church. However, I am beginning to take it less seriously as the usual draw of attractive young women and bundles of testosterone run counter to the ethics I have been instilled with, that is until my first encounter with God. My next door neighbour, with whom I have more-or-less grown up, has become involved with a local Christian youth group. So far I have avoided all her friendly invitations to go along, but this time she invites me to see a Christian film with her and I decide to go. Her mother takes us and sits with us.*

*As the film* (The Cross and Switchblade) *concludes, her youth leader, a young man in his early twenties, gets up on stage and asks us to bow our heads as he gives thanks for the film in prayer. I'm no stranger to prayer and happily do this. He then requests that we keep our heads bowed, and that if anyone would like to find out more about being a Christian, would they like to go to the back of the hall where someone will talk to them. Before I know it my heart starts to thump like it's going to jump out of my chest. All I can think of is, 'I'm OK, I go to church. I'm OK, I go to church.' The next thing I know is I'm on my feet, have kicked over someone's tin of Coke, and apparently (according to someone watching – I can't remember), have run to the back. There a local Baptist minister sits down on a table with me and prays with me. By this time the overwhelming shaking has started. As I reflect, with the benefit of hindsight, I recognise that I was quite simply overcome by the power of the Holy Spirit. I remember wanting to encounter God at the end of the film, the same way as the people portrayed in the film did, but I never thought it could be like this. For me this was when it all started, March 16th 1981.*

I was overcome by God, and the direction of my life was altered, something that God has gone on to do many times since. Yet, I also have to recognise that some Pagans claim similar experiences and I am not prepared to follow the fundamentalist route of simply labelling their experiences as counterfeit. All of us at times have doubts and for some of us it is the memory of these spiritual encounters that have held us on the path that we tread. For me, it is why I have remained a Christian, but it is important that Christians recognise that some people turn to Paganism because they felt called and had spiritual encounters with deities that go by other names. These encounters appear to seem just as real to them as mine did to me. The question it poses for us is: what shall we do with this knowledge? As I've said, many Christians use it simply to condemn Pagans as having counterfeit experiences, but who are we to judge? I think there is much more understanding and dialogue to be had, which is a part of the reason for writing this book in the first place.

## The painful experiences of Christianity

By far the greatest shock for me in speaking to Pagans in this country is that one story keeps repeating itself over and over again. A very large proportion of Pagans in this country are ex-Christians. I'm not going to try and put a figure to that in terms of a percentage, but in some groups, particularly in the forty-plus age group, I was surprised by how many seemed to have a story to tell. For some, as I mentioned earlier, it was simply a case of church not being spiritual enough. They tried it, perhaps grew up with it, but the services they attended were dry, cold and boring. For others they found that their free-thinking natures and questions were frowned upon by church leaders. Several told me that they had directly been instructed to stop asking questions and just accept what they had been told. Then it gets worse... I've been told stories of being on the wrong end of bullying, spiritual abuse and physical abuse. Over and over again I have heard Pagans tell me how they were once church-going Christians, but felt eased or pushed out of the church, or had to leave to preserve their own sanity. It was only after they left, and were still spiritually hungry, that they encountered Paganism. So, to Christians who are wondering why people are looking to Paganism rather than to Christianity, we need to consider the role that our churches play in the spiritual decisions people make. Anecdotally, at least, it seems we have pushed a lot of people away and we, therefore, need to ask questions about our own practices before criticising those of others.

## Notes for Chapter 2

1    diZerega G., *Pagans and Christians*, Minnesota U.S.A.: Llewellyn, 2004, 44.

## Chapter Three

# Wicca and Witchcraft

## Introduction

This book began by looking at some of the generalities about Pagan belief to help us build a picture of a very different approach to spirituality from that of those brought up with Christianity, or indeed any of the monotheistic world religions. We can now turn to the specific paths within Paganism, and in some ways the material that I'm going to present necessarily becomes a little more dense. I've decided to begin with Wicca and Witchcraft because they are the headline-grabbing Pagan paths which, sadly, are most likely to inspire fear and loathing on behalf of the public. This is something that I would very much like to see changed because, as with all aspects of Paganism, once one gets behind the tabloid headlines and meets the people, a very different reality emerges:

*We have very deliberately gone to St. Nectan's Glen for two reasons: first, I have been visiting this holy place since childhood and it's a special place both for me and for Alison. Secondly, after years in the doldrums, the Glen has been bought and is under new management. We've seen some of the publicity and it looks to us as if the slightly Pagan nature of the place that had grown over the last few years has become far more overtly expressed. We wander through the green and leafy woodland alongside the babbling stream, drinking in the steep-sided slopes and remembering how many times we have done this before when we reach the new sign. Its appearance is in stark contrast to the run-down nature of the one seen at our last visit and from here on in it is clear that far more care has been taken over the grounds, a care which becomes even more apparent as we reach the terrace where the outdoor café is. We walk through the gates and are greeted by a tall woman with a big smile who welcomes us, introduces herself as 'Gypsy' and invites us to take a seat. When she returns to take our order I notice that she's wearing a pentacle around her neck. She asks if we're on holiday and Alison responds with, 'It's complicated.' I explain that I'm an Anglican priest on study leave and that I'm trying to meet Pagans and find out about what they believe. She laughs warmly and says, in her broad West Country accent, 'Well I didn't burst into flames then!' We get on very easily and she tells us about her sisters, and only later does it become apparent that these 'sisters' are the other witches with whom she works and relaxes. They are closer than friends.*

*We explain that our journey around the country has been full of surprises and new friendships but, now we have arrived in Cornwall we've had rather more difficulty in getting anyone to talk with us about their beliefs. 'Wait here a moment', she says, as she disappears off into the shop. She returns with the custodian, Loz, a wonderful character who is initially a little intimidating as he sits down across from me at the table, leans forward and proceeds to question me closely about who I am and what I'm trying to accomplish. I realise that he is concerned that I may be some judgemental Christian fundamentalist about to tell him to 'turn or burn', and I try to reassure him that I am here only to learn. The questioning goes on for a few minutes and then he leans back, seeming to relax, and I breathe a little easier. If this was a test then I think I've passed. 'So then', he says with a smile, 'We've got a drumming circle on Thursday night. Would you like to come?' 'Can I bring my drum?', I respond. 'You play? Great! Bring it with you.'*

*Thursday night comes and after a wonderful evening of drumming we adjourn to the Cobweb Inn in Boscastle. It is here that Gypsy tells us what had actually happened when we arrived at the café. She had looked up, seen me, and had a momentary vision of a dog-collar.*

*The thing is, I wasn't wearing one and I know that I don't have the appearance that many people have in mind of a traditional vicar. I hadn't even taken a dog collar with me on study leave, yet that was what she had seen and that vision was what had led to the conversation which had opened the door to an encounter that went on to develop into a genuine friendship. I realise that Witches are not remotely like I had thought they would be, and that this is not so much about spells as about spirituality.*

I'll come back to the events around this encounter because it led on to so many other things taking place. One of the key things about it, though, was the beginnings of an understanding about the differences between Wicca and Witchcraft, and that, although they are intimately linked, they are not the same thing. This difference requires exploring.

## Wicca and Witchcraft

The confusion arises because the followers of both paths readily call themselves 'Witches'. The name 'Witch' has long been a term of abuse, but it appears that modern Wiccans are determined to rehabilitate it and give it a more positive spin, although I suspect that doing so will be an uphill struggle. So, what then is the difference between Wicca and Witchcraft? They are linked closely together; they are not one and the same. The link between the two paths is very strong and they merge into each other in places, but the key difference between them is that Wicca is a religion with its own deities, the Goddess and the God, whereas Witchcraft is a practice based around spellcraft which can be adapted to many different spiritual traditions. As I met more traditional Witches it became abundantly clear that not all who practise Witchcraft are Wiccans. Witchcraft revolves around the practice of magick to bring about change. (NB I have followed the common Pagan and occult practice of adding the 'k' to the word 'magic' to show the difference between stage magic, which is illusion, and magick which is used with the intent of bringing about a real change in the world by the imposition of one's will and/or the use of spirits to accomplish one's desires.) The practice of magick, however, does not require one to also be involved in any specific religious practice. Witches and the use of magick appear to have existed throughout recorded history. Wicca, however, is a religion that has a traceable history dating back only as far as the 1950s, although many elements were in place nearer the turn of the century.

This chapter, therefore, will begin with Wicca before considering Witchcraft as a second section. The third section will consider elements that are clearly common to both although, as with all Pagan paths, there are no specific delineations.

## Part One – Wicca

### A brief outline of the history of Wicca

The word 'Wicca' has rather disputed roots. Margot Adler[1] links 'Wicca' with 'Witch' stating that it comes from

> '..the Indo-European roots 'wic' and 'weik' meaning to bend or turn... A Witch would be a woman (or a man) skilled in the craft of shaping, bending and changing reality.'

However, d'Este and Rankine[2] suggest a number of different alternatives. They quote Leland from *Gypsy Sorcery* published in 1889 to suggest that 'Wicca' comes from 'witga' or 'witega', an Anglo-Saxon word for prophet, seer, magician or sorcerer. However, they also add the possibilities of the Indo-European root 'wek', which means 'voice', which could refer to a person who summons supernatural elements with their voice. For me, though, the one which seems most closely to reflect the religious nature of Wicca is the comment by Picton, writing in 1874, who suggested that the root of the word 'Wicca' may come from the low German 'wijck' or 'wicca' which means 'sacred', or 'devoted.' There may be some truth in all of these, but religious devotion and awe is something which I have, indeed, observed amongst Wiccans as being a defining characteristic:

*We are again sitting outside the Cobweb Inn in Boscastle. It's been another wonderful evening of drumming and now we're finishing it all off by sitting and chatting informally outside, drinks in hand, as we hear one story after another recounted by Gypsy who seems to have got herself into a variety of amusing scrapes and encounters with reality, such as when she worked in a local Christian bookshop for a fortnight before realising that it was actually a Christian shop! And then, in the midst of the laughter, someone looks up and sees the full moon, finally breaking through the dismal summer we've had. A hush descends on the group before one of them, Vicki, says, 'Isn't She beautiful.' They all agree, and for the first time I recognise honour, worship and awe amongst a group of Wiccans.*

For Wiccans the moon is the icon of the Goddess who is the object of their worship. When she is full, as she was on that night, anyone can see the beauty and the romance that she evokes. For Wiccans (and for Witches) the moon means far more. I suspect that the word 'Wicca' may have come from a number of places, but the honouring and worshipping nature that I have observed makes me think that the low German root word seems to be the one that most clearly describes the behaviour of a group of Wiccans.

Wicca as a religion may often claim to have ancient roots, and certainly many of its founding myths and stories can be traced back through history. However, the condensing of these ideas into a religion can be largely traced to a person called Gerald Gardner. Gardner was born in 1884 and became a well-travelled man, spending a great deal of his time in the Far East, largely in what was then Malaya where he developed an interest in folk customs and magick, eventually seeing himself as an anthropologist. Throughout the 1930s Gardner's interests in esoteric beliefs, folk religions and Paganism grew, and he spent a brief time with a Rosicrucian order in Hampshire. The turning point came when he was initiated as a Witch in the New Forest Coven in September 1939. He claimed that this coven was one of a handful of survivors of the ancient pre-Christian Witch-Cult of the British Isles, a claim that had been made by the author Margaret Murray in her book of 1921, *The Witch-Cult of Western Europe*. Gardner went on to publish *Witchcraft Today* in 1954 with a preface by Murray. In 1953 he initiated a young woman, Doreen Valiente, into Wicca who went on to become the High Priestess of his Bricket Wood Coven and to help him rewrite his *Book of Shadows*, the book which outlined the rituals practised within Wicca. (Valiente, herself, went on to play an extremely influential role in the development of Wicca.) Gardner had claimed that much of the book was ancient and fragmentary and so he had filled in the gaps with his own material and that of other contemporary sources, such as the infamous Aleister Crowley, the English Occultist and Esotericist[3]. What then became known as Gardnerian Wicca is based around the practices laid out in this book and Gerald Gardner is often referred to as 'the father of Wicca'.

However, there is more to Wicca than this very brief history suggests. The 1970s saw the beginnings of an historical re-engagement with the source material leading to a great many questions being asked about how much truth lay behind the idea of a surviving pre-Christian Witch-Cult. Piece by piece much of the historicity has been dismantled leading modern scholars, such as Ronald Hutton[4], to doubt that there is any factual evidence for an underground movement that survived by secrecy. Recent scholarship seems to suggest that Gardner was a good self-publicist, a contributing factor to his relationship with Valiente and others eventually breaking down, and that there is very little proof of any traceable connection to an earlier 'Old Religion', as Wicca is often called. And yet, regardless of how much truth there is to the mythology surrounding its birth, what cannot be denied is that modern Wicca has captured the Zeitgeist, the trend of thought of this day and age. What has been created, and continues to evolve, is a valid new religious movement that focusses on the belief that the ultimate deity is a duet of Goddess and God, and possesses a recognition of the importance of the divine feminine, something that is often absent from much of the overly masculine focus of God in Judaism, Christianity and Islam. This new religion finds its focus in the cycles of the moon and the seasons of the year and, therefore, as well as valuing women, it has an eco-centric spirituality in a time when the earth is undergoing violent exploitation in a way never before seen. Wicca sees itself as a force for good in these times and, given the caring nature of many of its followers, who can deny that? Whilst its history may be shrouded in rather creative modern mythology, it is evolving into a religion whose followers really seem to care for each other:

*As we sit outside The Cobweb Inn once again, soaking up the atmos-phere, I look around at the way this circle of friends, united by their religion, treat each other. They have told me stories about how not one of them is ever in need for long. When one was made homeless by circumstance another opened her doors and provided a room for as long as it was needed. I know it's not all perfect. I know there are disagreements and I know that some of the friendships are quite fragile. But the way in which many of the women treat each other like the sisters that they call themselves, and the way in which they have welcomed us in at face value is not what I expected to find. But, perhaps what has shocked me most, was realising that almost unconsciously I was comparing them to how Luke describes the early church in Acts 4 and how the disciples looked out for the needs of each other. It's not quite the same as what I see here, for example the disciples and early Christians held all things in common and were far more radical in the way they lived out their beliefs, but it is, nevertheless, a cause for some deep reflection...*

I am also aware that it isn't always like this! Communities do not always remain as loving fellowships, and I know of Pagan groups that have collapsed in recrimination and anger, usually when someone who is greedy for power tries to take over. One only has to look at the power struggles in early Wicca to see human frailties come to the fore, but I also recognise that I have seen and experienced similar things in Christian churches and organisations too. However, to those who try to deny Wicca's validity because of its newness, I can only respond that every religion had to start somewhere and at sometime. D'Este and Rankine[5] again capture the essence of its history with these words:

'One point we must make is that the further back in time we go, the less evidence there is for direct lines of descent for practices and beliefs. Nevertheless... there are techniques and references from the ancient world which parallel some of the practices found in Wicca.'

Wicca is not my religion and I am not tempted to join up, but it is an evolving religious movement that deserves our respect and a relationship that includes constructive dialogue. To that end, it's time to look a little more closely at some particular aspects of Wicca before we turn to Traditional Witchcraft. The place to begin is with the objects of their veneration.

## The Goddess and the God

As with so many other aspects of Paganism, the Wiccan understanding of deity is very different from those brought up within a monotheistic culture. For Christians, God is a Trinity: Father, Son and Holy Spirit and all orthodox Christians will share this belief, however they interpret it. Most Christians will have some form of creedal statement that they are at least mostly content to say. For Wiccans, however, there are generalities rather than absolutes. In Christianity there is one focus: God, and theology is there to better understand that one God. In Wicca there is a very different feel to the study of deity, with a much broader approach simply because there is a much wider array of beliefs. There are, however, some general truths that are shared by most Wiccans. Most believe in two principal deities, the Goddess and the God, but they can at the same time hold that in tension with being polytheistic, believing in many goddesses and gods. This apparent paradox is resolved by the statement I have heard many times: 'All goddesses are but one Goddess, and all gods are but one God.' In practice, I have tended to hear Wiccans talk about the different aspects of the Goddess and the God as each having a different name. So, for example, Aphrodite, goddess of love, is the love aspect of the one Goddess, except she may well be treated as a different goddess.

One of the most important aspects of both God and Goddess is their cyclical nature. Both are tied to the seasons, with the Goddess also tied to the lunar cycle, and are also tools by which the different stages of life are valued:

*Alison and I are sitting in the downstairs room of one of the Cornish Witches, Ruth. It is a beautifully decorated space which includes her own altar, many paintings and various musical instruments. Ruth and Vicki have been telling us excitedly for days about their vision to record an album. My wife, Alison, has her own recording studio and has offered to collaborate with them and so we're having this first meeting to listen to some of the chants and songs and to offer some suggestions for arrangements and rhythms. The evening goes well and at some point I ask them for the name of their group. They tell me that they have decided to call it 'Crone-Heart' to reflect their stage in life. None of them look remotely like the caricature of a*

*crone, so they explain to me that it is a simple description of a valued
stage in life, that as older women they are beyond child-bearing and
have moved into the third stage of womanhood – becoming a crone.*

This is a typically Wiccan valuing of womanhood, that even
though many of the aspects of youth have passed, and contrary
to the values of most modern western cultures, they value
themselves and are valued in their third stage of life. For women
they recognise three stages in life: maiden, mother and crone, and
these are represented by the three stages of the moon's cycle:
waxing, full and waning. Each has its own characteristics and
each is valued.

What is not always so clearly recognised is that it is not just
the Goddess who has a triple-aspect; the God, her consort, also
has three sides. He, too, is child, adult and sage, mirroring her
maiden, mother and crone. However, as discussed by Marian
Green[6], he also has three aspects that derive from the three
worlds he represents. In order to understand this we first need a
little background with an important point to underline. The God
is often called 'The Horned God' and is usually portrayed with
horns protruding from his brow. It is at this point that many
Christians begin to become paranoid that Wiccans are actually
worshipping the devil. I will say more of this in the section on
Witchcraft, but let me underline here that there are few modern
Wiccans who even believe in the devil, let alone worship him!
The idea of the devil having horns is a medieval Christian fantasy
where the Pagan images of Pan, wild god of the forest and
eroticism, were conflated with the devil in order to try and
frighten people away from Paganism. In other words, it was
Christians who invented the idea that the devil looks like a Pagan
deity, and then become paranoid when Pagans portray their
horned god as they have always done. It is rather ironic that
Christians have made something up and then used it to accuse
Wiccans!

Green describes the god's three aspects like this:

'His hairy legs and hoofs link him with the animal kingdom, as their guardian and shepherd; his human body from the waist up, containing his human heart, shows that he can feel for the humankind in his care, and is their Lord of Life. His noble brow, dark thoughtful eyes sparkling with humour, and above these his lordly antlers, show that he is Divine in his own right. These antlers are the symbols of the sun's rays, of the power of Light, of co-creation, and like the points on the earthly king's golden crown, they signify royalty.'

It is the way the Goddess and God change through the seasons of the year that form the root of most Wiccan and indeed much Pagan ritual. Of course, as with many Pagan stories, there are numerous variations on how this works, but a general outline follows the Wiccan (and general Pagan) eightfold year, (known as the 'Wheel of the Year'), which is:

Winter Solstice – Yule – December 19-22
Imbolc – February 1
Spring Equinox – Ostara – March 19-22
Beltane – May 1
Summer Solstice – June 19-22
Lughnasadh/Lammas – Aug 1
Autumn Equinox – Mabon – September 19-22
Samhain – October 31

The pattern they follow is of the God being born of the Goddess in midwinter at the Winter Solstice. The God grows in strength through the spring bringing life back to the land. At the spring equinox he is filled with desire for the Goddess and at the beginning of May they marry, hence the May Day celebrations that are filled with fertility symbolism. The God reaches his peak in midsummer and thereafter begins to wane as the days shorten. By the autumn equinox, when night and day are of equal length, he is aging and the Goddess mourns his coming death which takes place at Samhain (pronounced sow-een), before he is born of the Goddess again at midwinter. Intermingled with this cycle is also another story of the willing self-sacrifice of the God at harvest, cut down to supply grain for the land, as told in the folkloric story of John Barleycorn. The cycle for the Goddess is of maiden, mother and crone before returning back to maiden, hence the Goddess doesn't die. For the God he is first her son, then her lover who impregnates her with himself. He becomes elderly sage before dying and returning to the ground before being reborn of the Goddess again at midwinter. Numerous different stories surround this basic outline, but the key point is to understand that Wiccan beliefs, like many other Pagan beliefs, are very clearly tied to the seasons celebrating eight sabbats, and are deeply honouring of womanhood and also of masculinity.

Wicca, being a religion of the moon, is also tied to its cycles, called esbats, with Wiccans meeting at full moons for their celebrations, which are often dedicated more specifically to the Goddess. It is at these meetings that magick may be worked and a ritual called 'Drawing down the moon' may be enacted. This is a specific invocation to the Goddess to enter the High Priestess. Two renowned and well-read scholarly Pagans have stated in a meeting at which I was present how, on many occasions, they have seen the High Priestess glow with an inner light at this point in the ritual. Some Christians may baulk at this because at face value it sounds rather like inviting possession, but, once again, it is necessary that we compare it with our own practice of inviting the Holy Spirit to fill us at our gatherings. Indeed the language Mark uses at the beginning of his Gospel to describe the Holy Spirit descending on Jesus at his baptism is the language of possession, of the Spirit coming 'into' Christ. It's important that we understand the deeply religious and feminine centredness of this practice and recognise that in Christianity, and indeed Judaism and Islam, the feminine aspect of divinity has very little emphasis, thus disempowering and disenfranchising women. It is little wonder that in modern western culture many young women are looking to Wicca as a way to express their spirituality – for where else is there for them to go?

## Wiccan Initiation

*'You can guess all you like Paul, I'm not telling you my initiatory name,' she said with a big grin on her face as we chatted about her initiation into Wicca.*

So went part of the conversation between myself and Helen Woodsford-Dean who runs Orkney Pagan Weddings with her husband Mark. Wicca, like Christianity, is an initiatory religion, as I came to understand from our conversation, and Helen had taken a new name at her initiation in a similar way to the names that are sometimes given at first communion or confirmation in some Christian traditions. The difference for Helen is that only five humans know her initiatory name, so if she hears someone calling her by that name she knows it is her gods calling her. For Christians the rite of initiation is baptism and when Christianity was itself a new religion, baptism took place on profession of faith, although from early on if the male head of the household professed faith in Christ then the whole household could be baptised with him. Initiation into Wicca, however, is always done as an adult and is a very individual thing. One can self-initiate and it can be deeply filled with meaning, but the general feeling seems to be that it is taken more seriously if one is initiated by someone senior in the tradition to which one is drawn. There are numerous different traditions of Wicca with Gardnerian being only one, even if his was (arguably) the first. Different traditions have different emphases, so, for example, Alexandrian Wicca, (after Alex Sanders who split off from

Gerald Gardner following a disagreement), tends to be more ritualistic than Gardnerian, but both have initiatory systems.

In many ways you could think of the different traditions within Wicca as being treated similarly by each other as the different denominations within Christianity. In both religions, different traditions or denominations have come about as the result of a disagreement and, with the passing of time, there usually comes a point when they recognise each other's validity. Likewise, though, just as there can be some sense of superiority between Christian denominations, so there can also be between different Wiccan traditions, with some Wiccans placing a great emphasis on tracing their initiatory 'pedigree' back to see which famous Wiccans are in their 'family' history. This is a fundamental difference from Christian initiation since all creedal churches state that there is 'One baptism'. In other words Christians generally aren't remotely bothered who baptised them whereas some (certainly not all) Wiccans are very concerned that they have a good 'lineage'.

The initiation rites are supposed to have been kept secret, recorded only in a coven's Book of Shadows. The reality is that several of these Book of Shadows have been published over the years and so the initiation rites are readily accessible with numerous different variations available online. It is interesting to note the similarity in initiatory rites between Gardnerian Wicca and Freemasonry. This, however, should come as no surprise since Gerald Gardner was himself a Freemason and used the Masonic rites as a basis for the rites of his new religion. The point of the initiation is more important than the history of how it was constructed, and the reason for being initiated is that one is making a lifetime commitment to the Goddess.

A basic outline of initiation is as follows: The rite will probably take place at a new moon rather than a full moon to symbolise the beginning of something new, although the person being initiated will have spent some time studying beforehand to prepare themselves. Traditionally, this will have been a year and a day. Where the initiation is into a circle or coven a great deal of trust will have been built and will be expected, but contrary to what so many people think, sex is **not** a part of the initiation and from within their own tradition would-be Wiccans are warned that if someone tries to convince them that sex *should* be involved, then that person ought to be reported to the relevant authorities. The only place where sex may be involved, (where it is called 'The Great Rite'), is in some forms of the Alexandrian third degree initiation, but even there most people expect this either to be in private between a couple who are already committed to each other, or to be performed symbolically using a ritual knife called an Athame, representing the male phallus, and a chalice, representing the female womb, wherein the knife is solemnly dipped into the chalice as a symbol of the union of the Goddess and the God bringing fertility to the land.

In ordinary or first-degree initiations a sacred circle is first cast to provide the ritual space. In some covens and traditions the initiation may be carried out 'sky-clad' or naked, but this is by no means universal. Several Wiccans have told me, with wry smiles and much merriment, that the only person seeing them naked is their partner! I therefore assume that not all initiations take place naked, but where they do it is nothing to do with sexual expression, but is, instead, meant to symbolise one's willingness to stand fully revealed to the Goddess with nothing held back. The initiate is then usually blindfolded to symbolise their lack of spiritual knowledge prior to this time, and may be loosely bound to symbolise having been bound, prior to this moment, to the trappings of materialism in the world. They are then led to the circle where a password, 'perfect love and perfect trust', is given and a question is posed. It is highly unlikely that the initiate will know what this question is in advance. On answering this question they are taken into the circle where the ritual proper takes place which enacts a death and rebirth symbolism ending with the bonds and blindfold being cast off. This is a way of enacting in one ritual the whole sense of the Wiccan Wheel of the Year as described above, where the fertility of the Earth is revered through the seasonal cycle of life, death and rebirth.

Now let me suggest something controversial for consideration by the reader. Those who are familiar with full immersion baptism in the church will recognise that the intention behind the Wiccan ritual is similar. In baptism a person is baptised into Christ and into his death and resurrection. When a person comes up out of the water they are counted as reborn. Baptism is one of what the church calls a sacrament which means two things: first a sacrament effects what it symbolises, so the baptism effects a rebirth into Christ. Secondly, a sacrament is an outward and visible sign of something that God is doing within, so as we pour water on the outside of a person so we believe the Holy Spirit of God deeply cleanses the person on the inside. For a Wiccan their initiation is also a deeply special and important rebirthing experience. They arrive as one person who wishes for rebirth and acceptance by the Goddess, and leave as someone who has been reborn into a dedication to their path and acceptance by the Goddess who they may call, 'The Lady'. Although the word 'sacrament' is unlikely to be used, the sense (and often experience) of having been changed on a deep level is similar. Of course, one is being reborn into different paths, either into Christ, or into the Goddess and her expression through the seasons, but both are rebirthing rituals.

## Wiccan Ethics

In Christianity we have got rather used to what seems like an awful lot of prohibitory commandments. Our religion sometimes seems, especially for outsiders, to be all about what we're not supposed to do. The reality is that Christian ethics were summed up very neatly by Christ when he said these words in Matthew 22:37-40:

'Jesus said to him, "You shall love the Lord your God with all your heart, and with all your soul, and with all your mind. This is the greatest and first commandment. And a second is like it: You shall love your neighbour as yourself. On these two commandments hang all the law and the prophets."'

In Wicca, since there is no specific sacred text, there has not been a multiplication of ethical rules. There is, however, one simple commandment and it's called the Wiccan Rede:

'An' it harm none – do what thou wilt.'

This is not a licence to do what you want. It more or less translates like this: You may do what you want to do, specifically in order to grow spiritually, so long as what you do does not in any way bring harm to another. Some simplify this to, 'Harm none.' This is a very strong ethic which bears much similarity to the second commandment Jesus gave. There are, however, differences too. Jesus' commandment is both pro-active and other-focussed. The reason for this is the emphasis on love with the use in the original texts of the Greek word *agapé*. This kind of love cannot just happen, it's an active response to a perceived need. In other words, Jesus' second commandment begins with the other person, looking to what needs to be done to serve them. The Wiccan Rede, however, begins with the self, requiring of them that they keep an eye on the possible outcomes of their actions and ask themselves whether those actions will cause harm to another. This is, of course, a difficult task since there are so often unexpected outcomes to our actions, but its primary focus is nevertheless on the self. It asks the question, 'What do *I* want to do?' before it asks the question, 'How will this affect someone else?' Many of the Wiccans I know who are active in spellcraft and magick are most definitely focussed outwardly to the needs of others, but this is not a commandment, just a testament to their giving nature and moral standards. By the same token, sadly I know many professing Christians who seem never to have read the second commandment. In other words, the ethical standards people keep are not necessarily based on their beliefs.

Alongside the Wiccan Rede is another rule, not always stated quite so clearly, which is 'The Law of Threefold Return'. The belief is essentially that whatever the Wiccan sends out, they can expect to receive it back three times over. So, if Wiccans commit themselves to good actions then they will receive back within themselves the positive fruit of those actions. If a Wiccan chooses to curse someone then they should be prepared to receive the force of that curse back within themselves three times over. I will return to cursing below in the context of Traditional Witchcraft, but note again that the focus appears to be more on the outcome for the self.

## Part Two – Traditional Witchcraft

As I said at the beginning of this chapter, the confusion between Wicca and Witchcraft lies with both types of followers calling themselves Witches. A simple trawl around the internet suggests that some Traditional Witches are not at all happy with this. So what then is Traditional Witchcraft?

### Traditional Witchcraft

The basic difference between Wicca and Witchcraft is in terms of belief versus practice. Wicca is a reasonably well-defined religion with its own belief system and deities who are venerated, most specifically the Goddess and the Horned God. Witchcraft, on the other hand, is not a religion, venerating no specific deities, although many claim that they work with deities or spirits as equals. Witchcraft is, instead, a set of practices that can be a part of any religious system or stand-alone. It is thought of as a craft to be learned, like being a blacksmith, so with practice one can become magickally quite adept. Whilst Wicca is a modern religion with a traceable history, albeit drawing on ancient stories and beliefs, the practice of witchcraft dates much further back in history. Within the Judeo-Christian religion one does not have to look far before one encounters witchcraft. King Saul, the first king of Israel, dating back to a little over 1,000 BCE (before common era), encountered the Witch of Endor (referred to in some translations simply as a medium) before the battle that took his life as he used her to summon the spirit of the dead prophet Samuel as recounted in 1 Samuel 28:3-25.

So, what then is a Witch? There are numerous definitions available, but it seems to me that a Witch is someone who uses magick to effect a change on reality, either by imposition of their own will or by the use of summoned spirits. They may also claim a hereditary lineage. Wicca, being a religion, has a strong moral code. Witchcraft, on the other hand, is amoral. That is not to say it should be considered immoral, it is simply that magick is a tool for them in just the same way that one can use a spanner to undo a nut, or as a weapon to strike someone with. Different Witches will use 'the Craft' to different ends depending on their own personalities. Some have adopted Robert Cochrane's 'Witches Law' which states:

'Do not do what you desire – do what is necessary. Take all you are given – give all of yourself. What I have – I hold! When all else is lost, and not until then, prepare to die with dignity.'

This comes from Cochrane's sixth letter to an American Witch named Joe Wilson. The irony of this is that Cochrane's claims to be a hereditary, traditional Witch have little supporting evidence.

He was a contemporary of Gerald Gardner, although he claimed an older lineage, but the evidence suggests instead that much of his story was concocted[7]. Nevertheless, the first line of his Witches' Law, 'Do not do what you desire – do what is necessary', seems to have been adopted by at least some of those who call themselves Traditional or Hereditary Witches. There is no ethical code within this, which is meant as an observation rather than a criticism, but it does highlight the willingness of some Traditional Witches to do things by magick that Wiccans would not consider. Most are responsible and many times I have heard or read mature counsel against using a particular spell, for example a love spell, since it can backfire and make it rather difficult to get rid of the suitor at a later date if love doesn't last. Notice again, though, that the emphasis is on the self rather than on the ethics of enticing someone with a love spell. Inevitably, though, if we are going to think about the use of magick, we need to consider the difficult subject of cursing because it is an area that many people assume comes as second nature to Witches.

## Cursing

I owe special thanks to several Pagans who were very open to discussing this most difficult of subjects. They all said that they were quite happy to be associated with their comments as they felt that with something as serious as this they should be willing to take the flak for what they believe in and have sometimes done. I admire their courage and, indeed, following a discussion on this matter one of them went on to post some detailed comments about her experience of cursing on her public blog. However, despite their willing assent to being included by name here, I have chosen not to. I am aware from personal experience of just how strong the tide of public opinion can be, and whilst they are not afraid of this, having the courage of their own convictions, I personally don't want to have to take responsibility for bringing disrepute on to what should be untarnished local reputations. As I said in the introduction to this book, many of the people I've met in my journey to understand Paganism have become close personal friends. We may not believe the same things but, as I hope has become abundantly clear, I do not believe them to be evil and bear them no ill will whatsoever, and so I have chosen not to mention who has had these conversations with me in order to avoid any local difficulties for them that could otherwise be provoked.

In any book like this it is the most salacious parts that people will seize on, such as the subject of cursing, and so in writing about this I recognise that I am risking the possibility of under-mining my own aim, of helping people to understand Paganism. Yet to omit the subject would mean to leave out something important in the Witchcraft tradition.

The first point to make about cursing is that it begins with what I have heard from several sources, with wry smiles, as being about 'headology' (quoting Terry Pratchett)! What they mean is that if people think they can be cursed by someone then they have voluntarily ceded power to that person. In believing that they can be cursed they have opened themselves up to a third party having a degree of control over them. In other words, if you think someone has cursed you then you will behave as if you have been cursed – a kind of anti-placebo. Whilst one might argue that our logical/scientific culture has reduced this cursing ability, I would suggest that such opinions are normally voiced only by those who, in their enthusiastic acceptance of secularism, have disregarded humanity's innate spirituality. I suspect that the average person may be far more open to this kind of psycho-logical pressure than we might think. I was told (although have no reference with which to verify this) that a friend of one of my Pagan contacts works in an office in Malaysia where cursing is a recognised issue and that if someone feels they have been cursed then they will openly take time off from work to go and have the curse lifted without any fear of repercussion from their employer. In the UK that would be unheard of, but certainly in some other parts of the world it is an accepted part of life:

*'I have a piece of black card with a pentacle inscribed on it', 'James' explained to me. 'I've never given it to anyone, but have kept it just in case someone is really nasty to me. I know the effect it would have if I gave it to that person. They would begin mentally to associate every-thing that went wrong with that piece of card. I wouldn't actually have to curse them; they would do all the work themselves.' His wife chimed in that she had a friend who, if slighted in the pub, would wait until the person who had offended them went to the toilet and would then openly take out a fresh tissue, wipe it around the edge of the glass of the person who had been nasty to them, and then tuck it away in their pocket and leave. Inevitably word would get back to the person who had gone to the toilet of what had happened. Nothing was ever done with the saliva impregnated tissue, but the threat that the person who did this had power and could use it usually did all that was needed!*

We may well live in what we call a technological culture, but scratch away at the surface and a fear of spiritual consequences is not far down in the western veneer.

I ought also to mention that, contrary to what some might believe, cursing is not the sole preserve of those engaged in black magic. Another person said to me that she reserved the right to curse someone *in extremis* to protect herself. It seems unlikely to me that many of those following a Wiccan path would necessarily curse (or at least make a habit of it), especially given the Wiccan Rede, (the closest thing to a commandment), 'An' it harm none, do what thou wilt.' With Wicca being a religion dedicated to the love of the Goddess and the God and looking for recognition as an acceptable religion, cursing is not something that many would consider.

*Our conversation ranged over many subjects as we sat outside in the nighttime warmth of the summer. Eventually, it felt like we had talked around enough of our beliefs for me to venture the question, "Have any of you any thoughts about cursing?" There was a very short silence before they responded, almost as one, that none of them would ever, EVER consider cursing someone. They all believed strongly in the law of threefold return and just simply wouldn't risk it. Furthermore, it simply wasn't in their natures. As I got to know them better over the next few months I would have to agree with that. I simply couldn't envisage any of them wanting to curse someone else.*

Issuing a curse would be difficult for a Wiccan dedicated to the path of worshipping a loving Goddess, and they would be well aware of the effect it may have on them if they did curse. Witchcraft, however, is, as I've said, a craft which is open to any who wish to learn it, and cursing is simply a part of the craft. Two people have quoted to me word for word that, 'If you can't hex, you can't heal'. However, those who do curse know very well that they must also bear the consequences of doing so, and that cursing is a last resort. For that reason, even those who wouldn't necessarily think of themselves as Traditional Witches, usually baulk at the idea:

*We sat in the back of his shop which he had very generously closed over lunchtime in order to spend time talking with me. Although he wasn't a Witch himself, the Craft was certainly a part of his life. He was very good with Tarot, as attested by a mutual friend, and thought of himself as a Mage. He explained that a woman had come in whose husband had committed adultery. She wanted to pay him to curse the woman in question, specifically to have a car crash. He repeatedly said 'no' because it wasn't possible to control a curse, and so others may be hurt in the fallout. She hadn't thought of that. On top of all that, he explained to her, he didn't want to take the hit in terms of the three-fold return.*

Pagans take cursing seriously, and I know of one who relented once he saw the physical effect it was having on the person he had cursed, causing him to withdraw it. However, if nothing else has worked in sorting out an unjust situation in which they have been badly maligned, *in extremis* some will turn to cursing. So a scenario may be, as it has been explained to me, that someone has been done a very bad turn. Their first attempt at solving the issue, as with many people when wronged by another, will be to try and have a conversation with the antagonist. If this doesn't work they may even go so far as to seek legal redress. For the serious Pagan (rather than the uninformed dabbler) cursing is always the last resort to obtain justice simply because of the potential consequences for the person who issues the curse. One friend explained how she had cursed a woman who had systematically sought to do her and her family a great wrong. This is the only time she has ever cursed someone and now, several years on, she is still struggling with the psycho-spiritual consequences to herself and the guilt she carries. As to whether it had any effect, on that account she could give no answer; she simply didn't know. However, another woman explained to me that she has cursed several people for whom there was no other way to get justice for how she was wronged:

*Another meeting in another pub and I seem to be getting a taste for real ale. I asked her how she actually put a curse on someone. She explained, 'Usually I probe the spiritual realm around me, looking for something unsavoury and give it a direction, an address, how they can find the person who has hurt me.' 'So what happens next?' I asked. 'Usually they will have a serious illness or an accident.' She was not remotely flippant in the way she said this. She took it very seriously and was fully aware of the implications of what she had said. 'So then', I continued, 'What about the law of threefold return?' 'You take the hit,' she replied, 'If you're prepared to take responsibility for issuing a curse on someone then you have to be prepared for the fallout that comes as a result of it.' I was impressed by her candour as well as the seriousness with which she took the implications for herself. Taking responsibility for one's actions is important to them when magick of this type is being considered.*

What concerns me most is the nature of the spirits with which a person is dealing in bringing down a curse on someone else. Most Pagans will go to great lengths to protect themselves from unsavoury spiritual influences. The act of casting a circle before a ritual is designed for precisely this effect. Many Pagans, following rituals based on those written in the Grimoires, (ancient magick books often based on Jewish Kabbalist magick), will call on a number of archangels to come and protect them before they begin any ritual or spellworking. It therefore seems quite a dangerous practice to deliberately seek out spirits who would choose to harm rather than help. From a Christian perspective, orthodox teaching is that such spirits may even be fallen angels. Such beings are credited as being incredibly powerful and to seek to direct them to harm another would seem to be a dangerous thing to do. I am not convinced that fallen angels are the only spirits that someone can call upon, but given biblical stories of the feats angels are capable of, the thought of inciting a fallen angel to do harm concerns me because of the power that one may be unleashing on oneself. I would not wish to be indebted to such a being.

It's also worth mentioning that sometimes a more ritualistic form of cursing is done with the use of a poppet, which is a doll designed especially to represent a particular person. It may even incorporate something physical, such as a hair from the person it represents. Harm is inflicted on the doll in order that something similar is inflicted on the person it represents. (It's amazing how popular Adolf Hitler poppets were during the Second World War, even before Witchcraft was once again legalised in the UK!) A common practice would be to stick pins in the doll. Now to some this may sound like mumbo-jumbo but experience suggests otherwise:

> *As I approached the staircase in the museum I was increasingly struck by a sense of being ill at ease. One woman has already told me that she can't get anywhere near this part of the building without feeling physically sick or crying. For some, they might cite the power of suggestion, but all I can say is that as I went up the staircase it felt as if there was something truly nasty at the top. Sure enough, when I turned the corner, there was a glass cabinet in front of me that felt somehow vile, unclean, even from a distance of a couple of metres. When I forced myself to go over to the cabinet, I found that it contained numerous examples of cursed poppets. The palpable sense of darkness and evil surrounding them was unnerving to say the least. Some may say that this is all down to psychology again, but I would have to say that I am far from the only person to have difficulties being near this particular collection.*

A Hedgewitch told me that, in her opinion, such things should be burned rather than curated.

There is, indeed, a great divide in opinion amongst Pagans concerning cursing and Christians should take care not to assume that all Pagans curse. My experiences and conversations suggest quite the opposite; that very few do, and those that do take it very seriously as an option of last resort.

Now, one could argue that the belief in the power of cursing held by the practitioner is simply another example of the power of psychological suggestion. This time, however, it is operating in the opposite direction in that the person they cursed had something unfortunate happen to them quite by chance, but the one who cursed them interpreted it as meaning that their curse had been effective. Like all spiritual matters it is difficult to tell, and I've already explained my feelings regarding being close to a number of cursed poppets as justification for suspecting something is genuinely taking place. A common saying amongst Christians when faced with scepticism is, 'When I pray, coincidences happen'. Sometimes what takes place is genuine coincidence, and sometimes it is an answer to prayer, and between lies the grey space in which we simply don't know. I suspect the same happens with cursing. There will be occasions when it has an effect and there will be occasions when the effect is coincidence; but, for spiritual people, whatever their religion, we understand from experience that spiritual effects on the world around us are genuine, and I therefore believe that cursing can have an effect. I also admit to being more than a little concerned about it. This is the one part of the book that I have had to think very carefully about before writing in case I inadvertently encourage someone to try it. The counsel I would offer is that if there are any reading this who have considered cursing, avoid it. A desire for vengeance and retribution can eat away at the core of our being and change us, and that's before the potential backwash of dealing with spiritual powers far more powerful than we are.

So what are Christians to make of this? St. Paul gave his followers the command, 'Bless those who persecute you. Bless and do not curse.' Romans 12:14. Having said that, St. Paul twice calls down a curse on those who were misleading the Galatian church in Galatians 1. Christ was even more radical when he said:

'Love your enemies, do good to those who hate you, bless those who curse you, pray for those who abuse you.' Luke 6:27-8

This stands as a total opposite to the idea of cursing someone who has done us wrong. One can understand why because Christ's mission was to disempower hatred. When a person responds to evil with a curse, the amount of evil is magnified. When someone responds to evil with a blessing the force of hatred loses all power. One could make an argument that this is precisely what the cross of Christ was designed to do; to take all the evil that humanity could throw at it, and not to retaliate. When we do not respond to evil by cursing, then what we do is simply to make the world a better place because evil has not multiplied and has instead been replaced by good. Evil has a habit of snowballing to greater evils, but forgiveness stops that taking place. It's a shame that forgiveness is so hard for us!

I am going to risk venturing a personal opinion here. I admit that cursing is one of the most difficult subjects to write about. I felt uncomfortable when I spoke with Pagans about this subject, but then maybe if Christianity had been treated as badly by the press, institutional religion and the general populace as Paganism has been then I imagine I might feel a little more in need of ways to protect myself from the evil wished on my fellow believers and I. Christ commanded, 'Do not judge or you will be judged', so I am not about to start judging Pagans for this practice. I may not like it, and I would not want it to be a part of my spiritual armoury, but having spoken about it I think I can see why they feel that issuing a curse as a last resort is a viable option within their tradition. I am also reminded of how one prominent and open Pagan, who has always seemed to me as someone concerned to do the right thing, has been subject to vile statements of hatred in his village from a small number of local and visiting Christians who have been willing to blame him and his colleagues for any misfortune that takes place.

Of special interest, however, is that whilst we might differ on the subject of cursing, it is interesting that there is a related spiritual activity that Pagans and Christians share in common, and that is 'binding', the action by which the influence of something spiritual is stopped. For the Christian we look to the saying of Jesus to the apostles in Matthew 16:19: '...what you bind on earth will be bound in heaven'. The use of the Greek makes it clear that those things which are bound can only be the things that would be bound by God, i.e., one cannot bind something that is inherently godly through this kind of prayer. In terms of prayer, Christians will usually only seek to bind an evil activity, but will sometimes pray a binding prayer on a particular group or even a person if we think they are being used for evil purposes. We might ask Christ to bind them from the evil they're trying to do, which would be a prayer, or we might actually bind them ourselves in the name of Christ. In the latter case that is a spiritual utterance conveying power and should not be done without preparation and thought since, in doing so, we are voluntarily wielding the spiritual power entrusted to us by Christ himself. This is a serious spiritual act and should not be taken lightly. More controversially, I suspect that for a Witch they would struggle to perceive the difference between a Christian binding in the name of Christ and a binding spell since both are intended to produce the same outcome, the spiritual binding of an evil force or a person doing an evil act. For someone issuing a binding spell they might need to do something more ritualistic such as making a poppet of the person they seek to bind and then putting tape around its mouth. It seems highly unlikely that a modern Witch would invoke the Christian God in doing so, but in earlier times there were people who referred to themselves as Cunning Folk who may well have used magick in this way. In either case the intended outcome is the same: to stop an evil act.

Now, I am fully aware that there are some who would say something along the lines of, 'You cannot use the devil to combat evil, and a binding spell is nothing more than a demonic counterfeit of a Christian prayer.' This is hard to argue with because it is difficult to use rationalism in spiritual matters since we are dealing with faith in the unseen. My main response would be that Jesus said a good tree would bear good fruit and a bad tree, bad fruit (Matthew.6:17), so if a person is good, you can see it from the works that they do. If someone is seeking to do good and is actively pursuing a course of love and justice via magick we should be challenged by that rather than simply condemning it, and we should humbly recognise that maybe there is more good intent in the world that is not of Christian origin than we like to admit. I know that for many readers this is an evasion, but once again I can only apologise and say that my experience of Pagans has been one of meeting some deeply spiritual people who believe different things from me, yet who seem to be operating as forces for good in the world. I struggle to believe that, given all the barbaric tools in his armoury including western imperialist driven wars that are sanctified by, for instance, North American right-wing Christian fundamentalism, the devil, however we perceive him, is particularly more active amongst the Pagan community than he is amongst any other religious (or indeed political) community. Cursing carries huge risks to the practitioner and Christians are commanded not to do it, but I remain unconvinced that those who do must therefore be agents of the devil. Cursing is not a popular subject, but I am saddened by the way in which Christians tend to use it as an example of how evil Pagans are without applying the same standards to themselves. We tend to make ourselves feel better by judging someone as being worse than us, but to do so is not Christlike, it is worldly.

## The Man in Black – the devil

I have already made it clear in the opening chapters that the devil is not a figure that you will find in the lives of many Pagans. They believe him to be a fictional character made up within Christianity as it evolved into a dualistic battle between good and evil, and has nothing to do with their own spiritual path. So why write about him here? Purely because there are so many Christians in all traditions, particularly in the more conservative ones, who write off all Pagan practice, and *especially* Witchcraft, as devil worship. This unthinking dismissal is lazy theology and belies a lack of understanding, even within Christianity, of what is said about the devil.

There is, however, one exception to the rule that Pagans do not believe in the devil. Amongst *some* Traditional Witches you may find him referred to as 'The Man in Black' for example. Now before we embark on any speculations on satanic orgies within Witchcraft, it's important that we understand what Christians can say about the devil based on the biblical accounts, and perhaps first of all I need to say who he is not. The devil is not a character who plays pipes, has horns and goat's feet with cloven hooves. That character is a conflation of the Pagan god of the forest known as Pan, and the Horned God known as Cernunnos, and it was the idea of the medieval church to portray the devil in this way in order to try and frighten country folk away from the old religions. So the devil is not Pan or Cernunnos. Nor is the devil a creature created by God to live in hell and torment people who aren't believers. Dante and Milton *et al.* have a lot to answer for. In fact, the latter part of the Revelation to St. John seems to indicate that hell is a place reserved for the devil and his demons to be consigned to at the end of this age, where they are destroyed. This is, of course, made more confusing by the letter of Jude 6 where the writer refers to fallen angels, i.e., demons, being kept in everlasting chains until the day of judgement. If that were so, then we would have to ask where all the demons that Jesus and the disciples cast out came from; this kind of confusion shows that the Bible does not have a consistent picture or a complete revelation of who the devil actually is. This may partly be because the intent is to show that God defeats evil and therefore we shouldn't get too worked up about it. The model of the Old Testament is not, as some might imagine, dualistic, with a battle between good and evil. In fact, it becomes fairly explicit in its emerging monotheism that all things are under God's charge. When something goes wrong in the Old Testament no one blames it on the devil. Instead it is believed to be God acting in judgement. So when the devil appears in the Old Testament, usually under the name Satan, which means 'Accuser', he is actually an agent of God. You might like to think of him as the witness for the prosecution. Two examples spring to mind: in the Book of Job he is the one who brings Job to God's attention, but he has to ask God's permission to test him. And in Zechariah 3 we find a prophetic picture of Joshua the high priest standing before God while Satan is stood at Joshua's right hand side hurling accusations at him. Is he evil? It's difficult to tell. He seems to be doing a job, that of prosecutor, of accuser, but he is nevertheless rebuked by God when he does so.

Even in the New Testament we find similar things where Satan seems to be used as a tool of God. For example, the Synoptic Gospels all record the Holy Spirit taking Jesus out into the wilderness in order to be tempted by the devil. But, we also find verses like Luke 22:31-32 where Jesus says

'Simon, Simon, listen! Satan has demanded to sift all of you like wheat, but I have prayed for you that your own faith may not fail; and you, when once you have turned back, strengthen your brothers.'

The Greek suggests that Satan asked permission of God to do this. St. Paul also mentions Satan as a tool of God such as in 1 Timothy 1:20

'...among them are Hymenaeus and Alexander, whom I have turned over to Satan, so that they may learn not to blaspheme.'

So why then do we call him a fallen angel and where does this idea of his being in opposition to God come from? The answer is quite complex. I don't wish to negate the idea that there is a progressive revelation of who the devil is in scripture, but some suggest that the idea of him being an angel who fell because of the sin of pride is hugely influenced by dualistic religions in the geographical area, such as Zoroastrianism, which had opposing forces of good and evil. As I said earlier, Judaism is not a dualistic religion. That is not to say that there was no being standing in opposition to God, it's just that, as the opening of the book of Job makes clear, the adversary was himself subject to God and had to seek permission before acting.

Some interpreters, therefore, look at passages such as this from Isaiah 14:12-15 and say they are about Satan:

'How you are fallen from heaven, O Day Star, son of Dawn!
    How you are cut down to the ground, you who laid the nations low!

You said in your heart, "I will ascend to heaven; I will raise my throne above the stars of God; I will sit on the mount of assembly on the heights of Zaphon;
    I will ascend to the tops of the clouds, I will make myself like the Most High."

But you are brought down to Sheol, to the depths of the Pit.'

Now that certainly sounds like our interpretation of the devil being an archangel who was full of pride, but who was then thrown out of heaven and cast down to the earth because of that pride. That is until we read earlier in the passage where in verse 4 Isaiah says, "You will take up this taunt against *the King of Babylon.*" So is that meant to be a prophetic picture of what will happen to the King of Babylon in return for what he did to the Jews? Probably, because that's the context of this part of Isaiah. Could it also be about an archangel being thrown out of heaven? Well, yes it might be because prophecy often works on several levels. Certainly some of the prophecies we use about Christ in the Old Testament were not originally written about him. Even the idea that the devil is the snake in the Garden of Eden is an interpretation of a story. In the original story in Genesis the snake is just that, a wily talking snake. But the snake clearly acts to sift Eve, to test her, to tempt her, to lie to her, and she fell for it. The action of the snake is consistent with the action of Satan, but the story is still about a snake.

What I am trying to show is that the person of the devil, of Satan, is not as clearly described in the Bible as some people assume. Scripture is not written in that manner, and so it seems to me that the most important point we can make is that it is not God's intention for us to take too much of an interest in the devil. We have to be careful not to let early Middle Eastern dualism colour our interpretation of scripture too much. The picture seems to be of an accuser who, nevertheless, has to obey God and has to get permission before doing anything. He seems to be used by God, but I get a feeling that with time we get a creature who is steadily consumed with the accusations he makes. At some point his permission to enter heaven seems to be revoked, with Jesus referring to him falling, like lightning, to the earth, and John in his Revelation, chapter 12, inferring that he was cast down to the earth and as he fell he enticed a third of the angels to follow him. Ultimately, near the end of Revelation, we read of the devil, being described as the one who deceives, being thrown into the lake of burning sulphur.

How then does this Christian and scriptural account compare with the Witches' understanding of the devil? Well, the first thing to say is to underline what I've already said, that modern Witchcraft is not devil worship. It is extremely difficult to determine what part the devil may or may not have played in earlier times since most of the records were written by those who persecuted Witches and it served their purpose to portray Witches in this light. In modern times Witchcraft is far more to do with magick, charms, herbs and the like, using practice and the will of the Witch to try and alter reality in line with the Witch's purpose, either for themselves or for another. However, it is also the only path within Paganism where a *small* number of followers do cite the devil as being a part of their belief system, but even there it is a minor part of what they believe.

Perhaps the most important aspect for Christians to understand is that the Traditional Witch's understanding of the devil is quite radically different from what I've outlined above, being largely devoid of any dualistic battle between good and evil. The above story is how the Bible views Satan who Christians also call the devil. At some point in history Christians began to call the Witch's god 'the devil', and Witches have essentially accepted that epithet and used the title themselves. But the devil of the Traditional Witch is not normally thought of as the Judeo-Christian Satan. For many he represents the darker, more animal and uncontrolled side of human nature and is more archetypal than actual. For those conversant with Jungian psychology, the devil in Traditional Witchcraft could be expressed as being the Shadow side, those parts of us that we deem less acceptable but nevertheless should be integrated with the whole. This is also consistent with the Pagan belief outlined earlier that evil does not exist but is more to do with context. So rather than being an actual being, for some on this path the devil represents a part of themselves.

For other Traditional Witches the devil is the personification of the wildness of nature. For them the idea is that when one gives oneself over to the devil it is actually about allowing the full forces of untamed passion and primal desire loose within oneself. As such it is viewed by some as being about rebelling against the more stultifying aspects of some parts of the church and its views on the dangers of passion. In reality most spiritual couples would actually affirm that God-given passion for one's beloved can and sometimes should be primal.

From conversations that I've had it would therefore be true to suggest that some Traditional Witches will engage with the devil, also known as 'the man in black', 'Owd Scrat' (from the Old High German 'Schrat' meaning a hairy wood daemon according to Jackson[8]), or even 'Old Hornie', but that the practice should be differentiated from Satanism, which I will touch on below. One Traditional Witch explained that he was as happy to pray to the devil as he was to pray to Jesus, which suggests to me that Witches are content to engage with what they see as powers of darkness and light so that balance may be sought within the magick that they intend to weave.

For some reading this from a Christian perspective there is quite possibly a degree of confusion by this point. The ingrainedness of the Christian dualistic world view is so strong that it is difficult to recognise that other religious paths do not necessarily share this. The typical reaction is to dismiss any non-dualistic path, which includes most of Paganism, as being counterfeit; its followers being misled by demons. This view owes much to the ideas of C.S. Lewis as outlined in his novel *The Screwtape Letters* wherein a senior demon explains to a junior demon that one of the greatest ploys the devil can play is to convince the world of his non-existence. This idea is at the root of much Christian thinking about Paganism and especially Witchcraft, but, whilst it bears consideration, it is also not exactly what one might consider to be a part of Christian systematic theology.

One final comment needs to be made in this context, which is to say that there is indeed such a thing as Satanism. It is largely a hedonistic practice with far fewer followers than fundamentalists would have us believe, and it is actually only those who call themselves 'Theistic Satanists' who genuinely worship Satan. Let me make it clear that this is not a Pagan practice. It is a perversion of Christian belief, but genuinely has nothing to do with any form of mainstream Pagan practice.

## Part Three – Elements Common to Wicca and Witchcraft

### Spells, Magick and Prayer

Spells and magick are perhaps the prime focus for Traditional Witchcraft, but are also a part of the lives of many Wiccans, although not all follow these practices since their main focus is more towards devotion to the Goddess and the God.

A question you may ask, though, is why would I put spells and prayer together in one heading? Simply because for some Pagans they are counted as the same thing, or as one explained to me, to his mind they were both ways of getting something done. To explore this we begin with how one should define a spell. For many it is to do with the power of words to shape reality. If the correct incantation is spoken in the right way and with the proper intent (intent is vital), using the correct elements (herbs/candles/etc.), then it is believed that an effect will take place on reality. One can then begin to see why some who engage in spellcraft look at some forms of prayer and believe them to be the same thing. A good example of this is the Eucharistic Prayer in a communion service. As the priest prays the prayer, especially in a high-church context, she or he believes that something takes place within the bread and the wine. For the Protestant they believe in transignification, which means a sacramental change in the symbolism of the bread and the wine so that they no longer signify food, but instead signify the body and blood of Christ. For the Roman Catholic and some High Anglicans they will believe in transubstantiation, which means that the actual substance is changed into the body and blood of Christ. Although the whole prayer is thought of as consecratory, it is the part of the prayer called the epiclesis, (meaning to perform an invocation of the Holy Spirit or ask for the Spirit's blessing on the bread and wine), at which this action is thought to take place. It is notable that the words that are spoken by the priest must be exactly as those laid down by the ruling council of the church. The priest may add or write a preface to the prayer, but everything else must be word for word exactly as laid out in the prayer book he has been entrusted with. Given this information it is not difficult to see why a Witch would look at the Eucharistic Prayer and see instead a very powerful spell in the high magick tradition. (There will be more on high and low magick below.)

*'This is why some priests fall ill', so the online conversation went, 'They don't take account of the power that they're playing with.'*

Witches generally believe in the power of prayer because many have seen it in action. They may interpret it differently, but they also believe that it has an effect on the real world in the same way as spells do, and hence often equate the two. I suggest that there is a difference, but it is perhaps more subtle than we might imagine. Prayers tend to be *supplicatory*, that is they ask God to do something for us. The prayer in itself does not accomplish anything but asks, instead, for God to do something. Spells tend to be *manipulatory*, that is to say it is the spell itself that accomplishes the work in line with the will of the person casting the spell. However, these are only tendencies and are far from clear-cut. Many Christians believe that if they have faith in Christ then by that faith they can change reality. Jesus himself seemed to indicate this possibility:

'For truly I tell you, if you have faith the size of a mustard seed, you will say to this mountain, "Move from here to there", and it will move; and nothing will be impossible for you.' Matthew 17:20

*'What about Jesus?' I asked him. 'How does he fare in your beliefs?'*

*Without hesitation the Traditional Witch said to me, 'He was one of us.'*

This belief came about because the Witch knew that Jesus manipulated reality, healing the sick, raising the dead and casting out demons, and in his view he did that by magick.

The other counterpoint to this is that not all spells are manipulatory. Some appeal directly to a higher spiritual power to achieve what is being asked, and in this case are clearly supplicatory. One cannot even say that it is to do with intent because most of the spells that I know of people casting were to accomplish something positive in the life of someone else. Perhaps the clearest distinction is in whose name a prayer or a spell is said. For the Christian, if they are wise, they will ask if this is something that Christ would will, and if so would pray the prayer in his name. For the Witch they are more likely to wish to take the responsibility for their own actions and hence the spell would be in their own name.

So, we might ask, how does one cast a spell? That depends entirely on the type of spell that one is trying to cast. It is almost akin to asking, 'How does one pray?' The answer is, it all depends, and a full discussion of the different types of magick falls outside of the remit of this book. In order to get some degree of understanding, however, perhaps it is best to start with recognising that there is low magick and high magick. If we remain with the idea of spells and prayer one could equate low magick with being akin to the kind of prayer that one prays when asking for something in one's own words. High magick is more ceremonial, requiring careful practice and attention to exact wording and is therefore more akin to the liturgical practice surrounding the Christian Eucharistic Prayers within a high Anglo-Catholic tradition, requiring training and learning to pray them properly. Or perhaps one might think of low magick as being the magickal equivalent of low church, where there are few candles and statues and much of the 'liturgy' is made up on the spot. High magick is more like high church, where the worshippers need in themselves a degree of ceremony, robes and the like, simply because that's the kind of people they are. It is not that one is superior to the other; they are simply different.

However, there are differences in the understanding of what is taking place. In low magick the practitioner is dealing more directly through the elements and is therefore focussed on the cares of the everyday: money that's needed; the desire to fall in love and other practical matters. This is the kind of magick that one is more likely to find in Witchcraft and Wicca. It is more earthly and consequently more attractive to Pagans for that reason since Pagan religions are very tied to the earth. High magick, although practised by some Pagans, is more in the realm of the occultist. It is always ceremonial, requires absolute adherence to the text being used, and intriguingly will often engage with the spirituality of mystical Judaism or Christianity, although other ancient religious forms also have their adherents. The high magick practitioner will tend towards a more intellectual approach and is likely to think of him or herself as plugging in directly to the Source of the power. To put it in very twenty-first-century terms, a low magick user might see themselves as the person who knows what they want to accomplish on their smartphone and seeks out the right app to achieve it. The high magick practitioner is more likely to see themselves as the one who has committed themselves to learning the software on which the phone runs, and knowing how to rewrite it to get it to do what they want.

## A life between two worlds – using the examples of Hedgewitchery and Mediumship

A Hedgewitch is most simply defined as one who practises her or his Craft as a solitary:

*She explained to me that when she began her explorations into Paganism she had begun first with Druidry. But she soon found that the group she joined behaved more as if they were playing at Paganism. She wanted to take it very seriously and for it to be life-changing so ultimately she decided to leave the Pagan group. She then made contact with a local Witches' Coven and asked to join. However, before too long, she found again that with this particular coven, they were a strong draw on her resources, and it felt as if she was giving far more than she received. Ultimately, she decided that the only way forward for her was to become a solitary practitioner, a Hedgewitch.*

Different people come to Hedgewitchery by different routes. For some it is simply that they are introverted by nature and would prefer to work alone. Others, such as my friend, have just had less successful interactions with other Wiccans or Witches and hence have decided to go it alone. However, there is also more to being a Hedgewitch than this. Traditionally, the hedge was the place where the village and farmland gave way to the forest. Wise men and women, also known as Cunning Folk (because of the negative connotations of being labelled a Witch), would often live at this boundary and be sought out by the locals in need of spellcraft or simple herbal cures. But the action of living at the boundary was not purely their physical location; it was also their spiritual location. Hedgewitches, if you like, walked the boundary between physical and spiritual and in this way also had a Shamanic role. We will consider Shamanism in depth in chapter 6, but suffice it to say here that this would have meant communicating with other spirits on behalf of people who asked for their help. All of which leads to the last consideration, that of Mediumship.

Many in both the Wiccan and Traditional Witchcraft communities also claim to be Mediums, that is those who contact the dead on behalf of the living. Not all Mediums are Pagans and not all Witches or Wiccans are Mediums, but it is a common practice. What's more, they don't necessarily seek out the spirits of the dead; sometimes they are sought out themselves:

> She explained to us that she had gone to stay with her son and daughter-in-law and that they had given up their bedroom so that she and her husband could sleep there. However, in the middle of the night she was woken up by a lot of whispering in her ear that went on and on. 'Go away' she'd said – to no avail. So she tried to think who might be talking to her, before remembering that her daughter-in-law's father had died. She decided that it was probably him, but that he hadn't realised that it was someone else sleeping in the bed, not his daughter. So she told him straight, 'I'm not your daughter, she's asleep in the room above us. Now go away and let me sleep.' The whispering stopped...

This is the kind of story, often with this amusing edge, that I have heard on many occasions. The thing that one notices is just how matter-of-fact most Wiccans, Witches and indeed many Pagans are about the spirits of the dead. There are numerous different ideas about the afterlife, some complimentary and some contradictory, but there seems to be a general acceptance that the spirits of the dead sometimes wish to communicate with the living. For many Witches and Wiccans, therefore, Mediumship is simply a natural part of their practice. Christians will tend to have a variety of reactions to this, from those who accept the possibility that some of the dead have not yet found rest and may need human intervention, through to those who recognise the Old Testament prohibitions against Mediumship on the grounds that one really doesn't know exactly who or what the Medium is *actually* communicating with. That may well be based as much on experience as anything else. For example parish priests are sometimes called upon to do a 'house-cleansing' where something or someone is interacting with the residents on a spiritual level. Anecdotally, some priests have suggested that some of their experiences have been of a human person who had somehow become 'trapped' and needed prayer to allow them to leave this world. My own experience and reason for an open mind is rather more personal; this comes from my journal written in 2009:

*It is two years since Helen* (my eldest sister) *has died. Yet somehow she seems close. I can't explain it because I have no frame of reference and it goes against all my research training of having some proof. All I can say is that somehow this feels like Helen being nearby in a reassuring, 'It's OK little brother, all is well' kind of way. The experience lasts for a couple of weeks. She, if it is her, will understand if I merely acknowledge her presence with gratitude rather than attempting the two-way communication that she knows is not in my tradition. It feels like a special time. And then, after two weeks, the feeling is gone. I, however, feel like I have reached the end of the hardest stage of grief.*

## Not so dark

This, then, is a basic outline of Wicca and Witchcraft. Wicca seems to be growing more popular in Pagan practice in the UK, particularly amongst younger women, and I believe it is essential that, as with all religions, we understand what they actually believe rather than what we think they believe. Press bias has often tainted those who follow these beliefs with dark stories of Satanism and ritual abuse, whilst those I have met have, instead, been open, honest and friendly, living lives which they hope will do good for others. My hope is that this chapter has opened up a better level of understanding and has provided a basis for further discussion and dialogue.

# Notes for Chapter 3

1   Adler M., *Drawing down the moon*, London: Penguin, revised edn., 2006, 10.

2   d'Este S. and Rankine D. *Wicca – Magickal Beginnings*, London: Avalonia, 2008, 31-32

3   Crowley was popularly known for his use of sex magick, his saying 'Do what thou wilt shall be the whole of the law' (which is actually concluded with the words 'Love is the law, love under will', but this is often forgotten) and for being called 'The Great Beast', referring to the creature of the book of Revelation. In reality he was a complex figure of great influence within occult circles but not a Pagan. Nevertheless he is linked to them and is potentially, therefore, one of the reasons why people react badly to Paganism.

4   See for example Hutton R., *The Pagan Religions of the Ancient British Isles*, London: BCA, 1991, Chapter 8, and Hutton R., *The Triumph of the Moon*, Oxford: OUP, 1999.

5   d'Este S. and Rankine D., *Wicca – Magickal Beginnings*, London: Avalonia, 2008, 239

6   Green M., *A Witch Alone*, London: Thorsons, 1995, 20.

7   Hutton R., *The Triumph of the Moon*, Oxford: OUP, 1999, 314.

8   Jackson N. A., *Call of the Horned Piper*, Chieveley: Capall Bann Publishing, 1995, 24.

## Chapter Four

# Druidry

## Introduction

*In the midst of this summer, which has not been a summer, we seem to be fortunate to be gathering in the dry again on this early August day. I have been once more taken aback by the openness and welcome of the Pagans I am meeting. I knew nothing of this ritual until I was contacted on Facebook by a friend of a Pagan with whom I had been conversing. She heard about my travels and my research and invited me to attend this Lughnasagh ritual. So here I am, feeling a little unsure of myself for I know absolutely no one here, making my way through the earthworks and past the little ruined church at their centre to stand just beyond its east end where the ritual will take place.*

*People quickly greet me and are pleased that I have come to take part and observe. Like many gatherings the mixture of Pagans is eclectic but dominated here by Druids for this is their ritual, and mid-afternoon is their time as we meet by the light of the sun. Some of the women are dressed in beautiful semi-medieval long dresses, made by one of the participants. Others wear ordinary weekend clothes, and several of the men wear white robes, very similar in shape to my liturgical alb. Two wear tabards with large red crosses on and several carry staffs.*

*Before we begin the leader speaks to various different people to assign tasks and roles within the ceremony. Then, as with the other rituals I have been to, we gather in a circle which is then cast by calling in the quarters, north, south, east and west, to create the sacred space within which the ritual is offered. From then on there is a strange similarity to my Church of England background, although still quite informal. The leader has a liturgy in his A4 file which he follows closely. Rather than a Bible reading we have an enacted story of John Barleycorn, an archetypal figure who represents the first fruits of the harvest that we are here to give thanks for. The different players deliberately ham-up the story to make it fresh and fun, and a mother and young daughter, who have been watching at a distance, come over to join us and are welcomed in. We continue with a very moving and beautiful meditation by the woman who contacted me in the first place. The ritual concludes with giving thanks for the first fruits of the harvest as food and drink are shared around as well as bread that has been specially baked for the occasion by the ritual leader, himself a master baker.*

*Afterwards, we stay for ages talking about not just what has taken place, but also about who we are and what has brought us here. I am taken aback when one of the Druids produces a handmade staff that he himself has crafted, and he simply gives it to me. 'I can't take this', I stammer, 'It's such a beautiful piece.' 'Nonsense', he replies, 'I said to my wife this morning that I was going to give this staff away to someone at the ritual and I would know who when I got there. That someone is you.' I am deeply moved by this unexpected gift and then, before I leave, the ritual leader comes over to me and presents me with a sew-on badge for their Grove (a Grove is the name a particular group adopts). They all want to stay in touch, and indeed via Facebook that is exactly what we have done. I look forward to joining them again.*

Each group that I have met within Paganism has a different 'flavour'. It would be very easy to over-generalise this, but whereas Wicca is inclined towards being more feminine and intuitive in the way it presents itself, Druidry somehow seems to portray a public face that is at times (though by no means exclusively) more masculine and has a more studious (sometimes openly academic) feel to it. This is not remotely to suggest that

Druidry is dominated by men, but it has been in the past and there remain orders today which are male only. It is more a sense that the intuitive is more closely woven with, and tested by, research and study. Many public rituals have liturgies within which an Anglican like myself can feel at home because of the sense of familiarity. However, as I discovered whilst researching this chapter, this is by no means the whole story. Whilst this more public face of Druidry as an academic discipline is often the face that most people, including myself, see first, as one delves deeper other groups become apparent, such as the Auroch Grove led by Druid Blogger and writer, Nimue Brown. Following her reading for me of an earlier draft of this chapter where I concentrated far more on the more rigid liturgical and intellectual aspects of Druidry, Nimue invited me to meet members of her Grove and explained to me that they were by no means unique. I began this chapter with a Druid ritual, thought by many to be the norm because it is what most people see. The Auroch Grove was quite different:

*I arrive at Nimue and Tom's house under leaden January skies. This has proven to be one of the wettest and stormiest winters any of us can remember and this afternoon is clearly going to continue the trend. Immediately, I see the difference between the Auroch Grove and the other groups I've witnessed. Here there are no white robes and no sheets of paper with liturgy. Instead there are stout walking boots and full waterproofs and a wonderfully windswept and conversation-strewn forty-five minute walk up the hills behind their house in Stroud, smiling at their son who is delighted with every dog we encounter along the way. At the top we meet up with two other similarly dressed members of the Grove and find our way to a sheltered spot in the shadow of the long barrow at the hill's summit. From there we gaze out across the Gloucester hills, sharing hot ginger tea that someone has thoughtfully provided from a thermos. And then we become still...*

*We watch the way two winds from different directions collide over the distant River Severn, as the far hills disappear under a stormy onslaught. Gazing out at the land, we simply allow it to 'speak' and a gentle 'voice' whispering human insignificance becomes apparent. Perhaps almost Quaker-like observations are made. Nimue speaks of the thin veneer of humanity that we can see, occupying such a small space in the landscape. She explains how, when faced with a difficult problem, the simple act of coming up to this space and looking out puts it back into its perspective as something tiny amongst the hills and valleys. I notice how easily all human signs are wiped from our vision by the approaching storm, and gradually it dawns on me that today's lesson from the earth is one of humility. On this occasion, on the one hand I don't have the sense of a spiritual experience per se, but on the other it feels just like my own practice of prayerfully walking the countryside surrounding the parish I serve and allowing God to speak through my senses.*

*Within the Auroch Grove is one who attends Quaker meetings and another who leads a contemplative Druid group, and amongst them what is important is a simple sharing of a spiritual space together with a growing bond. I recognise here a welcoming inter-faith space created by a lack of insistence on a particular practice or set of beliefs. As Nimue explains to me on the way back down, those who attend come from all sorts of backgrounds and no one stands in judgement on any other. For them it is about the landscape and the senses, not about liturgy or robes. Words are few, hierarchy is entirely absent, and the contrast with my earlier experiences of Druid practice is profound.*

Alongside these different models of practice within Groves comes a most surprising observation regarding the breadth of different beliefs within Druidry. Whilst Wicca tends towards the honouring and worshipping of the Goddess and the God, Druidry uses deliberately open language in public ceremonies, which may also be more likely to include references to The Great Spirit, or, as I have described above, as little language as possible. Whilst polytheism is very common, so monotheism has a place too and I have been surprised at how many Druids I've met who are also involved in their local churches. Indeed, one of the people I met at the ritual I described at the beginning of this chapter preaches in her local church.

Perhaps this sense of familiarity can be traced back into the re-emergence of Druidry and, especially, its constructed 'history'. I use inverted commas because, like Wicca, whilst the modern history is well documented, some of the revivalist Druids made claims about early Druidry that can now be seen as difficult to substantiate. However, Druidry has a very strong inclination towards scholarship and such inventions could therefore in no way stand the test of time. So, before we venture too far into the beliefs and practices of Druidry, it will be helpful to have a look at its history.

## The History of Druidry

Writing a short history of Druidry is an almost impossible task and all I can hope to do here is to give a sense of it. Those who avidly read the pages of the internet dedicated to this subject would do well to look to the more scholarly works first. To my mind the currently definitive version of this history is *Blood and Mistletoe* by Professor Ronald Hutton[1], himself a regular speaker at Druid events, but this runs to almost five hundred pages. It's not, therefore, possible to include a full account in this chapter! However, in common with Wicca and Witchcraft, there have been many myths propagated over the last few hundred years which have been found to have no basis in fact so it's important to have at least a basic understanding of how Druidry has evolved into what we see now in the twenty-first century.

As with Wicca and Witchcraft there is a lack of a reliable written record by the Druids themselves. However, there are at least some records of the early Druids written by others, but they too are not without their problems. It is often said that history is written by the victors and the same may be true here, so accounts need to be read within what we know of their context when written. What we do know is that when the Romans invaded these islands there was a group of people already in existence within the British, Irish and Gallic cultures called the Druids who appear to have fulfilled the role of learned priests in the religion of that time. Almost anything beyond that is speculation. Although Druids of today feel a strong affinity to stone circles and henges, the original Druids were not responsible for their construction (which took place much earlier, largely in the Neolithic period). That being said, one cannot in any way rule out the possibility that the original Druids used these places for their own rituals. We simply cannot know.

The first written record, describing the Druids as the holy men of the Celts, comes from two Greek sources of about 200 BCE. Both are now lost, but were quoted some four hundred years later by Diogenes Laertius. After that we hear nothing more until Julius Caesar, writing circa 50 BCE. However, he was writing from the point of view of a military commander and so one can make a strong argument that anything he wrote may have been written from a propagandist perspective of justifying a military campaign to civilise what they wished to portray as a barbarian nation. For example, Caesar made much of recording that a part of the Druids' priestly function included human sacrifice, usually (but not always) of criminals in a burning wicker man, something the so-called 'civilised' Romans would never do. Yet despite the question marks over the historicity of Caesar's writings, the overall picture gained is of a learned and well-trained vocational class within society that regulated the worship of the gods, believed in reincarnation, arbitrated in disputes, and held great power in society. One might argue that they held a position similar to that once held by the medieval church. However, unlike the church, they kept no written records, leading to the need to rely on alternative 'second-hand' sources of information, and these sources had their own agendas, hence the need for caution.

Lest we dismiss Caesar's writings as invention, three other writers, Strabo, Diodorus and Pomponius wrote accounts over the next hundred years which held sufficient common ground with Caesar's descriptions to give weight to the impressions he left. It was not long after this that the force of feeling against the idea of human sacrifice led to the Romans suppressing Druidry, culminating in a great battle on the Isle of Mona (probably the place now known as Anglesey) in the early 60s CE, as recorded by Tacitus. Again, question marks arise about the historicity of the account. However, the Roman suppression appears to have been successful because the religious and political power of the Druids shrank rapidly from the historical record as Roman rule took hold in their homelands. There are, of course, numerous tales of Druids in literature, and some suggest that their teachings and practices were ultimately subsumed into the church, but it seems more sensible to hold to historical accounts, even with their likely biases, if we are to have any kind of picture of what really took place. To all intents and purpose the power of the original Druids seems to have been broken by this Roman oppression, with the consequent rise of Christianity in the British Isles giving birth to a new priesthood filling many of the gaps left by the absence of the Druids. As with Wicca and Traditional Witchcraft, there are numerous stories of an underground secret continuation, but there is scant evidence in the historical record to confirm this.

However, events took a new turn as national identity interests in European history began to grow around the turn of the sixteenth century. Hutton [2] is of the opinion that the people of that era felt that since the Druids were the only indigenous religious leadership revered by the Romans and the Greeks, then they must have been worthy of respect, and hence each nation wished to lay claim to them as ancestral. In the British Isles the revivalist retelling and re-imagining of the stories of the Druids was under way by the beginning of the seventeenth century. Numerous colourful figures took turns at describing mytho-logical histories as fact, such as Stukeley's (1687-1765) affirmation that the ancient Druids were Abrahamic missionaries. Foremost amongst these more creative writers was the Welshman Edward Williams (1747-1826) who took the Druid name Iolo Morganwg. Williams can be credited with founding the Welsh national Gorsedd, yet despite, or maybe even because of his knack of inventing histories, he was one of the key figures in the revival of Druidry as a modern spiritual path. George Watson MacGregor Reid followed in his footsteps at the dawn of the twentieth century with the founding of The Universal Bond as a form of Druidry that could unite other spiritual paths. As an active movement for social justice The Universal Bond gradually evolved into the Ancient Druid Order.

Just as the Wiccan movement had its founder in Gerald Gardner, so his contemporary and friend, Ross Nichols, developed modern Druidry, first as the chairman of the Ancient Druid Order before leaving to found the Order of Bards, Ovates and Druids (OBOD) in 1964. This order has gone on to become the largest and most influential Druid order in the world with a lengthy course of assessed study required to work through the grades from Bard to Druid, in keeping with the historical scholarly nature of Druidry. Under his guidance Druids have almost universally come to follow the same eightfold path of the year as Wiccans, which may be one of the reasons why so many of the Druids that I have met will also mention a Wiccan part to their journey and vice versa.

## Druid Symbolism

*It seems strange, after being outside for almost every ritual I can recall, to be sat in a theatre as the opening ritual is played out on the stage in front of us. The gathered are hushed as the white-albed Druids of the Cornovii Grove quietly walk in from the wings. A circle is laid out on the floor in flags of the different peoples within our land. I note the Cornish flag amongst them. As the leaders take their places around the circle I see that on both sides are stands showing the now familiar symbol of Druidry, the Awen, and I reflect that like so much else within this tradition it can be interpreted in so many different ways. Yet for each person their understanding is special to them, as I remember seeing it tattooed almost daintily on a young woman musician's forearm. So subtle and to the untrained eye it means nothing, but for Druids it is an instant symbol of recognition, of being a part of something greater than themselves.*

The Awen is the key symbol for Druidry and consists of three concentric circles. Within this there are three dots at the top and three lines radiating out downwards from them and, as I mention above, like so many aspects of modern Paganism there are a myriad of ways of interpreting it. One of the more traditional interpretations is from the folklore of how the Bard, Taliesin, came to be, and is a story that bears retelling. It is a legendary tale with many different variations of how a young boy, Gwion Bach, was tending a cauldron of inspiration for the crone, Cerridwen, for a year and a day. The mixture in the pot was intended for her unbearably ugly son, Afagddu, that through it he would become wiser than any other man in the land. Unfortunately, right at the end of the process, three drops from the cauldron, the three drops of inspiration, spattered on to young Gwion's finger and he instinctively put his burned finger into his mouth, thus inadvertently stealing the magic intended for Afagddu. (In some tellings Gwion's actions were anything but inadvertent!) In her rage, Cerridwen pursued Gwion and they both shape-shifted several times until he hid himself in a barn as a grain of corn. But Cerridwen turned herself into a hen and ate him, becoming pregnant as a result of having done so. Her intention was to have the reborn Gwion Bach and to kill him at birth, but when he was born his brow was so radiant, (Taliesin means 'radiant brow'), that she couldn't bring herself to do it. Instead she put him into a basket and, with echoes of the story of Moses, she cast him adrift on the waters. He was found by Elphin, the son of Gwyddno Garanhir, who brought him up to use his preternatural gifts as a bard in the court of King Maelgwn Gwynedd. Whilst numerous myths and legends surround Taliesin, there is ample evidence of a sixth-century bard by that name. Here then the three points and three lines represent the three drops from the cauldron and the wisdom that emanated from them.

However, as I said, the Awen symbol can mean many things. For others the three dots represent the triple aspect of Deity. Again, how one wishes to interpret that is up to the individual. For the Wiccan this could be the Maiden, Mother and Crone aspects of the Goddess. For a Christian Druid they might think of it in Trinitarian terms as Father, Son and Holy Spirit. The three lines radiating down and outwards from the points may be thought of as three rays of light wherein the light is the light of inspiration and of truth that comes to the seeker from above, however one wishes to interpret that. Awen, then, is essentially inspiration from beyond oneself, probably, or at least possibly, of divine source, and indeed the word comes from the Welsh word for poetic inspiration and appears to have its roots in an ancient word for 'breeze' leading to the idea of it being indicative of 'flowing spirit'. Emma Restall-Orr[3] goes further, though, as she expresses that for her Awen is '...spirit connection in absolute truth.' Emma is writing in the context of two people/beings engaged in an intimate connection and for me I wonder whether her ideas can also be expressed within the context of a relationship with the in-dwelling of God. You might like to think of it like this:

*I sit at my desk in front of a blank screen looking out of the window in front of me at an ocean of green growth. Yet this time the trees and bushes bring no ideas and no peace. I have a sermon to write and all I have are the readings, sitting on my screen, glaring at me. But there's nothing coming; no trace of an idea and re-reading the text again continues to draw a blank. In desperation I turn to the web to see what other people have written about this passage. And then it happens. I see a phrase in someone else's sermon and suddenly the whole idea unravels in my mind and the point that needs to be made becomes bright and clear in my head. I start writing, but my thoughts bear no resemblance to the other writer's sermon of which I had read very little. It was just that phrase, that short set of words, not even a sentence, which acted like a key to unlock my mind. The words flow freely, as if they are writing themselves, and within half an hour the sermon is written, complete and in its entirety. Not for the first time I ask myself, 'So where did THAT come from.' Knowingly, the Spirit within smiles and I grin too. All I needed was the start, the leading, and the rest followed.*

When I first began to understand the idea of Awen it quickly became clear that for me it is a simple description of what inspiration feels like, but it puts a personal context into it in terms of my own beliefs. Awen is a reminder that inspiration comes from One who is greater than I am, yet with whom I enjoy an intimate relationship. This One intended to communicate a deeper truth than I would have grasped if left just to my own devices. Now I'm no poet, but a significant portion of the work I do as a priest is based around writing and presenting material related to spiritual growth and on several occasions people have asked me where the ideas come from. I have to say that they simply come. But I imagine that what I've described above is exactly the kind of experience that many writers and preachers can testify to, sharing the creative gifts of poets, composers, choreographers and storytellers; that of starting from almost nothing, searching for some kind of inspiration, then being surprised by how, once it starts, the ideas just flow out almost (and sometimes completely) fully formed. It is this process to which the Druids attach the name, 'Awen'.

My intent in framing the description like this is, once again, to try and take some of the fear of the unknown out of acknowledging a branch of Paganism. What the Druids describe as Awen seems to me to be what I and other Christians would refer to as divine inspiration. Those of us in any form of ministry, which requires teaching or creative expression, utterly depend upon it, whatever we choose to call it. Without it our expression of what we believe becomes cold, dry and merely academic.

## Nemeton – The Sacredness of 'Place'

I mentioned above that particular groups of Druids who meet regularly tend to refer to themselves as 'Groves'. One often finds that the Groves will meet repeatedly at the same place, always outside. It may be in the midst of trees, on a hillside, or at an ancient monument such as some kind of earthworks or standing stones. Once you know what to look for it's not difficult to ascertain whether a particular place is being used in this way by the presence of 'Cluties'. This word, which I'm told originates in Cornwall, refers to the tying of some kind of offering, most often a simple ribbon, on a tree branch, and is a practice not restricted to Druidry, but one which is a part of many Pagan and New-Age practices. A Clutie may be thought of as a kind of prayer or spell, with the sense that you wind your request into the ribbon and tie it to the sacred place. As the ribbon biodegrades so the spirits of that place will grant your request. I should add that a number of Druids I have met are somewhat scathing of this practice because of the way it marks the environment, and will remove Cluties if they find them, whilst for others it seems to be a valid part of their practice. Either way, if one finds a tree with a number of Cluties tied to it then you can be fairly sure that someone treats that as a sacred place, and the word that describes that in the Druidic tradition is 'Nemeton'. Some of these are in quite surprising places:

*Loz, being his usual amiable self, is sat at the table with us at St. Nectan's Glen. We're talking about how so many people treat it as a sacred place, and how it is often heard that there is a peace there which one feels when standing in the water looking at the Cleeve. 'There's somewhere else you ought to go', he says to us. 'On the road out to Launceston from here there's a little road off to a place called St. Clethers. Behind the church there is a little path off to St. Clether's Well and Chapel. That's a really sacred place!' Neither Alison nor I have ever heard of it, despite having driven the Launceston road many times over the years. So the next day, a beautiful warm early September day, we pack our rucksacks, load Alison's travelling harp (since this sounds like a wonderful place to play), closely look at the map to find where this village is, and set off. It quickly becomes apparent why we've never found it before. St. Clethers is not a village that you drive through on the way somewhere. You have to go searching for it. After driving exceedingly slowly around numerous winding Cornish single track roads, we finally find the beautiful little village of St. Clethers. Parking in front of the church we walk along its south side, through the graveyard, and easily find the marked path to the chapel.*

*It takes ten to fifteen minutes to walk the path to the chapel and well and as we do so the track winds its way into a beautiful river valley. As we gently meander along the side of the valley we see the tiny chapel ahead, surrounded by a wooden fence to keep the animals out. We arrive at the gate, open it and walk in, to be greeted instantly by a deep sense of peace and tranquillity. The valley is beautiful, green and fertile, but this, this crossing a threshold, was rather unexpected, transcending the natural surroundings, being touched with something from another 'place'. Without doubt this is a sacred place. It is not until later that I understand the word a Druid would apply is 'Nemeton'.*

Many Christians will be quite at ease with an understanding of what I've just described, although perhaps in a different context, with holy places tending to be sites where something important took place in the life of a saint or of Christ himself. Those who follow a nature-centred path may be likely to respond by suggesting that a nemeton occurs naturally at a place where sacred mysteries are earthed in the natural world and would therefore say that a nemeton is something that has to be discerned rather than created. However, I am not so sure that the distinction between the two is as simple as that. Certainly many of us would be able to talk about arriving at a place in the woods, on a mountainside, near the sea or a lake, which somehow feels holy. Yet, I also believe that places can become sacred with use, not just because something important took place there. For example, the parish that I look after meets in the church of St. Mary Magdalene in the village of Tanworth in Arden. Parts of the building may date back one thousand years. People have been praying in that space for so long and that sense of sacredness seeps into the fabric of the place. Numerous people have told me of how they have walked in and found such a deep sense of peace there. It strikes me, therefore, that the only real difference between that and a Druid nemeton is largely to do with nemetons usually being outside. The chapel and well at St. Clether manages to bridge the gap as a nemeton because it was not just the tiny building, but the surrounding grounds which also felt so sacred, and indeed several of the trees enclosing the space had numerous Cluties tied to them.

From what we observed and what Loz had said to me, St. Clether's Chapel and Well are sacred to people of a variety of beliefs. Certainly as Christians we felt right at home there. The well itself is just outside the small building and waters feed it from a stream that runs down the hill above the chapel, through the rear of the chapel behind the stone altar where the reliquary with several bones of St. Clether once lay, to a little pool outside the chapel. The waters once ran over some of the saint's bones and so the pool was said to be sacred as waters for healing or baptism. We may think of this as superstition, but don't forget the stories at the beginning of the Acts of the Apostles in the New Testament where, in chapter five, Peter was regarded so highly as a healer that people would place their sick in the streets so that his shadow would fall on them as he passed by. St. Clethers has that sense of a place that has become sacred and it is intriguing how that sacredness transcends any particular doctrine or dogma. Celtic Christians would refer to such a place as a 'thin place', meaning that the veil between heaven and earth was thin there, whilst Druids would use the word 'nemeton', but I suspect that the same sense of sacredness is felt by both.

The origin of the word 'nemeton' is, as with so many aspects of Paganism, subject to various different interpretations. It may be related to an ancient tribe called the Nemetes who once existed in what has become Germany and who followed the goddess Nemetona. However, a potential question mark hangs over this because of the lack of evidence that Druidry was ever active in Germany. 'Nemeton' may also be related to the Latin word *Nemus* which refers to a small collection of trees, although there is no sense of sacredness to the Latin word. What one does find is that a number of place names in England incorporate a version of the word 'nemeton', or a modern version of its Old English equivalent, *Bearu*, (now usually Beer) into their names. Examples in Devon include Beer itself, or perhaps Bishop's Nympton, known as the manor of Nimetone in the Domesday Book. However we wish to look at it, it becomes plain that the concept of a sacred space is deeply enshrined in British history.

## Bards, Ovates and Druids – the Different Orders within Druidry

After much reflection on this chapter, I realise that I first need to add a disclaimer before describing and discussing the different orders because, although in one sense the three orders are very real and are important for many on the path of Druidry, for others they are an almost artificial addition; a distinction where there is none. Earlier in this book I mentioned the sometimes anarchic nature of modern Paganism, that many of its followers often react against any form of hierarchy, and a similar observation can be made about Druidry. In essence, anyone who seeks a kind of spiritual wisdom through the natural world, and most especially through trees, can call themselves a Druid. One does not need to have any formal kind of training, although it would be wise to at least do a lot of reading about what other Druids believe. It seems to me that there is a clear parallel here between Druidry and Christianity. Any person who is a follower of Christ can call themselves a Christian, but within that title there is a vast array of belief and understanding. Ultimately, all that is required is for one to follow the way of Christ. However, there are many who wish to understand their faith better and who therefore choose to study it, and amongst those there are some who are called to the office of Deacon, Priest or Bishop, all of which are present in the descriptions of the early church, and each of which has some kind of specific public role. You could think of it like this. Peter wrote the following to a group of exiles scattered across several countries in 1 Peter 2:9:

> 'But you are a chosen race, *a royal priesthood*, a holy nation, a people for God's possession in order that you may proclaim the mighty acts of him who called you out of darkness into his marvellous light.'

The key phrase in there is the words, 'A royal priesthood...' What he means is that collectively Christians are meant to be go-betweens, forming a link from the world to God, praying for those in need and making a practical difference to the lives of those who are struggling or searching. This is the model the church is meant to follow. So collectively all Christians together form a priesthood. That, however, is not the same thing as saying every Christian is a priest. Some are then called to train for the office and work of a priest (or whatever denominational name we might apply) whose public role is specifically to be focussed on helping others to develop spiritually. I believe that the same principle can be applied to Druidry. Anyone who wishes to follow a Druidic path can call themselves a Druid, but amongst that group there are those who feel drawn to what we might call the office and work of a Druid, or of a Bard or an Ovate. Those who have achieved those grades, which require a great deal of commitment and work, are more able to fulfil public duties for those seeking their particular spiritual skill set, but trying to draw a distinction between them can sometimes be somewhat artificial. This is recognised by some within the Druid movement in this country, so whilst there are the formal Druid orders such as the Order of Bards, Ovates and Druids, or the British Druid Order, there are also organisations such as the Druid Network which has no formal learning structure but which simply welcomes all who would wish to call themselves, 'Druid'. With this in mind let us move towards those descriptions.

I've heard it joked that Druids do everything in threes, reflecting the three drops of inspiration from the cauldron of Cerridwen, and the same is true within the structure of Druidry. The largest Druid order, the Order of Bards, Ovates and Druids (OBOD) has its own study course through which one may study, for perhaps a lengthy period, to find one's place within the structure as a Bard, an Ovate or a Druid. However, I would be hesitant to compare these with the threefold ministry within the established church denominations of Deacon, Priest and Bishop since, as will become clear, the gifts and work of each order simply do not correspond to church titles. I will, however, argue that when taken together those who have trained for one of the orders within Druidry form a kind of priesthood. I have already described my own concerns about the division into three classes and there are others within Druidry, such as Graeme Talboys[4], who also believe that such a clear division is an artificial one and that in its original form the three titles may even have been merely three amongst a multitude. It is therefore necessary that we approach these three different orders as helpful delineations rather than as necessary absolutes, and that there may therefore be significant crossovers between them.

Bards are perhaps the easiest for us to come to terms with because the title 'Bard' is still in the modern English language, perhaps largely thanks to Shakespeare, so we know that it has something to do with the creative arts using music, song, poetry and story. But, a Bard is more than a singer, or than any of those things:

*He spoke clearly and gently, yet with a quiet authority that was his alone as he addressed the conference. The gathered audience from around the country (and beyond) listened appreciatively as he spoke of the ways in which Bards should tend their craft and practise, practise, practise. It was insufficient for someone simply to write nice songs. Being a Bard was a calling, not just an innate ability. Being a Bard required study and vast amounts of work perfecting their abilities to do them justice. One should not use the title of Bard unless one had honed abilities that were valued by others in the community. It began to dawn on me that one vast difference between New Age beliefs and Druidry is that there is a sense here of a group of people who do not flit from one practice to another as soon as they become bored and need a different spiritual high, but instead are committed to learning, to wisdom and to their creative abilities. In essence, they are committed to the path they are on, and not forever looking to try something new.*

Whilst in some Druid groups one can simply call oneself a Druid if one wishes, in OBOD one has to study to achieve each grade, reflecting the historically attested practice within ancient Druidry of a lengthy period of learning that takes many years. For the outsider it needs to be understood that it is not simply a case of having the learning rubber-stamped and being given the title. I have one very good friend whose final piece of course work was not deemed sufficient and who had to do further work in order to be able to move from the Bardic grade to the Ovate grade. The order of Bard is a prerequisite for going on to Ovate or Druid, but it is valued in and of itself, not just as a stepping stone to something greater. At its most fundamental level the Bard is simply the keeper of stories and histories. In a time before the internet, and even before books and the general use of the written word, the Bard was expected to have an encyclopaedic knowledge of stories and myths gained from many years of study. You might like to think of this as the Celtic equivalent to the Hebrew practice of studying to become a Rabbi, wherein the study required the commitment to memory and understanding of the stories and writings of what Christians call the Old Testament alongside the commentaries by other Rabbis. In both cases this is the knowledge of the ancestral histories and teachings of the tribe. But a Bard was expected to be more than just the memory of the tribe. Drawing deep on a well of creativity was inherent to the calling, as indeed it is now. Not only should the Bard be able to recount a wide array of stories, poetry and song, but also should be able to add to them. Deeply embedded in this, therefore, is an ability to see the world differently and to be able to communicate this to others so that they can observe through Bardic eyes that which was hidden from them:

*We are walking along a well-trodden path. This is a dog walkers'*
*paradise and I suppose it is only because we are approaching*
*twilight that we have the space to ourselves. The Bard I am with is*
*a musician whose creative abilities touch hearts. What happens next*
*is quite enlightening for me. Our walk begins on a tarmac track to a*
*farm, although as the track turns off to the right we continue*
*straight up the hill on the older footpath, but first we pause. We're*
*about to climb a stile and go into a wooded area when the Bard stops*
*for a moment. I know what she's doing because I've been with her on*
*previous occasions when she has done the same thing, and it no*
*longer seems remotely odd. She is simply honouring the space we are*
*about to enter. It is almost a seeking of permission and I understand*
*why as we cross the stile and begin to trek up the hill.*

*'Lots of people walk through here', she reminds me, 'yet this is*
*someone's home.' Quizzically I look around. She points out a*
*squirrel hopping from one branch to another. Over to our left is a*
*bank, 'And that's where the local rabbits live. Often I hear a buzzard*
*calling although she's not here tonight.' I'm getting the idea, and*
*then she says, 'Come on. I want to show you the Rhino Tree'.*
*Intrigued, and with the light failing, we hurry on up the path. She*
*stops again, although I sense we're not yet at our destination. 'This*
*is one of the Old Ones', she explains as she lovingly lays her hand*
*on the trunk of a very mature silver birch. Again there is a sense of*
*honouring the space, but now I notice something else, and it's*
*difficult to put this into words. The only vocabulary that fits is*
*'rapport'. Here a sense of ease within this woodland feels like a two-*
*way conversation. She is happy to be here and it feels as if the*
*residents are happy to have her here. This may just be my imagi-*
*nation, and I'm sure some would say so, but I realise I'm beginning*
*to see this through her eyes. Then with a bright smile she playfully*
*points to the right-hand side of the path, and with an impish grin*
*says, 'And there's the Rhino Tree'. Instantly, I see what she means*
*as a weather-beaten tree comes into view, a tree that has lost most of*

*several branches which were growing out one above the other. It does indeed look like horns. A Rhino Tree indeed.*

There was a delightful sense of playfulness embraced by a deep respect for her environment in this encounter. But this particular Bard had precisely the kind of gifting that I am almost jealous of, that through her abilities to see the world in a different way, and through the poetry and song that flows out of her, she was able to let me see the world through her eyes and in a different way. She has not yet written a song about this woodland like those she has written for other places, but each time I listen to her I see the world in a different way. The Bardic gift has the potential to change people in positive ways by expanding their horizons.

As a personal aside, I lament the way this gift is not treated with the respect it deserves in much of the Church, whilst at the same time feeling a sense of stirring at the changes that seem to be taking place at the grassroots of the Church. As a priest in the Church of England I am supposed to use only authorised liturgies, yet for me so much of the phraseology we are compelled to use in our worship lacks the poetry which takes us out of ourselves and allows us to see through another's eyes, being, instead, tied up in the minutiae of trying to accurately convey correct doctrine. The Bardic gift is not confined solely to Druidry by any stretch of the imagination, but it is they who seem to value it as a calling and a valid part of a spiritual path far more than other parts of our national culture where instead it is little more than a vehicle to fame. But I digress...

The second order within Druidry is that of Ovate. Whilst Ovate is not perhaps a word that is in familiar usage, we don't have to delve very deeply to see a common root with the Vatican, the place in Rome, now the centre of the Roman Catholic Church, which was once the place where the Pagan oracles dwelt. Ovate, or simply 'Vate', has the same root as Vatican. This oracular, or seer role is at the heart of the Ovatic path. (When I use the word 'seer' in this context I am not necessarily referring to someone who sees the future, but rather as someone who sees a spiritual perspective that others miss.) The Ovate is perhaps the most mystical of the Druidic paths:

*As she walks on stage to address us an awed hush descends. She is well known in Pagan circles, and although she claims no particular title for herself, there is a sense of darkness which seems to fill the stage around her. Yet this does not feel like an evil darkness, but rather the spiritual sense of 'unknowing' that surrounds her. On occasions when she, Alison and I have sat in conversation, the dark stillness of unknowing yet deeply questioning has been inspiring, (and sometimes quite exhausting as I have tried to keep up with the many twists and turns our discussions have taken). She is an influential figure by virtue of her engagement with a spiritual world that few people can even begin to comprehend, and everyone gathered knows that. She bears within her a wealth of encounters where she has walked the path between this world and some unseen other place. I know within myself a sort of unease, not because I think of her as someone who has touched evil, but simply because her experiences are so far beyond any that I have had. She embraces a world that I know little about. As she speaks so she reminisces, recalling an occasion when Pagans of a multitude of paths engaged in a ritual together. She describes how each one brought their own deities leading to confusion and conflict in the spiritual realm because not all of the gods know how to be in the same place at the same time with each other...*

In this particular instance I am left with many questions, as I imagine that you, the reader, would be. How we understand her experiences will depend upon the belief construct with which we have begun this book. It may be, as some will suspect, that this person is dealing with malevolent spirits masquerading as deities. Or it may be that on some level she, as a mystic, is attuned to the differences in human spirit between those of differing beliefs, picking up on the unspoken disagreements between those with different ideas about deity. Or it may be that you come to this book with the belief that there are indeed either many deities or at least many unseen spirits and what she sensed was close to the reality. We must remember that even the most ardent of mystics come to their experiences with belief constructs, and so the interpretation she gave of her experience is based on what she brought to the gathering herself. Nevertheless, her description of what took place is helpful within this context. She doesn't claim the title of Ovate, nor Druid for that matter, so this is a good illustration of what I said earlier, that the distinction between the paths is blurred. However, what she demonstrated on this occasion falls within what we might think of as the Ovate stream and I recognise that her spiritual ideas are so different from my own that I find I just have to listen and try and understand what she is 'seeing'. This is one of the gifts at the heart of being an Ovate; being a seer. Within Druidry this is related to Shamanism, and we will look at this connection in Chapter 6 when we consider that path.

However, the role of seer is not confined to any particular path, and the Bible is also littered with stories of seers. A seer is purely 'One who sees', in any tradition, but from a spiritual perspective. So, within the Old Testament, for example, Isaiah was a seer. In the first section of that book one can read how the first prophet to take the name Isaiah, (there were probably three whose writings were all collated under the one name of Isaiah), could see God's judgement on the nation of Israel for the ways in which they were oppressing the poor, the weak and the vulnerable. As a prophet, Isaiah was able to then go beyond simply seeing and declared what God would do about it as a warning. Within Druidry the Ovatic role of seer is related, but may refer to any deity or to many, depending on the beliefs of the

Ovate. Again this is difficult for those who are monotheists to understand. How can a spiritual path with people who have such a variety of different understandings and beliefs have seers who can speak of what they have received spiritually to the group as a whole? There is no simple answer to this, but I suspect that those who are seers within the Ovatic tradition would speak prophetically mainly to those who share their own beliefs. Having said that, within Paganism it is also possible to receive a word from a respectful person of a different tradition from one's own. This is because most Pagans will talk about many different, and equally valid, paths ascending the same spiritual mountain, at the peak of which one finds God, God and Goddess, gods, enlightenment, or whatever the individual is searching for. Many times I have heard it said that although we have different perspectives and understandings, we still travel the same ascending route. Regardless of whether or not one subscribes to this philosophy, my own experience of this certainly made me think deeply:

> *This is one of the first encounters I've had with a Pagan and I recognise that she is a very busy person, so it felt like a huge privilege to be able to meet to chat over lunch. As she, Alison and I sit down to order I thank her for giving up her time like this for someone who knows so little about the subject he's chosen to research. She smiles as she explains to me that she doesn't do much of this kind of thing these days. Why then did she agree to on this occasion I ask? Her answer has an impact that still reverberates two years later: 'Because my gods told me that I should.'*

The conversation that afternoon threw up far more questions than answers, but that one single statement was perhaps the most important in changing my perspective on Paganism. I felt called by God, as a Christian, into this journey and here was someone saying that her gods were telling her to respond to me and to talk with me. This ability to state something simply that challenges someone deeply is a part of the role of the seer. I have never really felt that I knew how to respond to this comment and so have felt the need to take it at face value. She went on to tell us the names of the two deities, in tradition local to the part of England where she lived, and so it seems to me that she believed this was who spoke to her and I should honour that in the same way that she was honouring my beliefs that I felt called by the one God, since any kind of dialogue must be built on this kind of respect. She believed that the deities to whom she gives honour and respect instructed her to take part in the process that I felt called to do as a Christian. How we respond to that will, I suspect, depend once again on the belief construct, as I discussed in Chapter 1, which we bring to the discussion. If you believe that all Pagans are fundamentally being misled by the devil then you will probably believe that this woman's comment was intended to lead me off the Christian path into believing in or being affected by her gods which you think are, in reality, demons. If you believe, instead, that all spiritual paths lead up one mountain then you may well believe that she and I worship different gods, all of which are trying to help us make our way up the mountain. If you are a monotheist and believe there is only one God, but that we know that God by many different names, then you will probably imagine that both she and I heard the same God speaking, trying to get us to talk to each other so that we both come to a greater depth of understanding of the breadth of God's nature. I will leave it to you, the reader, to draw your own conclusions, but this example serves to show that the role of the Ovate is one that can see a different perspective and speak that perspective into a spiritual situation regardless of whether all participants actually believe the same thing.

Other Druids have related similar stories of where someone of the same Grove, yet with very different spiritual beliefs, can still challenge them because they possess a seer's spiritual perception. A seer can do this because it is within their gift. Their ability to challenge is far less dependent on the beliefs of the individual whom they address than that person is necessarily comfortable with. Those who read this from within the Christian tradition will know this from experience. If someone has what we call a 'Word of Knowledge' and communicates that to another, if that word is from God it will challenge the other person, regardless of their beliefs. A good example of this can be found in Chapter 3 of John's Gospel when Jesus encounters a member of the Jewish ruling council called Nicodemus. That encounter, and the words of Jesus, had such a profound effect on Nicodemus that by Chapter 19 we read that Nicodemus was one of those who approached Pilate to ask for the body of Jesus after his crucifixion. Christ's words as seer had changed the spiritual reality of Nicodemus. Numerous other examples abound in scripture and experience of how someone who has the gift of being a seer can speak words of spiritual wisdom and knowledge into a situation that leaves people challenged and perhaps changed despite their differences in belief. Within Druidry this is thought of as the gift of the Ovate, but it may be demonstrated by others since, as I have mentioned previously, the distinctions can be somewhat artificial.

I've made much so far of how some aspects of the Ovate tradition are similar to those found within orthodox Christianity and another example of this is the importance of ancestry in both traditions. In the first instance this can be simply a recognition of, and a listening to, the voices of one's own familial ancestors:

*We're sat in my grandparents' living room, looking through old photos that date back several generations to the early and very posed black and white pictures whereby one had to sit still for maybe a second or more. In the midst of these is a photo of my paternal great-grandfather. My sister suddenly exclaims, 'His eyes, I have his eyes! I look like him!' For many years it has bothered her that, although there is no doubt she is my sister, many of her facial features look nothing like our parents or grandparents. But here she has found an ancestor to whom she bears an astonishing resemblance and it means a great deal to her sense of self-identity.*

Finding out about and understanding our own ancestors can give us a real feeling of belonging, as my sister discovered. When we were small children she had often joked about whether she'd been adopted because she didn't think she looked like our parents, and I suppose that until we saw a photo of our great-grandfather whom we'd never met, I hadn't appreciated how important this was to her. For some there can be a sense of belonging when one re-examines one's family history, as not just physical but personality traits resurface. So, familial ancestry is important to many people, not just to Druids. However, there is more to Druid ancestry than purely family.

I am trying to give a flavour of different traditions within Druidry, from the deeply contemplative to the highly intellectual, and in choosing a path to follow; Druids will also choose the ancestry of that path. It goes yet further because, for many in the tradition, ancestry is not simply about human ancestors, it is also about ancestors of the land, of the place to which one feels one belongs, which may include both human and non-human ancestors. Again this will vary immensely from one individual to another. For some it is the history of animal life within a place, but for others it is the spirits of the land whom they honour. Although there is no straightforward analogue within Christianity to which this can be compared, there is an acknowledgement that not all that exists can be seen:

'For in him [Christ] were all things in heaven and on earth created, things visible and invisible, whether thrones or dominions or rulers or powers – all things have been created through him, and for him.' Colossians 1:16

This is a difficult verse to take in isolation. but it seems to leave open the possibility of unseen spirits and may well have much to speak into the dialogue between Christians and Pagans, at the very least being an acknowledgement that there is more to the universe than we often understand. In the Judeo-Christian tradition one does not, in general, consult other spirits for advice simply because if one is looking to their creator for help, why look for help amongst other created beings? However, one might consider the Roman Catholic example of praying to the saints to be similar in some senses, even though these are human ancestors. We will revisit this topic in the next chapter on Animism where we will consider who or what is being consulted.

Surprisingly, to some extent there is also an analogue to the reverence of ancestors in Christianity. Whilst it may not always be apparent because of the numerous disagreements between denominations, the Church in theory understands itself as one family under the Fatherhood of God in the Brotherhood of Christ (and some may add under the Motherhood of the Holy Spirit or perhaps the Motherhood of Mary). However, this form of ancestry is not one of blood and genes but of faith. It is more akin to the Druids who choose the ancestors of their tradition than to those who follow their ancestors of blood. So we, too, celebrate and are inspired by our forebears and may look to those declared saints, or Christians and Jewish Patriarchs and Matriarchs celebrated as wonderful examples of faith, as being our ancestors in this one big family. We may read about their lives and be inspired by their actions.

Those outside Christianity may be surprised at some of these examples such as a prostitute named Rahab who became famous for her decision to put her faith in Israel's God, living as she did in the then unconquered city of Jericho in the time before Israel had completed its takeover of the land of Canaan. When Israelite spies came to examine the extent of Jericho's defences she hid them, thus putting her faith into action. Furthermore, within the

Judeo-Christian tradition our spiritual ancestors are generally revered 'warts and all'. For example, David was the great King of Israel but he was also an adulterer. Moses was a murderer who initially said no to God. Peter was called 'The Rock' by Jesus despite going on to deny him, and Paul appears to have had a truly bad temper and had persecuted Christians until his spiritual experience on the road to Damascus. These examples of ancestors are useful for Christians because they remind us that God's grace is sufficient so that whatever lifestyle one leads, faith is always possible. The beginning of John's Gospel is a good example of this:

'But to all who received him, who believed in his name, he gave power to become children of God, who were born, not of blood or of the will of the flesh or of the will of man, but of God.'

One key difference in the understanding of ancestors is that within Druidry the emphasis is more likely to be placed on the individual and the choices that they make. Within Christianity we come back to this comment by Christ to his disciples:

'You did not choose me but I chose you...' John 15:16

This is a typically Rabbinic model where the Jewish teacher chooses their followers from the prospective candidates, but it serves as a reminder that if one is a Christian one gets less choice in ancestry. I may well struggle with many of the lives of the saints and their sayings, but I still need to honour them as people who trod the same faith path as I seek to.

Within Druidry, however, there isn't a sense or specific teaching of all being a part of one body in the way that there is within Christianity (even the difficulties that many Christians have living out the beliefs in practice). Each person within

Druidry can look back down their lineage at the gifts that members of their families had, and then draw upon those gifts and talents as they are found within themselves, or they may seek out the stories of the ancestors they choose as inspiration for the gifts they wish to develop. I should add that this is not limited to just Druidry either, since I have also come across it within Traditional Witchcraft which places a great emphasis on one's own family lineage (whereas in Wicca, as we discussed in the last chapter, it is more the initiatory lineage which is valued).

Up to this point there is little about the valuing of ancestors within Druidry that the Christian could disagree with, since we can all recognise the value of knowing where we came from and who we are like. However, it goes rather further than that within Druidry and this is where aspects of the work of the Ovate would be difficult for many Christians to feel comfortable with. This is because within certain Druid traditions it is felt that one can converse with one's ancestors, asking them for advice. (Within some streams of Roman Catholicism this could be akin to praying and listening to the Saints.) An Ovate, in particular, may be sought out because within their gift is the ability to converse with the ancestors of another; that is they can speak with the dead. As I wrote in the previous chapter, mediumship has a large role to play in Wicca and Witchcraft and the Ovate may fulfil a similar role within Druidry.

Within Christianity there is a strong sense of being ill at ease with this practice because one does not know to whom one is speaking and one could, therefore, be misled. Indeed, many will believe that conversing with the dead is more likely to be conversing with demons. There is also a sense among Christians that people who follow this practice do so with no recognition as to whom they are speaking and the dangers that are inherent in their practice. This was one of the questions that I raised with Emma Restall-Orr about this part of her own path in the context of being a medium within Druidry and, in particular, how that might link with the prophetic calling within Judeo-Christian circles in which the prophet may be called to warn someone. In a polytheistic context, would a similar thing take place? Emma's answer was intriguing:

'First, if I am asked by someone to be a medium between themselves and a god, spirit or ancestor, then I would (if I were able) tell them what I was told. The responsibility for the request, and thus to a greater extent the content and its consequences, lies with the person who has requested I work as the medium for them... If I hear a warning, or guidance, or even a blessing, for someone, my task is primarily to work out who has given me that message. In a pluralistic universe, populated by many gods, many minds, many aspects of the whole, I cannot make an assumption about where the message comes from. It may not be helpful. I can understand that if your belief is about one loving/judging deity, then all messages should be relayed, but if there are understood to be countless demons, ancestors, spirits, gods, countless coherences of mind, countless souls and not many of those human or friendly towards humanity, then messages need to be filtered. The dead sometimes retain a coherence through the sticky nature of emotion, and such messages are thick with emotion – patterns of fear and anger that crave iteration. Many warnings seem to me to be of this kind. The medium becomes responsible for the consequences of passing on the words.'

'If I am given a warning for someone, I am not likely to tell the person that it is a warning that I've been given from the otherworld, an ancestor or god. I would guide them, person to person, so they are able to see the potential problems and address them their own way. In other words, the authority must stay with us. We can't look to god, or the dead, as our authority and abdicate responsibility for our communications, our actions, our part in the fabric of being.'

Whilst we differ in many ways regarding our understanding of the spiritual world whose reality we touch, one can see from her response that in order to operate with wisdom and care the Ovate must bear a heavy weight of responsibility for what they do with what they discern. Emma went on to explain to me that she has sadly seen occasions (and had to pick up the pieces) where a Pagan has loudly proclaimed something that showed little discernment and was more to do with their own ego than a genuine message from an ancestor. This is something that we do have in common, having had to do exactly the same thing in a Christian context where leaders, who should really have been better trained, have sometimes said the most painful things to people, believing themselves led by God when the trail of destruction left by their words would suggest otherwise. The seer's gift requires wisdom and handling with care, whatever spiritual tradition one is from.

The art of divination is also within the role of the Ovate, and this too lies on the cusp of acceptable practice within Judeo-Christian circles. Divination is normally thought of as some kind of ritualistic way of ascertaining the will of a divinity, to read omens or to tell the future, perhaps through reading tarot cards or scrying (the art of staring into a crystal ball or other reflective surface in a trance state to induce visions). A face value reading of the Bible will lead to a straightforward condemnation of the practice because that is what we find in Deuteronomy 18:10 which reads

'No one shall be found among you who makes a son or daughter pass through fire, or who practises divination...'

However, further consideration opens the discussion up a little more since one could consult a Levitical Priest who would use the Urim and Thummim to discern God's will. We know little of what the Urim and Thummim actually were, but it seems to have been that by asking questions which could be answered 'yes' or 'no' one could determine the will of God by what appears to have been a form of casting lots. Also, before the coming of the Holy Spirit recorded in Acts 2, we read in the first chapter of how the disciples prayed and then cast lots to see who would replace Judas as the twelfth disciple, with the lot falling to Matthias. Most Christians would now look upon this practice as inferior to the prayerful listening to seek out God's will in the power of the Holy Spirit, but it nevertheless, at least at one point, had the appearance of a sanctioned form of divination. We might also ask why other forms of divination seem to be so roundly condemned in the Jewish and Christian traditions. One possibility is that there may simply be knowledge that God chooses not to reveal and divination could be seen as a means of trying to circumvent that divine decision by inquiring of other spiritual entities who may use the giving of knowledge, either true or false, to their own advantage. Sometimes the future is hidden for a reason. For example, if God had revealed to me that I was to be ordained priest one day when I was only a child, then I might either have run in the opposite direction or alternatively have thought I should have a particular kind of religious education rather than the scientific one that has served me so well as I've found my way around the study of theology.

It is therefore possible that divination may actually limit our choices and take away some of our capacity for freewill by guiding us down a path before we are ready for it. I am fully aware that there are many Christians of a more conservative tradition than I who roundly condemn all forms of divination as consulting demons. Personally, I am not at ease with that simple formulaic response since, were that universally the case, then I would expect to see a deep corruption of the souls of those known to me who practise divination. Certainly, as many Pagans know themselves, not all those spirits who they consult mean them well, but for me this is a practice that I would not wish to take part in because of the ways in which my own experience has reassured me that when I *need* to know something, God will tell me since he has done so in the past. I need only remember to listen through prayer and find the deep silences where I can discern his voice of stillness within the noise of the world which we inhabit. For me this is sufficient and it helps me to develop trust.

Nimue Brown explained to me that divination is not always about discerning a path forward into the future. It may also be a tool for re-examining the past in order to make sense of the experiences happening in the present. An experienced practitioner may use it when accompanying the path of another to help them to understand what route they should take by looking closely at their heart. I imagine that this could take a form similar to that which some of us have known through receiving counselling or therapy, wherein we are asked questions that help us to see the truth for ourselves rather than simply letting someone else tell us what to do. In this way divination becomes a psychological tool for the benefit of another. However, I would still wish to add the same note of caution, that all spiritual tools, in whatever tradition (including my own) need to be used with a great deal of care because of the ease with which we can be misled, either by ourselves or by an outside influence.

The final part of the Ovate's work that I will cover here, perhaps linked to the model of mediumship, is to do with time and the fabric of the universe. The scientific and Christian understanding of time tends toward it being linear. Although science indicates that time is malleable and the rate of its passing depends on gravity and velocity, it nevertheless suggests that time has the appearance of flowing like an arrow, having a direction such that one is unable to revisit what has already taken place. You might like to think of it as concrete that has been poured, with many fluid possibilities until the moment arrives and the actual event sets into reality. For many Druids (and indeed many Pagans in general) time is viewed differently, as being cyclical, a view that is perhaps inspired by the cyclical nature of the seasons. This has the effect of making past and future seem far more accessible. Hence, through visionary experiences, the Ovate may tread these paths on behalf of themselves or another who seeks wisdom.

On this matter of wisdom though, the one who seeks to access these strands of time is expected to understand that if time is cyclical then it will contain many different pasts and possible futures, all of which are fluid and changing dependent upon decisions made in the present. Reaching this kind of understanding is one of the reasons why training traditionally takes many years. Christians may themselves scoff at this belief, yet there are certainly cycles that can be seen even within the linear model. In terms of basic upbringing, many parents will testify that when they tell their children off they hear their own parents saying the words in their voices. Genetics and nurture select for repeating patterns within families that may linger for generations, and so although time passes, cycles seem to repeat. One who can in all wisdom see these cycles, however we may interpret them, may gently guide someone towards a change of behaviour that can break a destructive cycle of behaviour to prevent it being passed on to the next generation. In fact, I would go so far as to say that if Christians allowed their linear understanding of time to be influenced by the Pagan cyclical understanding, this could benefit how they grow and develop in freedom by looking at familial patterns of behaviour that need to be broken. In this model we might think in spiral terms, where time cycles through seasons and repeating patterns of behaviour, yet with a definite direction down which we are unable to reverse where patterns of the past may influence us unless that influence is broken.

The remaining and most senior order within Druidry is that of Druid. Where the Bardic path seems to be about the artistic talents of the recollection and retelling of stories, the singing into being of new understandings, and the Ovatic path seems to be about developing a mystical perception of reality, so the Druid is called to be immersed in philosophical wisdom based on a life lived in intimate connection with the natural world. The word 'Druid' seems to be a composite word which has its roots in two early Celtic words, 'dru' and 'wid'. Most sources agree that these two words have at their roots the words for oak and wisdom, knowledge, seeing. Together they suggest one in whom the wisdom of the natural world has taken a deep root. We often picture Druids as elderly men with long white flowing beards, rather like the way Gandalf from *Lord of the Rings* is usually portrayed. Whilst there may be a significant literary and romantic input to this vision, an important part of it is down to the age to which a person had lived, and the knowledge which they needed to have acquired before the title of Druid could be applied. In our modern culture, where spirituality is often treated as merely another consumable, one finds people calling themselves a Druid far more speedily than would have been the case amongst the original Druids. This is recognised amongst the more serious modern Druid orders, such as the Order of Bards, Ovates and Druids, or the British Druid Order, both of which run courses that incorporate a great deal of learning and practice before one can claim any of the above titles.

To give some idea of the length of time required to train as a Druid, a fairly good approximation would be the training to be a priest in my own tradition. First there are fourteen years of formal education, starting at the age of four and finishing with A levels at eighteen. The minimum time from there is a further three years in college gaining a degree in theology for ministry and then four more years as a curate. That process of education has taken twenty-one years. Although the route is obviously different, this is remarkably close to the period of nineteen to twenty years that much folklore and the writings of Caesar suggest was the training period for a Druid, although one might speculate that their formal schooling probably began a little later than the four-five age group that we begin with in the UK. Either way there is a clear recognition here that in order to reach the rank of Druid one must acquire through education and experience a great deal of wisdom. In a conversation it was suggested to me that we should think of Bards as the ones who listen, Ovates as the ones who observe, but Druids are the ones who live out what they have heard and seen, and that is a process that cannot be rushed, and it seems to me that this is a commonality in the leadership of any religion. So whilst Bards are the ones who listen to the world and learn the stories to be recounted, and Ovates are the ones who have learned to see the mysteries that transcend time and space, it is the Druids who live out this acquired knowledge and wisdom, encompassing within themselves the sanctity of the natural world.

It is for this reason that an important observation one can make about Druids is a sense of deep and intimate connection to the land. Our culture has become so rapidly mobile that it is rare to find modern people of any tradition who are deeply earthed in their own landscape. In my own practice as a priest in a largely rural community, there is often a clear distinction between those whose families have been here for generations and those who have moved into an area because they see it as pretty. Yet even those who have settled for generation after generation may only see the land as a commodity, something to be farmed and used. Druids go further than this, seeking to put roots deep down into the land itself, to seek its spirituality (although different Druids will understand this differently depending on whether they are monotheist, duotheist, polytheist, pantheist or atheist), and to engage deeply with it. One practitioner (who wishes to remain anonymous) sent me some of her reflections on the land which she and her husband felt compelled to move to. I was stirred by the active way in which she had theologically, academically, practically and spiri-

tually tried to understand her place and its history. As an archae-
ologist and storyteller she feels that she is becoming deeply
bound to her locality, and although she has not yet attained the
rank of Druid, this is a distinctly Druidic practice. One should not
underestimate the personal cost in following this path as it forces
an individual into a place of self-knowledge that those of any
spiritual path could profit from having.

There is a very important distinction that needs to be made
here between Druidry and most traditional forms of Christianity
as expressed in the western world, and that is the distinction
between natural and supernatural. There is a tendency within
western Christianity to distinguish between the spiritual world
and the material world. In part, this is probably a legacy of the
Renaissance and the ways in which Christianity has often tried to
see itself within a culture, such as today's scientific and logical
culture, as opposed to finding a voice to challenge it. The result
of this is that, although this is far less so in the Celtic re-
imaginings of Christianity, for the most part Christians value that
which is spiritual whilst assigning far less value to the physical
world, making a fairly sharp distinction between the two. This
probably goes some way to explaining why Christians are rarely
at the forefront of the ecology movement, with those who adopt
a conservative viewpoint assigning barely any value to the
natural world because of their belief that it will be destroyed by
God soon in what they see as the coming judgement at the return
of Christ. Within Druidry, almost regardless of the philosophical
or religious standpoint of the individual Druid, this dualistic
division does not exist. This is hardly surprising given that the
wisdom gained is taught through interacting with the natural
world. So, for them, the world is prized and valued because it
contains within it, both seen and unseen, all that is necessary for
spirituality and wisdom. Indeed the world is both spiritual and
material at the same time and in such an intertwined way that to
try and introduce an artificial distinction would be an anathema

that an adept Druid would fail to recognise in their practice.

## Druidry as Priesthood

I mentioned earlier that there is a case to be made for Druidry as a form of priesthood, and here I am thinking of all three grades, Bard, Ovate and Druid, working in concert, although it is primarily those who have reached the grade of Druid who are charged with leading public ritual. Before I go too far into this though, I do need to underline once again that not all who call themselves Druid have undergone any kind of formal training. Those who have worked their way through the OBOD scheme, for example, will have had to submit to many hundreds of hours of teaching, study and assessment. Even then one has to face the possibility that someone who has completed all of this is still not the kind of person that should be working in any kind of priestly role because of a lack of self-awareness with respect to issues of using people for their own power needs. As I made clear earlier on in this book, Pagans do not normally have much regard for formal structures and, consequently, there is no clear mechanism by which unsuitable characters can be weeded out, although there is a very good informal network and word soon gets around about an inappropriate practitioner. That, however, is only of use to those within those networks, and there is plenty of anecdotal evidence that the ordinary person in the street is gaining confidence in asking for help or advice from someone who appears spiritual, whatever their tradition.

In order to consider this we need to ask what we think priesthood actually is and also how this applies to other Pagan paths. First, it is important that I make it clear that for many within the Pagan paths, being priests or priestesses is a given; this is how they think of themselves and some would be curious, if not taken aback, that it is even necessary for me to write a justi-fication and reasoning behind what they see as being a defining role of the path that they tread. It is often said that everyone is their own priest/priestess, needing no one to intercede for them to the gods. Whilst I acknowledge that, what I am considering here is more of a public role to those who do not yet feel spiritually engaged and who may be asking for help. For many outside Paganism, specifically in one of the Abrahamic religions, the idea of a Pagan priestly function is either something not considered, or it brings to mind dark imagery of sacrifice. The truth, however, is quite intriguing in a more eco-aware world.

Priesthood is generally defined as a human go-between who communes with the cultural understanding of deity on behalf of the people. In many cultures that have a Judeo-Christian background this will have been thought of as originally being the role of the Levites, one of the twelve tribes of Israel, who were set aside to work as priests between God and the rest of the Israelite, and later Jewish, people. Ultimately, under organised Judaism, these were the only people who were permitted to perform sacrifices to God and these sacrifices could only take place at the temple in Jerusalem. Of the priests in Jerusalem one would be designated as the High Priest and he was the only one permitted into the inner sanctuary of the temple, known as the Holy of Holies, the place where the glory of God was said to dwell. This place was screened off by heavy curtains. The High Priest could enter the Holy of Holies only once a year, and then with a rope tied around his waist so that he could be pulled out if he was overcome by God's presence.

With the advent of Christianity a new understanding of priesthood came, with a belief that there was only one High Priest, Jesus Christ, who being both human and divine was the ultimate go-between because he held both God and humanity within one being. However one interprets what took place at his death and resurrection, the intent of the Gospel writer Matthew, writing in Matthew 27:51, was to show that something new had taken place in the divine human relationship:

'At that moment [the death of Christ on the cross] the curtain of the temple was torn in two, from top to bottom...'

Matthew was indicating the Christian belief that the presence of God was no longer bound within the temple's inner sanctum, but was instead now let loose in the world through the high priesthood of Christ. The understanding of the early church became one of seeing all Christian believers, when taken as a whole rather than as individuals, as a type of priesthood, mediating between God and humanity, led by Christ as High Priest. Whilst this belief has not altered, it has been attenuated in many of the established churches by church leaders who are ordained as priests and whose primary role is to lead Christians in their overall priesthood to the world as they help people to engage with Christ as the way to God.

One might ask how this Christian understanding might relate to Druidry and I would suggest that it is to do with a growing eco-awareness within western culture. Christianity has been guilty of portraying God in more transcendent terms, as somehow separate and away from the natural world, that one has to *go* to Christ who, as High Priest, leads you out of this world to the place where God dwells. I do not personally believe this to be the case, believing, instead, that God is immanent, present in every breathing moment throughout all creation, as well as being also separate and transcendent and, although I would suggest that this is the orthodox theological under-standing of God, it is not the popular one (although it seems to be regaining ground). It appears that because of the lack of Christian engagement with the natural world, spiritual people have begun to look elsewhere. In Druidry what one tends to find in several of the orders is a well-schooled group of people who have been through lengthy training and now dedicate a signif-icant portion of their time to engaging with the spirituality of the natural world. The training, particularly in OBOD, can take many years of learning and self-reflection, but ultimately a dedicated person may emerge with the title of Druid. Acting in concert with those who know the stories and the traditions, the Bards, and those who have a deep spiritual acumen, the Ovates, the Druid may act as a priestly go-between for those who seek to connect with or through the spirituality of nature.

Now there is almost a sense of romanticism about Druidry here, that in some ways it is a return to how Druids of old would have been the priests for the Celtic people, and there are some who think of themselves in terms of recreating this role. Just as some churches romanticise the early church as having got it right and so the modern church needs to return to its roots, so Druids may feel that they need to emulate the original Celtic priesthood. Neither point of view bears up to scrutiny. Christians often look longingly at the early church, but those who actually study its history can tell of the many, sometimes bitter, disagreements and controversies that took place from the very beginning. There was never a golden age because we are only human and we have to deal with our petty squabbles and power struggles. Although there is no written history for the Druids, I have no doubt in my own mind that there would have been just as many arguments then as there are now. Anyone who spends any time amongst the modern British Druid community will know that there are sometimes disputes, some of which can be very public, about who is right or wrong, with online spats every bit as difficult and painful as those that are seen between and within different Christian denominations. Sadly, following a spiritual path, whichever one it is, does not preclude our own desires and ambitions from getting in the way. We all know it shouldn't be so, yet this is what so often happens, particularly amongst those who wish to lead. My argument that Druidry is a modern priesthood is not based on a view that they are any better than any other religious group. It is simply this: that in a culture that is turning more to valuing and understanding its environment, so it is the

Druids who are better placed and better trained to be able to help people make the connection between themselves and the spirituality of the natural world. If God, or however one wishes to define divinity, is speaking through the natural world, there are far more Druids who are aware of it and able to mediate that presence than there are Christians because most of the major denominations have surrendered that position, perhaps in part due to suspicion. There are, of course, disagreements about what communication with the divine entails and to whom one is talking (which I will examine in the next chapter, on Animism), but it is the Druids who have the training in how to engage spiritually with the natural world.

One cannot consider Druids in isolation, however. Priesthood as a model is also present in the other Pagan paths. Within a Wiccan coven, for example, one would expect to find a priest and priestess. In Shamanism the role of the Shaman is to be the go-between for the one seeking help from other spirits. Both of these are clearly priestly roles as we have defined it, yet to my mind they differ from the Druidic priesthood, although only in terms of emphasis. Within Druidry the primary emphasis is on the land and its spirit(s). Although the other Pagan paths are also tied to the land, it seems to me that the emphasis is subtly different. For example, in Wicca, which is far less centralised than Druidry tends to be, one is seeking to connect to the Goddess and the Horned God. Whilst both of these are seen as immanent rather than transcendent deities, and both are affected by the seasons, the manner with which they are engaged does not seem to always be quite so immediately concerned with the particular piece of land on which the ritual is taking place. Within Wicca, the priestly role is to help others engage with their deities, whilst within Druidry it is far more difficult to find clear separation between the deity and the land. As I say, it is a matter of subtle emphasis, yet there appears to be a difference.

## The Future for Druids

It was an intriguing thing to hear some of the concerns raised at a Druid conference I attended in 2013 about Druidry being an ageing path. There are some within the movement who believe that their path is gradually making way for Wicca to become the dominant Paganism within this country, as Wiccan groups seem to flourish within towns and cities, whereas Druids tend more towards rural areas. This may well be responding to a cultural shift with rural life becoming an unaffordable luxury for many. On top of this, Druidry requires lengthy study and culturally we live in an era that values immediacy and struggles with lengthy commitment. These may be some of the reasons why Druidry has a tendency towards a more intellectual edge, because those who have been able to move out of the cities into the country are more likely to be those whose jobs have provided them with sufficient funds. Many Druids have to make do with travelling from the urban sprawl to the country, but most would prefer to dwell there the whole time. Wicca seems to flourish everywhere, but seems to be more prevalent within towns and cities. It would also appear that the age profile of Druidry is older (although the Druid gatherings I have attended have had plenty of young people present). This may also reflect that Wicca is sometimes tied to Goth fashion, especially amongst young women, and is a way of self-empowerment, whereas Druidry is more of a path requiring study. For all these reasons I think I would concur with the Druids who have discussed this, that currently Wicca seems to be in the ascendency, but this doesn't mean that we should conclude that Druidry is going to fade away; it is perhaps more a matter of culture and fashion.

## An inspiring model?

It probably comes across that I have certain sympathies towards Druidry. Whilst I have significantly different beliefs, especially regarding the afterlife, there is much in my Celtic Christian heritage that resonates with the Druidic approach, especially regarding a connection to the earth and its spiritual connection to its creator. Both the liturgical and contemplative practices of Druidry seem similar in style to my own tradition, and the open language it uses allows me to bring my own beliefs as a Christian without feeling excluded.

It is unfortunate that there seem to be so few Christians who seek to develop a deep eco-awareness, perhaps because of a fear of being labelled as Pagan, because I believe we are missing out on something very deep and very beautiful which I will examine in more detail in the next chapter. I personally believe, following my own engagement with the natural world through the medium of Forest Church, that Christians can learn their priestly role again in helping seekers to engage with God through God's presence within the natural world, but I know from conversations with other Christians that there is a deep suspicion here that we are engaging with spirits other than God. I can only point such sceptics to Psalm 24:1:

'The earth is the Lord's and everything in it...'

*Alison and I stand under our beloved cedar looking up through its branches at the misty full-moon, trying hard to lighten our way through a thin sky of broken cloud. We turn to each of the four directions, giving thanks to God for the different ways in which God reveals God's self in this world. Our feet are planted firmly in the ground, our fingers entwined in the soil. I am a brother of Christ through adoption, but I am also a son of Adam, man of dust, of dirt, of soil, and I think we would do well to remember this, to regain some humility. I believe with all my heart that there is more to come, but for now, with damp grass coiled around my fingers, I feel home, connected to the earth from which I was crafted as I recall the poetic beauty of Psalm 139. The sense of God's presence through all of this is so tangible I feel I can reach out and touch it, only to realise that it is already touching me. Is this how my Celtic Christian ancestors felt? How did we lose touch with this precious gift from God?*

## Notes for Chapter 4

1   Hutton R., *Blood and Mistletoe*, London: Yale University Press, 2009.

2   Hutton R., "The Origins of Modern Druidry" in *The Mount Haemus Lectures*, Vol. 1 2000-2007, Lewes: Oak Tree Press, 2008, 8f.

3   Restall-Orr E., *Living Druidry*, Piatkus, 2004, 79.

4   Talboys G.K., *The Way of the Druid*, Winchester: O Books, 2005, 49.

## Chapter Five

# Animism and Panpsychism

## Introduction

Of all the different Pagan paths, Animism is perhaps the most readily misunderstood, caricatured and dismissed. The reality, as I hope to be able to show, is far removed from the notion of people who think all rocks have souls and can be talked to as if they were people like you or I. Instead, modern Animism, with its more philosophical twin, Panpsychism, is often a deeply thought out and experienced alternative understanding of our surroundings which begins by placing an inherent value on the natural world. This is not an easy task in a modern scientifically rationalistic culture where we take the natural world as there mainly for our exploitation.

For many an appreciation of the values of Animism begins when they discover within themselves a simple acknowledgement that everything in the natural world has a right to exist because everything has its own inherent value, regardless of whether or not it can be used as a resource for humanity. Later on in this chapter we will see how Animism stands as a challenge to rethink the command from Genesis 1 to '...fill the earth and subdue it'.

It quickly becomes clear, therefore, that Animism, perhaps more than any of the other Pagan spiritualities, is a way of thinking about nature that crosses over and speaks to a wide variety of paths. Many people believe that life consists of a body and soul dualism in which the soul can exist separate from the body, and this is often found amongst Animists, just as it is found amongst Shamans, as we will see in the next chapter. In the Judeo-Christian tradition, it is not so much that you *have* a soul but that you *are* a soul. For me I have so far tended more to think of 'soul' as being related to mind; it's an aspect of who I am rather than something that can escape my body when I die. I think this is why I have found the language of Panpsychism so challenging because Panpsychism is more concerned with mind than with soul, and with different levels of awareness possessed across the spectrum of complexity found within the natural world. This will allow us to bring some scientific consciousness studies into play later on in this chapter to show how the claims of Animism and Panpsychism should not be easily dismissed and may, instead, have important things to say about the natural world and how we respond to it, as well as asking us questions about the supernatural world.

Whilst myth, story and narrative play a large part in the other Pagan paths, Animism and Panpsychism require of us that after we engage with the stories, we go far beyond them to think about real-world possibilities. In terms of trying to write a single chapter here, whilst books have been written on the subject elsewhere, I think that the easiest way to deal with such a complex subject is to divide the chapter into two linked parts. In the first part I will speak about Animism as a Pagan belief system, whilst in the second I will begin to link Animism to Panpsychism through some of the science of consciousness. I recognise that in some ways this will appear reductionist, that I am trying to explain spiritual experiences through scientific studies, but my concern here is twofold: first, I believe the division between spiritual and material to be an artificial one by those who deem that the rationalist and materialist model is the only one that makes sense of the world. Secondly, I want to suggest that of all the Pagan paths, some of the claims of Animism and Panpsychism deserve to be tested because they seem able to have a noticeable or measurable impact on the physical world as we experience it. In the second half there will be a significant amount of speculation, but that speculation is based on scientific principles. I have no desire to add another layer of pseudoscience around some new religious movements, so I have tried to make it clear in this chapter when I am speculating on possibilities rather than reflecting on evidence.

Animism probably has more in common with Druidry than with any of the other Pagan beliefs, and many Druids would also count themselves as Animists. This is why this section follows straight after the chapter on Druidry. Animism is also a vital component for Shamanism, which is why that chapter follows from, and builds on, this one. Intriguingly, as I will explain, many of the experiences found in Animism, with respect to the natural world, can also be understood through the lens of Trinitarian Christian theology. But, perhaps more than any other field of Paganism, Animism asks that we consider its claims about the actual world in which we live. This is what we shall do later in the chapter, but first we need to look at the nuts and bolts of the subject.

## Definitions and Discussions

In thinking about what Animism is, it is actually helpful to begin by saying what it is not. Harvey[1] quotes Hume, writing:

'There is a universal tendency amongst mankind to conceive all beings like themselves, and to transfer to every object those qualities with which they are familiarly acquainted, and of which they are intimately conscious... and if by a natural propensity, if not corrected by experience and reflection, ascribe malice and goodwill to everything that hurts or pleases us.'

This is one of the reasons why Animism is often thought of as a primitive religion, because many think of it in the same way that they have a fond childhood memory of nice furry caterpillars and horrible thorny brambles. Caterpillars were obviously nice because they were soft and furry and pretty, whereas bramble bushes clearly don't like us because they hurt us. In other words, people disdain Animism as being childlike because it confers a consciousness on to something else entirely dependent on how it affects the observer. Curiously, I would have to say that Christians actually sometimes do this towards God:

> *It's a beautiful summer Thursday evening in Cambridge. We have had our evening service in the theological college, followed by supper. As I walk across the quad two students are relaxing in the warmth. The service had been good and the evening meal was delicious, and one of them turns to me as I walk past and says, 'Isn't God good.' I was disquieted at the time and now, years later, I understand why. That comment was based on how the student was feeling in herself, not on any objective reality. If the service had been boring and the food abominable, would she still have affirmed God's goodness? God is good regardless of how we feel because he is real and separate from us.*

This natural tendency to think of any agent as being like us is more to do with a lack of awareness of 'Otherness' and seems to me to be deeply rooted in a childish, rather than childlike, appreciation of the world. It begins from that place that we all inhabit as children where everything we encounter is conceived of as an extension of ourselves. I can still remember the moment when, as a small child, I realised that everyone is an 'I', just like me, and all capable of thinking their own thoughts that are different from my own. Yet, even though most of us discover this, we rarely seem to develop to the point where we not only appreciate that difference, but actually *value* it and allow it to transform us. Christians can sometimes be heard to say something like, 'God keeps breaking out of the boxes I put him in.' This is the first step towards a greater understanding that even though Christians may claim that humans are made in God's image, God goes far beyond us and our understanding. My two friends, the students in the story above, were transferring their human values and contentedness on to God. They felt full and happy and that informed their understanding of the nature of God. In other words, they felt good so God must be good. This simple trans-ference seems very similar to the ideas about primitive Animism, that it is no more than unconsciously projecting our feelings and consciousness on to an object. However, I want to suggest that modern Animism is far removed from this. It contains within it a sense of playfulness, of wonder and of mystery, and for many this is overarched by a feeling of connectedness to that which is wholly 'Other' than human.

Graham Harvey[2] describes Animists as:

'...people who recognise that the world is full of persons, only some of whom are human, and that life is always lived in relationship with others.'

*As we share lunch, he begins to tell me about his daughter. I've met her on several occasions, with her delightful yet always quizzical manner, and as I write this she is still at the pre-school age. She is already the kind of child that many would call 'Fae' in that she seems enchanted by the world around her and interacts with it in a way that many city-born children seem to miss. She's lucky that her parents are bringing her up amidst mountains, valleys and streams. To watch her in the natural world is a thing of wonder for us and he explains to me that she is teaching him all about Animism. To her the world is alive with persons and to learn about it, all he needs to do is join in with her.*

In the relationship between humans and the rest of the natural world, it is interesting that children seem able to embrace, where adults are filled with scepticism. I have often heard it reflected that children are natural monotheists because of the ease with which they pray, but they are also natural Animists because of the way they see the world. Christians tend to be quite happy with the idea that children have a natural belief in God, but I suspect would be troubled by a natural Animism, yet both types of belief have the possibilities of growing beyond their childish theologies. As adults we are expected to retain the former belief in God, but reject the latter Animistic beliefs as not being rational. Animists beg to differ. However, it would be far too simple to imagine that an Animist world view is a childish one. Instead, as we look closer at Animist beliefs we find a world that is filled with life, but devoid of the romantic pre-Raphaelite imagery of nothing but pure and beautiful spirits. There is a recognition of the spectrum of behaviours across the natural world, just as there is within humanity as a single species.

## Seen and Unseen

The first point of contact with Animism requires of us that we understand the limitations of human senses, and that the world might therefore be populated with persons that we can't see alongside those that we can. We need to be careful not to become overly dualistic in this, but the categories of seen and unseen help us to understand what Animists believe.

Amongst the 'seen' is essentially anything that is physically 'animate'. However, the perception of 'animate' may differ from the rationalist world view. As I've said, Animists are often carica-tured as people who talk to rocks, but the reality is that for some Animists certain rocks or twigs or mountains, etc. are spoken to and treated as persons because they are perceived to have behaved, at some point in time, in an animated way. Animists don't think all rocks are persons, but they might think that some are, based on the evidence they have seen. Knowing the place where you reside is vital, so one Animist cannot walk into a new place, with which they have no relationship, and point to a particular rock and say, 'That rock is aware.' Instead, there must be time and relationship with the local environment as the Animist begins to engage on a profoundly observational and spiritual level.

The effect this has on an Animist is to make them good listeners to, and observers of, the natural world. All creatures are treated with respect and as of equal value to humans, with points of view and abilities to make choices that are just as valid as human ones. It is important, though, that I underline that a modern Animist does not anthropomorphize. To treat another creature as having a valid opinion is not to treat it as having a human consciousness; remember that the definition of 'other than human persons' includes the word 'other' and this concept is taken extremely seriously. In fact, it is this very 'otherness' that has led me into the Trinitarian reading of Animism that I will describe at the end of this chapter.

Yet despite this otherness, Animists believe that we are able to live in an interactive relationship with the natural world, a relationship in which animals respond to us and our overtures. A rationalist might think that this would be akin to birds learning to come to food put out for them on a bird table because of instinct, but for an Animist it is more than this because of the observational evidence of what seems to be unusual behaviour displayed by some animals in response to human overtures. In this context, from a Christian perspective, it is perhaps interesting to recall some of the stories told of St. Francis and his relationship to the world around him. Foremost is the way he was once known to preach to a flock of birds which came and stood around him, apparently listening intently to his charge that they must sing the praises of God. Despite his close proximity, that they were in actual physical contact, the story that is told is of the birds staying with him until he blessed them and sent them on their way. Though firmly based within a Christian perspective, there can be little doubt that the response of the creatures around him to his overtures is consistent with some of the experiences of Animists. This story of St. Francis bears a remarkable similarity in terms of avian behaviour to those recounted by Harvey[3]:

'...owls and herons are not rare in Britain, but I have witnessed them fly in ways that have been taken to indicate participation and benediction on Pagan celebrations or activities.'

That the two different traditions both testify to animal interaction suggests that the honouring of animals as persons in their own right is a claim that should be taken seriously, regardless of religious belief, and this is one of the reasons that, with respect to the seen world, Animism seems to be less of a religious path and more a different and equally valid way of engaging with the natural world. This does, of course, make us wonder whether this raises a difficult issue for Animists, which is the one of food. If another creature is also a person, isn't eating them a form of cannibalism? Once again, this is our tendency to anthropomorphize coming to the fore. An Animist recognises that some animals eat other animals, that is simply the way of the natural world, and consequently as a part of the natural world humans sometimes eat other animals. What you do tend to find, though, is a sense of honouring that which is being eaten. Whilst Christians may say a prayer of grace before a meal, thanking God for the food, an Animist may say a thank you to the animal for the gift of its flesh. It is this concept of honour that informs the food choices made by an Animist. For that reason it is unlikely that one who takes their beliefs seriously would eat factory farmed food. I have also met a number of Animists who find that in all good conscience they cannot eat any meat products.

Thus far we have dealt purely with animal life, but Animists may well go further to consider plant life too, particularly for those with a more Druidic perspective. In the previous chapter I wrote of my Bardic friend and her relationship to several of the trees in the woodland she visits most days. To her they have names and characteristics:

*The Bard and I have climbed through her favourite woodland again, but this time we've gone through the trees, following the route up to the fields beyond. Here the muddy footpath turns into a rutted and distinctly soggy farm track, lined on one side by trees, most of them horse-chestnuts. There's a particular tree that she is drawn to more than any of the others, and she wants to show it to me. When we arrive the mature tree has its boughs reaching right down to the ground. It is as if the trunk is protecting itself, but given that we are in the depths of winter there are no leaves, just a bare, expectant skeleton. We pause before the veil of branches and I realise that she is asking permission to enter. After a moment she moves in between the boughs and I follow her. Together we meander around the enclosed space, simply getting a feel for it. She smiles when I comment that I was never any good at climbing trees as a child, but this one makes it easy.*

*Respectfully, I stand on one of the larger boughs that reaches almost to the ground and begin gently bouncing, filled with a long forgotten childhood urge to jump and swing around the branches. And that's when I become aware of what she feels in this tree, and I feel it with her, because there is a sense of being welcomed into play, almost as if by one who misses a generation who prefers technology to the natural playground it offers. At the risk of anthropomorphising a very different type of being from myself, for a moment it is like a shared joy between three friends.*

An over-active imagination? I don't believe that there is a risk to my soul from re-engaging with my childhood joys and wonders, and I have many happy memories of an old oak tree, (just called the 'old tree'), which was, by turns, a ship on the ocean, a space ship or a den, depending on how we felt as children. However, this and several other similar experiences, has left me pondering whether there is more to our seen world than Christians in a rational age are usually comfortable with.

Up until this point in the chapter we have engaged with the spiritual side of the seen world, of animals and plants, and maybe even of rocks, each as being of value and potentially having a spirit of their own, spirits with which humans, as one part of the seen physical world, can interact. This interaction is different from that which we have with other members of our own species, but is possible nevertheless. But we now need to turn our attention to the unseen world, and we need to recognise that it is here that many Christians will become uncomfortable. Within many forms of Christianity, a semi-dualistic world view has evolved based on the evolution of beliefs that seems to take place through the Bible when read in historical order. The Hebrew people appear to have begun with a henotheistic view, that the world was populated by gods and Yahweh was simply their god; one amongst many. This gradually evolved through revelation and experience to a monotheism which did not preclude other spiritual beings, but Yahweh was in absolute control. From there, in the midst of questions about suffering, grew the concept of a created oppositional force which eventually, within Christianity, took on the mantle of the devil, a fallen angel of great power who would ultimately be defeated by God. This is not true dualism as seen in some other world religions because the forces of evil are not evenly matched with the uncreated God. However, it is often perceived, especially amongst those of more conservative beliefs, that this battle between good and evil forms the entirety of the unseen world. It is fairly easy for us to understand, therefore, why for many Christians the unseen world divides neatly into forces on the side of God, and forces on the side of the devil. They are either angels or demons. But the question I wish to ask is: is that really fair and what evidence do we have that angels and demons form the entirety of the unseen world? Whilst in my own mind and in my own experience as a Christian priest I have no disagreement with the belief in angels and demons, I am no longer convinced that they tell the whole story:

> *For an observer this would have seemed an unlikely gathering. The Anglican priest has invited Alison and me to meet four of her friends who are a mixture of Witch and Druid. The priest and one of the Witches both have Irish heritage and have both spent time there with relatives. Tales multiply through the evening of spirits of the unseen dead that the witch has encountered, and the priest counters with stories of her own, rich in the influence of the folklore of her homeland. The story which most attracts my attention, though, is when their stories converge on tales of the Bean-Sidhe or Banshee, known to come and announce when someone is about to die. They explain how in Irish tradition she announces herself either with a form of otherworldly wailing or by knocking loudly. Both the priest and the Witch have had similar experiences in Ireland with the Bean-Sidhe and on both occasions people within the household died during the night.*

There are numerous different unseen creatures within Animism, and their names and characters will depend to some degree on the country of origin. Britain and Ireland are no different and have a wide-ranging folklore concerning inhabitants from an unseen world, who become known to humans through some form of interaction, either intended or accidental. It would take a book in its own right to begin to engage with this vast array of beings from folklore. Yet even though there are many different types in popular thought, it is the Faeries who take a prominent position, and certainly, in my limited experience, this is the group that have generated the most interest and who are referred to in the story above. Intriguingly, they are also the race in the unseen world that is sometimes linked to the Bible and the stories of angels and demons. This combination means that we should spend a moment looking at them in particular.

The Sidhe (*'Shee'*) are at the forefront of the stories of Faeries that are told and Bean Sidhe translates more or less from Gaelic as 'Woman of the Faery Mounds'. The Sidhe are, however, far removed from the pretty Tinkerbell type creatures of popular Disney-influenced imagination. Instead, they are usually thought of as a quite separate and powerful race of beings with an Irish mythology that places them as the original inhabitants of Ireland before the Gaels came. They were known as the Tuatha De Danaan, 'The People of the Goddess Dana'. Stories tell of how the invading Gaels defeated them in battle leading them to retreat underground. Whilst some myths describe them as being short in stature, they are generally thought to be of tall, elegant and beautiful appearance and hence are often known as The Gentry, The Fair Folk, or The Good People, yet are also believed to be extremely powerful and knowledgeable. They are not normally thought of as divine, but certainly as being supernatural, and whilst they can die, it is not usually of old age but instead in battle. In terms of the part they play in Animism, they are thought by some to be the spirits of nature. As I've mentioned, others would put such 'Elementals' in a different category and shy away from the idea that all the unseen are Sidhe of one kind or another. They are, however, universally treated with respect by experienced Animists. They fall outside a dualistic divide of beings into the categories of good and evil, and instead are considered to be powerful creatures who make decisions in the same way that we do, but who have a different moral perspective from our own. Some Animists will try not to attract the attention of Faeries because of their power and one explained to me that it could be considered similar to our relationship with hedgehogs. We do not go out of our way to harm them; it's just that sometimes our actions inadvertently do so, such as the clearing of a hedgerow for farming purposes that can kill a hibernating hedgehog. Likewise, an Animist might believe that the actions of the Sidhe may not be intended to cause us harm, but it can happen anyhow simply because we are in the way. If one attends a Pagan ritual that begins and ends with 'Calling in the Quarters' (where one speaks words of welcome to spirits/energies of the four points of the compass), then it is quite possible, depending on tradition, that for some of those present they may intend their words of welcome to be addressed to the Sidhe.

As I have intimated, it is worth noting that there have been attempts to link the Sidhe with the Judeo-Christian story. Yeats[4] imagined them to be akin to fallen angels, cast out of heaven by God in their rebellion led by Satan. However, the Sidhe were not thought of as being evil in the same way as demons, but simply as ones who would not submit to God. This might also be tied to the mythology that sometimes surrounds Elves, a type of Faery, of wanting to return to their homelands, but being unable to. I have also read numerous attempts to link the Sidhe to the stories of the Nephilim from the Old Testament, suggesting that the Nephilim are a Middle Eastern example of Sidhe, and that the Bible gives their origin as the offspring of fallen angels and human women:

'When people began to multiply on the face of the ground, and daughters were born to them, the sons of God saw that they were fair; and they took wives for themselves of all that they chose. Then the Lord said, 'My spirit shall not abide in mortals for ever, for they are flesh; their days shall be one hundred and twenty years.' The Nephilim were on the earth in those days—and also afterwards—when the sons of God went in to the daughters of humans, who bore children to them. These were the heroes that were of old, warriors of renown.' Genesis 6:1-4

This is a rather obscure passage and many commentators[5]

believe that it is an ancient tradition from the Middle East that the writer of this part of Genesis has included as one example of a great evil that has overtaken humanity, leading to God's judgement and the flood. How we understand this passage depends entirely on how we interpret the phrase 'sons of God'. We cannot know for sure what was intended by the original writer. Certainly, this idea of divine beings mating with humans is often found in the mythologies of various countries and it's quite possible that the writer was seeking a rational reason for the existence of such large men as Goliath within the inherited mythologies from when Israel invaded Canaan. 'Sons of God' is a difficult phrase to interpret because it can mean angels, demons, kings or godly men, depending on which part of the Bible you are reading. However, the way in which a contrast is made between the male 'sons of God' and the female 'daughters of men' does seem to indicate that the intention was an understanding of the male beings as spiritual and of divine origin. Rationally, we might want to question whether a proposed union between a spiritual being and a human woman could actually possibly produce a physical offspring, yet at the heart of the Christian story is a belief that God's Spirit did something similar by creating a union with Mary that produced Jesus, the Son of God.

I think it would be unwise to draw too many conclusions about this, but it is certainly interesting to note that other cultures across the Middle East have mythologies of a race of beings which were far taller than humans, and explain them as having been a union between something divine and something human. This may well be a red herring, but it warranted inclusion because some kind of link between the angelic and the Sidhe appears to be fairly popular in modern mythologies and it is a postmodern phenomenon to mix and match ideas from different origins. My hope is that this will be a useful background for deliberation.

Animism is a vast subject that is of personal interest because of my own rural location and the ways in which, over the last ten years, the natural world has seemingly come alive to me. But I also recognise that I have come to this understanding through many years of working as a scientist, and that my naturally enquiring inclination means that I have attempted to examine some of the experiences and consider whether there may be some evidence in science for the kind of interactions that many Animists feel they have with the natural world. Although others are coming at this from a different direction, as Anathaswamy[6] reported, it is becoming apparent that some serious scientific inquiries are now being undertaken regarding plant consciousness. It is important to understand that as we move into the next section I am considering here far more the ways in which we engage with the seen world rather than with the unseen and rather more supernatural world.

## Panpsychism and Animism – Understanding What We Mean about Consciousness and 'Mind'

Emma Restall-Orr[7] defines Animism as:

'...a monist metaphysical stance, based upon the idea that mind and matter are not distinct and separate substances but an integrated reality rooted in nature.'

In this statement she draws us from the more speculative nature of the first half of this chapter towards a more philosophical appreciation of the natural world. In order to understand this better I think we should start with what we mean by 'mind'. At the beginning of this chapter I indicated that the Judeo-Christian understanding of being is non-dualistic; that we don't *have* a soul but that we are a soul. I suspect that soul and mind may be two sides of the same coin that emerge from, but do not remain dependent upon, our physical nature. The most difficult issue surrounding this is that, despite numerous attempts to study and understand it, we still don't know what consciousness actually is. Mainstream scientific opinion suggests that 'mind', the awareness of self, is something that arises in the brain but cannot be definitively tied to any specific part of the brain, as behavioural scientist Robert O. Duncan[8] states:

'The difficulties we have assessing self-awareness demonstrate that it is a complex trait and support the idea that no single brain area is dedicated to it.'

This line of thinking has led to the suggestion that consciousness may be, at least in part, spread throughout the body, or possibly, in a more esoteric model, that consciousness does not arise within the body, but that the body, and mainly the brain, is the transmitter through which it is mediated in its engagement with the world. My suspicion, as I hope to show here, is that the truth resides somewhere between the extremes, that consciousness may emerge from the physical, but can then transcend it and act upon that from which it sprung. However, the limitations of the scientific method suggest that when it comes to understanding our minds and our awareness, we are, for the time being, in the very early stages. One thing which seems to become clear is that human consciousness is not necessarily how we perceive it to be:

*I lie in bed in the warm darkness. The heating pump rumbles away quietly in the background and I am deeply aware of the sleeping presence of Alison beside me. The alarm has broken my slumber and I have switched it off. As consciousness returns I remind myself of all that I have to do today, and it's going to be yet another busy day. I keep trying to rouse myself, to move from under the duvet, yet I remain there. And then I find that I am moving and standing on the cool carpet, wishing that the heating was more efficient. Strangely, I am not sure who made the decision to get up. I am not conscious of having chosen to do so, yet here I am, standing. Where was the real free choice of consciousness...?*

This is a part of the so called 'hard-problem' of consciousness. Bricklin[9] quoting James, uses this idea about how hard it is to get out of bed on a cold morning, something that most of us have experienced, to illustrate how decisions are actually made and how little real choice actually takes place. He suggests that what's actually going on is an unconscious struggle between the different inputs from the body's senses. I wanted to get out of bed, but the bed was comfy and the room was cold. Then I became aware that the day was getting away, but the bed was still comfy and the room was still cold. Then suddenly I was up and the probable reason, he suggests, was that a mental distraction, that I had to get on with the day, meant that the impression of the room being cold disappeared for long enough for the wish to get out of bed to override the understanding that it would be cold. That moment in which I was not aware of the cold meant that an unconscious override could take place and activate my body to get out of bed. It would appear that I did not consciously make the decision to get up at a particular point in time, but actually became aware that the decision had been made and that I was now up.

At first sight this seems like a nonsense, but Benjamin Libet[10] conducted experiments that were able to show that we appear to become conscious of a decision to move about 200 milliseconds after the body has actually started to move. These and other similar experiments have led to the rather disquieting claims that freewill is actually an illusion and that what we call 'mind' is merely something that floats on the surface of actions that are completely determined and without free choice. This more materialist way of thinking can eventually lead to dismissing the possibility of the existence of the soul. There is also new evidence, as described by Spinney[11], which suggests that the brain puts together a sense of the present moment in 2-3 second portions. Anything that falls into a smaller time period than this, such as Libet's experiments, may well be below the threshold at which we can resolve what the brain can actually experience. Therefore, if we are going to take Animism and Panpsychism seriously we need to look at this problem of consciousness since, as philosopher Mary Midgely[12] put it:

'...the theory that says that what happens in our consciousness does not affect the behaviour of our bodies. Our experience is just... idle froth on the surface, a mere side effect of physical causes.'

She goes on to suggest that if this theory is true, then consciousness is unique in nature in that it is caused and exists but doesn't actually *do* anything. Anyone with any understanding of evolution can see that this is a problem, since something which is of no use is usually discarded. What we might call 'one way causality', i.e., that which is caused but has no value, doesn't make it into the next generation because it confers no genetic advantage – being simply a waste of energy. So it seems to me that consciousness must be more than just some kind of meaningless 'froth'. The intriguing thing is that once we begin to look at how consciousness might arise, we can begin to see how there are the beginnings of an argument that some of the claims behind Animism, at least with respect to the seen world, may well play more of a part in the universe than we might have imagined.

Another good indicator that Libet's experiments do not tell the whole story comes from the work of Schwartz[13] who claimed to have shown a measurable change in the behaviour of patients suffering from obsessive compulsive disorder (OCD) by treating them with cognitive behavioural therapy. This won't come as a surprise to some readers who may well have been treated with similar techniques. What makes Schwartz's work so intriguing and relevant to this subject is the neurological studies he undertook that showed excessive metabolic activities in specific regions of the brain in OCD sufferers. This, he believed, gave rise to what has become termed 'false error messages', e.g., simply seeing something dirty compels the sufferer to wash in case they have become contaminated.

During the first stage of treatment the subjects were taught how to describe their symptoms in a manner which expressed a separation between their experience of the compulsion and their perception of self, thus externalising the feeling of compulsion. Practically, Schwartz[14] describes how this would work out as patients ceasing to make statements such as, 'I feel like I need to wash my hands again', and replacing them with statements like, 'That nasty compulsive urge is bothering me again.' Following the first stage of treatment, two thirds of the group showed notable improvement with their symptoms becoming less severe. More importantly, in this group it was shown that there were significant decreases in the above-mentioned neurological metabolic rate.

In the next stage of treatment, sufferers were taught to refocus their attention on some other activity when under OCD compulsion, thus altering their behavioural response. In so doing Schwartz[15] reported that:

'...significant changes are seen in the activity of [brain] circuitry...'

These results would therefore appear to suggest that, contrary to the beliefs of many that consciousness is just some meaningless 'froth', not only can the conscious mind have a genuine effect on behaviour, but it can also have an effect on its underlying neuro-logical chemistry and structure. What makes that so important is that it shows us that mind, whatever it is, can affect the structures from which it arises. Or to make this more clear, the mind, which is a non-material phenomenon, appears to be able to affect the material from which it arises – the brain. We need, therefore, to consider the only model of consciousness that we can readily experience – our own – and use that to speculate about Animist beliefs concerning the mindfulness or ensouled nature of the rest of the world and the potential effect on the world of this.

Therefore, if mind can have an effect on reality, where does mind come from? I believe the answer to that is critical to our understanding of Animism, which is that mind emerges from the physicality of the brain and body, but cannot be reduced to being nothing more than a property of the brain and body. What is more, once the property of mind emerges, it can then affect that from which it has emerged. The technical name for this is 'supervenience'. The mind, (consciousness) arises from the physicality of our being, but cannot be reduced to it, and can have an effect on that from which it emerges because it supervenes it. Now, you might ask, why is this important for Animism? It is simply this; we do not know how consciousness arises in humans, but it appears to do so when a level of complexity has arisen that permits it to do so. Whether the brain is the originator of consciousness, or its transmitter from some other 'place', is more or less a moot point. Conscious mind appears to arise as a property of biological matter and can then have a direct effect on that matter from which it has arisen. In other words, once mind has emerged it can then affect its own surroundings. Animists believe that the world is full of persons, only some of whom are human, and if by 'person' we mean a being that has consciousness *of some sort*, then this belief that consciousness is an emergent property suggests that it may indeed be possible for there to be other minds at play in the world, provided, and this is key, that we do not superimpose on them a belief that human consciousness is the only valid form of consciousness. The human mind is likely to be individual to our species and so we can only readily communicate with ourselves. (Even then it is not without some difficulty as different cultures may share a common language yet infer different meanings to words.) For several decades scientists have speculated on the levels of consciousness of the higher primates, dolphins and whales, but the question they seem to be asking is more whether their minds are sufficiently like ours to be counted as valid, whereas the Animist is more likely to say that their minds are valid regardless of whether they are enough like us to permit communication on human terms.

I recognise that so far this is a fairly reductionist approach to Animism, in trying to give a degree of scientific speculation about whether the phenomenon of non-human mind is real or not. However, given that of all the Pagan paths Animism is the one with the most coherent philosophical partner in Panpsychism, I think this approach is valid in order to get us to think about possibilities, even if this argument can only be made with regard to the seen world. But do we need to simply stay with the seen world, or can we speculate a little further? If mind/soul is linked to spirit, then considering that the surrounding natural world may include minds other than our own permits us to consider whether there are spiritual presences other than our own that are also rooted in reality. Most Pagans, not just Animists, take this for granted and will often say that spirits and divinities within the world are themselves affected by the natural world. To illustrate this, let's return to a story that I merely outlined in Chapter 1:

> She explained to me that she had been out for a ride on her horse through some woodland where tree-felling had been taking place. There, standing next to a fallen trunk and weeping, she saw a Dryad (tree spirit). She enquired of it as to what had upset it so much, and it explained that its home had been destroyed and it had

*nowhere to live. The Druid invited the Dryad to come with her and she would find it a new home. Together they searched the woodland and found another tree which was to the Dryad's liking. The Druid then used a ritual to 'rehouse' the Dryad and it took its place amongst the forest once more.*

What are we to make of a story like this? Well, the answer is that it all depends on who you are and what you believe. I have had another Animist say to me that she felt this story was completely at odds with her own beliefs. Others would have no problem whatsoever with the idea of spirits within nature, without needing to classify them as good or evil, angel or demon. Yet, if we think of the consciousness model I've been describing here, there is another potential way of understanding this and similar stories, provided we recognise that, although I have used science to describe some aspects of consciousness, what comes next is most definitely speculation.

You will recall from earlier in this book that I wrote of the vision I received as a teenager of two angels in the church where I was an altar server. The question which that experience begs is, if I had my eyes closed, how did I 'see' angels? I believe that the answer to this and to any communication with God through prayer is that my spirit discerns that which God's Holy Spirit is saying or revealing. But I am a physical being and so any communication must be understood in terms of my physical senses; there can be no other way. So, in terms of seeing an angel whilst my eyes were closed, this can only have happened by my perception of a spiritual reality being mediated through the optical part of my brain. In other words, that part of my brain which processes visual information 'translated' the spiritual information into something that I could understand. With that in mind, and with all that we have said about emergent consciousness, we can turn back to the rehoused Dryad story and begin to speculate on another way of understanding the events.

Trees are complex forms of life. They react to seasons and conditions. Recent research by Dr. Monica Gagliano[16] has shown how the reactionary plant, Mimosa Pudica, known for closing its leaves when touched as a defence mechanism, learns not to react to water droplets and appears to retain that memory. Professor Richard Karban[17] has demonstrated rapid chemical communication amongst sage bushes when an attack against one prompts a warning response that leads to defences being mounted by its neighbours. The general scientific approach has been to declare that these and other similar experimental observations are all automatic evolutionary conditioned responses, yet, until relatively recently, precisely the same charge has been levelled against all animal life. As we are discovering that animal consciousness is more complex than previous generations had imagined, could we not at least speculate that some kind of very different awareness may be present amongst plants. I realise that this is a colossal leap and without much hope of experimental verification, but let's stay with this speculation because it may cast some light on the Druid's experience with the Dryad. Think of it like this: if a tree forms some form of consciousness, and if that emergent consciousness has similar properties to human consciousness, then we could speculate that what the Druid perceived was the dying of a host body over which the consciousness supervened. She could not 'see' a Dryad, but as a Druid her perception of the natural world was finely attuned and was shaped by her beliefs and imagination so to some degree she anthropomorphised and 'saw' what most people are simply unaware of and was able to interact with what she saw. We may wish to title this 'Dryad' or simply think of it as an awareness generated by the tree which was failing as a result of being felled. We shouldn't think of this as like a human awareness, yet for the one who perceived it, this was the only doorway through which it was possible to perceive. Once we start thinking in this way we realise that the language that assigns the words 'soul', 'mind' or 'spirit' may be breaking down. There is only the 'person'.

I am aware that this is hugely speculative, but I am also aware that many people who engage with nature on a deep level have experiences which are difficult to explain to others who have not had them. These are easily dismissed by those who think themselves as rational so I think it's important that we consider experiences from a rational perspective purely in order to inspire ourselves to be less dismissive. If we don't play the game of 'what if', we box ourselves into a very monochromatic world. As I said earlier in Chapter 1, how we understand our experiences will depend on what belief construct we have. But within that model we have to remain open to our beliefs being challenged by new experiences if they don't fit into the construct that we have. This can lead to a modification or a complete discarding of the construct.

So far I would have to say that none of my own experiences have been in conflict with my beliefs as a Christian, but I have certainly had to modify and enlarge my beliefs about the nature of God and the universe God has created. I think it's only fair that we recognise that some experiences may be purely imaginative, but the complexity of consciousness and the difficulties in understanding it suggest that we should be open minded to other possibilities too. We should also not rule out the possibility that there are other spirits abroad in nature. The knee-jerk Christian response is normally a dualistic one, that every spirit is either of God or of the devil, but I don't believe that there is a strong argument that can be made there. It is quite clear for those who hold the Bible as important that it teaches that God creates both the seen and the unseen. If this is so, and we are indeed engaging with the natural world in ways we might not have considered, then it is helpful if we can have a Christian understanding of what is taking place. I have stated that I have no problem with being a Christian and encountering the natural world in a new way, inspired by the experiences of my Animist friends. How then do I understand this in terms of the Father, the Son and the Holy Spirit of Christian belief?

## A Theology of Encounter

'Arboreal exchanges of affection may occur'.

This comment, written by Bruce Stanley to describe an aspect of 'The Grove', Forest Church's presence at the 2013 Greenbelt Festival, brought many wry smiles to the faces of the participants. Those who have taken active roles in the ecology movement have long been ridiculed as being nothing more than a bunch of tree-huggers, and now those of us who are involved in forging, or at least acknowledging, a spiritual connection with the natural world are having to face the possibilities of similar ridicule along with spiritual suspicion. Christians with a more conservative theological stance have a tendency to dismiss new ideas as diluting the truth and so now we need to take a deeper and more theological look at the possibilities of 'arboreal exchanges of affection' in order to understand some of what might actually be taking place. My hope is that by putting this within the context of Trinitarian theology I might be able to allay the fears of some whilst provoking debate amongst others. It is also important to add that, as within any shared experience, the conclusions that I have drawn from what has taken place are not necessarily the same as others who were present since, it is wholly possible for the same experience to speak to different individuals in different ways and on different levels.

## Understanding the Difficulties

Ancient Arden Forest Church is one of many Forest Churches across the country which meets to engage with God in the outside world. Our group meets under the canopy of a delightful cedar tree in the vicarage garden looking across a meadow.

Gradually, the cedar has been taken to the hearts of the participants and is now often talked of as the 'guardian' of the space we
use. But what do we mean by this? Many people name their cars
and even assign personalities to them. Is that what we intend by
adopting our old cedar? Is it just a friendly mascot that we have
anthromorphised into something it could never be? Or is there
something taking place at a much deeper level? Some within
Christianity view such a possibility as being tantamount to
communing with demons, but for others who have a genuine
experience, rather than a superficial dismissal of anything
outside their narrow theology, there is a sense of connection,
almost of companionship, with the natural world both within
and beyond the animal kingdom. A form of Animism can often be
found lurking not far beneath our logical scientific culture. Jenny
(not her real name) is an elderly parishioner whom I have known
for some time. She has a lively and active Christian faith which is
quite conservative in nature, yet she talks to her houseplants and
has affirmed to me that her companionship and friendship helps
them to grow. Jenny would never dream of attaching the label of
Pagan to herself, so this serves as a simple example of an intuitive
'feel' that many people have. If this connection is genuine rather
than imagined then we need to explore two difficult questions:

1. What/who exactly are we communicating with?
2. How can we be communicating?

In order to understand just how difficult the first question is to
answer we need to turn our attention to answering question two.
Picture this scenario:

*Alison and I are sat at a dining room table with some acquaintances.*
*The dinner topics range over a wide array of subjects. As I start to*
*raise something of interest to me that I would like their opinion on*
*there is a micro-second glance from my wife. No one else would have*

*seen it, nor noticed the subtle change in tack from what I had origi-*
*nally intended, but that tiny glance communicated Alison's*
*awareness that this topic might be more difficult to speak about, that*
*it touched a raw nerve I had been unaware of, and that I should*
*tread very carefully, and preferably in the opposite direction. Our*
*guests remained oblivious to the unspoken words between us.*

Like many couples who have been together for years, Alison and I understand each other deeply. No one knows us like we know each other because the depths of intimacy, the time we have shared, and the sacramental bond we have nurtured means that we can non-verbally communicate more with a glance now than we could have said in an evening when we first met. Language, although not transcending words, often has little need for them. Yet it has taken us more than two decades to have reached this state of relationship; that's two decades of the day-to-day togeth-erness of two complementing members of the same species, bonded spiritually by the knitting of two souls in marriage. We can often know what the other is thinking, but then you would expect that to happen. I do not pretend to have this kind of relationship with other friends, let alone acquaintances, where a glance can communicate a sentence. Yet despite this knowledge of the difficulties of non-verbal communication within our own species, we almost blithely accept that we can somehow commu-nicate with other members of the natural world. Indeed, this is at the heart of the Pagan beliefs and experiences surrounding Animism and I find myself concerned that there is almost an arrogance in questioning the experiences of others. However, there remains inherent in this a puzzle and the question we have to ask is, how can we be communicating? The answer to that question is dependent on us recognising the need to reject, or at the very least, question some of the assumptions Christians have historically made, whilst at the same time challenging our notion of awareness, all of which leads us to try and deal with question one.

I've described the non-verbal communication with my wife, and we are all aware of the ability of humans to transfer ideas by the written word, provided a common language is shared, but what about across the species divide? Obviously, the written word is beyond us since writing is a skill possessed only by humans, but verbal and non-verbal communication can certainly take place between us and other members of the animal kingdom. Anyone who has shared their living space with a dog will know of the seemingly almost telepathic abilities that they have to comprehend our emotions. Clearly commands can be learned, but dogs seem to be able to go far beyond this to astonishing levels of empathy. Romero, Konno and Hasegawa[18] have observed empathic yawning by dogs in response to yawns by their human partners. Intriguingly, a canine response was not demonstrated when the human yawns were faked or when yawns came from strangers in a room, regardless of whether they were real or fake. This is just one of numerous scientific studies that show that we connect on some level with other non-human animal species. Yet, when one is considering a spiritual connection with nature, this is only the first step.

We are going to journey through three stories, taking what I have outlined above, in order to set out a theological mechanism for how the connection may take place. The three stories are all personal ones rather than borrowed from another source, and they outline a progression from that which falls within orthodox Christian theology to that about which we can only speculate. Each has an arrow, a direction, which conveys something of who appears to have initiated the experience. The first is about a divine-to-human experience; the second is about a human-to-nature experience and the third *may* be a nature-to-human experience. I am far more speculative about this third example for reasons that will become clear, but for the sake of completion it needs to be included. This is also the chronological order in which they took place, which suggests to me a divine leading that has been aimed at overcoming my own inner misgivings, coming as I do from what was once a fairly conservative theological standpoint. In a sense by writing this I am inviting you along to see a part of how I feel I have been led by God into recognising God's all-pervading presence within the natural world, whilst recognising that the thoughts and ideas shared here represent a snapshot of my own developing theology regarding the world of which we are a part. These stories reflect some of the steps that I have taken on what I refer to as the Shaken Path, and the first one is a more in-depth description of an event which I mentioned in Chapter 2.

Story One: the Divine-Human encounter:

*Alison and I have gone on a journey into the forest. For me this was with an express purpose of experiencing the presence of God in the natural world, whilst for Alison it was a part of a spiritual exercise. We begin by following one of many pathways, but after a while, following Alison's intuitive lead, we leave the path and walk into the trees. We stop to scatter some seeds for those we sometimes call the 'Little Friends', those for whom this forest is their natural home. They don't need our seeds, they have plenty to forage for here, but whenever we visit the homes of our human friends we often take a gift like a bottle of wine or a box of chocolates, so it seems only friendly to do the same here. We then embark on a form of prayer walking – a way of treading slowly and carefully, listening out with all our senses, trying to become attuned to the song God is playing within creation.*

*After a while we come to what simply seems like the 'right' place. It seems right purely because we have been walking slowly and quietly and have become aware of some noise up ahead which seems to be coming in our direction, so we crouch down and wait, listening as the disturbance comes towards us. Within moments the forest is filled with the sound and vision of squirrels chasing each other. Neither of us has ever seen so many squirrels in one place at one time. Usually, they seem to be single or in pairs, and just occasionally we have seen three, but here there are many more, running after each other up and down trees, across the ground, circling and chasing excitedly. Then almost as soon as they have arrived they disappear, vanishing off into the forest, leaving us alone.*

*Yet this sense of being on our own lasts only momentarily. We stand up slowly, then with just a hoot of warning, a huge owl sweeps down in front of us, maybe no more than an arm's length from our bodies, before sweeping up into the trees and, as she sweeps past us, there comes to me a very clear sense of divine presence. I have known God's presence on many times in my life, but never like this. As I reflect now I think of Elijah's encounter when God was not in the earthquake, wind or fire, but after they passed there was the sound of stillness which was the presence of God. That is how this feels, an unmistakably divine sense of presence and welcome. God was not in the squirrel nor the owl, they were just heralds, trumpeting the coming One. What is so unusual for me, though, is that whilst the presence seems to me to be unmistakably God, for the first time in my life it is also very feminine. I simply cannot explain this – it must be experienced for there to be understanding on the part of another, but this, and a similar experience in another woodland just a fortnight later with exactly the same sense of presence, though encountered elsewhere, convinced me of both the genderfulness of God (that we are created in God's image, both male and female), and the presence of God throughout creation.*

From an Animist perspective this kind of experience is not uncommon in ritual. Harvey[19] notes:

'More than once animals from the wood's edge or neighbouring fields were encountered in the depths of the woods, or acted in unusual ways seemingly indicative of welcome intentionally offered.'

And[20]:

'Merely flying past a celebrant... might seem significant only to that person or their friends. However the unusual physical proximity that sometimes occurs in encounters between particular birds and particular humans can be considered to be deliberate acts of communicative intimacy.'

For an Animist, the encounter I have described might be thought of as a show of welcome and acknowledgement from the forest to Alison and me, and that in itself may be true, but I think it's probably only part of the story. What has led me to this belief is that an identical sense of welcome, as if from the same person, took place in another forest many miles from the first encounter, and with none of the unusual animal activity. The second 'welcome' took place in a moment of silent appreciation as we stood on a path gazing at the beauty of a different woodland. Yet the sense of presence was the same, and I recall saying to Alison, 'She's back', which is of course a nonsense. 'She' never left, it's just I became aware of this aspect of God through an unexpected and undeserved revelation.

This experience changed my understanding both of the natural world and of God. I know we are created in God's image, as affirmed in Genesis 1, and that the image is contained by both male and female together. It logically follows that God must have aspects that are what we would define as feminine, yet up until this point all of my encounters with God have felt powerful or gentle, yet always masculine. Here, though, in the forests I encountered God as 'She'. I experienced for myself what I had affirmed theologically for many years. The 'head-knowledge' became 'heart-knowledge' because of God's initiative within the natural world, using some of its elements and residents to draw us nearer.

This, however, was not the end of the journey. Whilst the above described encounters convinced me that the natural world was a place of divine and animal encounter, the second story takes us deeper into a place which is not normally considered within orthodox Christian theology. In this second story there is a sense of human-to-nature interaction, or, as our friend Bruce Stanley has put it to us on a couple of occasions, 'When you stare at nature – nature stares back.'

Story Two: Human-to-Nature Encounter:

*The Wyre Forest near Kidderminster is close to our hearts and a delightful place to walk. In the winter of early 2012 Alison and I went for a wander through the Forest. Towards the end of our walk we chanced upon an unusual pairing of trees. Much of the woodland through which we had walked was oak with the occasional yew in their midst, but we found on this occasion an ancient yew tree with an oak growing up and enveloped within her boughs, their union so intimate that their trunks rested against each other. To us, knowing how poisonous the yew is, this beautiful pairing read like nature's way of affirming the possibilities of reconciliation. We left the forest that day with a real sense of wonder at having found them.*

*A few months later I embarked on my sabbatical study leave, touring the country, living in a caravan and talking to Pagans to learn about their beliefs in order that I could work in this interfaith space from a place of knowledge rather than speculation. As we settled back into some kind of routine on our return in the early autumn, our thoughts returned to the oak and yew in the Wyre forest. Having not visited for more than six months, we returned, wondering how we could ever hope to find that unique pairing again. The leaves were full on the trees giving the whole forest a different appearance from our last visit. So we stood on the edge of the forest, on a path that we knew was not the one we had taken the first time, and we simply 'listened'. By this I mean we tried to still ourselves to heighten our awareness of our surroundings through our senses. The Wyre Forest is criss-crossed with numerous paths and so it was not long before we came to one such crossing, giving us three choices.*

*To understand how difficult this is for me you need to consider that I have absolutely no sense of direction whatsoever, and so if the sun is not visible (such as in a thick forest) I have no hope of finding my way around. Alison had gone to look at a little brook, so I stood at the crossroads with my senses as tightly tuned as I could, 'listening' for the direction. Gradually, it seemed as if the birdsong was louder in one direction than any other, and that had a sense of rightness, almost invitation, about it. When Alison returned I tried to explain which direction we should take. She was slightly bemused, knowing how hopeless I am with directions, but agreed to go with my impression. This was how we continued, with both of us 'listening' closely at each division of paths, and throughout the journey there were little encounters with the natural world as we followed our impressions, confirming a sense of rightness to the paths we took.*

*We passed a ring of wild mushrooms that seemed to be centred on a tree; a deer in the mist to our left; and then finally, as we came towards a bend in the path, a large black stag ambled across the track in front of us. We felt a growing sense of excitement and sure enough, as we rounded the bend, off to the left of the path was the thickening of the trees consistent with a yew, but not just any yew. This was the yew embracing her oak. Starting from what we knew was a different path, and simply by 'listening' closely to the cues from the natural world around us, we had walked straight to them.*

As Christians, what are we to make of this? We explained this to two friends of ours, both on the Druid path, and took them to the oak and yew pairing. We now knew the way, but even so they picked up on little signs such as a bird that seemed to sit and wait for us, then fly on ahead and wait again as if to say, 'Follow me, I know what you're looking for and it's this way.' This, of course, is to anthropomorphise outrageously! Nevertheless, our friends, who are far more adept at this than we are, were not at all surprised at what we explained had happened. They took it in their stride, but I was left with the query that, coming from a Christian metaphysic, what was I to make of what had taken place? Before answering that we turn to our third encounter.

Story Three: The Nature-to-Human Encounter:

Even as we affirm the possibility that we may listen to how the natural world speaks when we ask a question, so we also need to recognise the possibility that the connection may be two-way. What follows is, perhaps, rather more speculative purely because it challenges me more than any other encounter when I take into account both my scientific and theological background.

*We have observed a rather unusual 'happening' around our 'Guardian' cedar. I record this incident with some trepidation because my scientific training wishes to affirm that nothing can be proven unless it is repeatable, whilst my spirituality affirms that there is rarely anything repeatable in the paths we seek to tread within the Christian faith. It is about relationship, not science. God is personal, not some experiment that must always respond in a repeatable fashion. Therefore, it is necessary sometimes to observe apparent 'coincidences' and allow them to ask us probing questions. Since we began Ancient Arden Forest Church a rather curious thing has taken place. At face value it may mean nothing, but the imagery is important. Out of the roots of our cedar, and right up against its trunk, two new trees have begun to grow, a small oak tree and a small holly tree. To the casual observer this may be nothing more than happy coincidence, but within British folklore the oak tree and the holly tree play a major part in the cycle of the seasons. The oak represents the Oak King, who rules from midwinter until midsummer whilst the holly represents the Holly King, who rules from midsummer until midwinter and whose presence has found its way into many Christian practices such as bringing sprigs of holly into the house as decoration for Christmas. In folklore, they battle it out each year with the Oak King reaching the height of his strength at the summer solstice before being defeated by the Holly King, who reaches the height of his strength at the winter solstice before being defeated by the Oak King. It is, for us, an intriguing observation that the arrival of these two plants seems to have coincided with the advent of Forest Church and its practice in the space under the cedar. We are, of course, aware that in order for a plant to grow there must be a seed that is planted, yet having an oak and a holly growing out of the northern faces of our cedar, on the north western and north eastern sides respectively, at this time and in this place, has given us all pause for thought.*

These stories are just a very limited representation of experiences of connecting with nature spiritually, yet, as I have said throughout, there is a genuine question of the difficulty in imagining how this could take place. Unless we strongly anthropomorphise the natural world, assigning, for example, the presence of tree-spirits (dryads), with whom we can readily communicate, there must be an almost insurmountable difficulty in understanding how we can connect with consciousnesses which, if they exist, must be extraordinarily different from our own. Across these three stories are three different ways of connecting with nature. In the first we have little difficulty in incorporating it within a Christian framework because it was, for me, so rooted in a divine-to-human encounter taking place within the natural world and we have biblical examples, such as Moses and the burning bush (Exodus 3), or Elijah in the cleft of a rock (1 Kings 19), where similar encounters have taken place. However, the second and the third encounters become progressively more difficult to understand, leading us to the point of having to make a choice between four options: we can adopt a wholesale Animist approach; we can reject them as purely speculative coincidences; we can reject them as dangerous encounters with demons, or we can recognise that it is possible to describe a theology of what took place, and is taking place for many of us, which can be described using biblical ideas. Whilst I have some affinity for the first option, the way in which a sense of identical divine encounter took place in two different locations leads me to want to further investigate the theological possibilities within my own tradition.

## The Panentheistic Connection

Panentheism is a compound Greek word made up of 'pan' (everything), 'en' (in), and 'theos' (God). It literally translates as 'all things in God', but is also often understood to mean 'God in all things'. It is quite different from a Pagan understanding of the world as 'pantheistic', which means 'all things *are* God', suggesting that you and I, and all that can be observed and/or perceived are part of one divine whole. I suspect that most people within the Forest Church movement, or who would think of themselves as Christians within the Celtic stream, would affirm their belief in panentheism which describes how God is present to us because God pervades all that we are, but, at the same time, God is also separate from us as One who is both immanent *and* transcendent. To me this means that God's presence can be observed within the natural world because God pervades the natural world, and indeed I would go so far as to suggest that the natural world and the whole created order exists only because it exists in God. Were God to remove God's presence, it would simply cease to exist.

I choose to recognise this as another manifestation of the Holy Spirit, that the Spirit is present throughout. Now lest we over-romanticise this, as modern Celtic Christians have sometimes done, we have to accept and be challenged by the reality that if God is in the beautiful mountains and hilltops, then God is also in the volcano and the tsunami, (which is a different book for a different time). However, if we affirm the presence of the Spirit of God within all things, then we have a mechanism for under-standing what is actually taking place within these encounters; for understanding how the connection is taking place and for comprehending the 'connections' felt within Animism. The answer is there for us in the words of Christ in Matthew's Gospel:

'Are not two sparrows sold for a penny? Yet not one of them will fall to the ground unperceived by your Father. And even the hairs of your head are all counted.' Matthew 10: 29-30

I have queried throughout how it can be that we can interact with elements within the natural world around us if they possess types of consciousness different from our own. Here is a possible answer: we connect through the Holy Spirit, defined by John V. Taylor as 'The Go-Between God'[21]. In other words, what I am suggesting is that, although we may feel as if we are connecting directly with the natural world, logic suggests that we cannot do this across the species divide because whatever awareness exists beyond humanity must be a different, and in some cases profoundly different, kind of consciousness because it exists within a very different physical medium. Therefore, we cannot be directly aware of the consciousness of an other-than-human life, but what we *can* be aware of is God's perception of that consciousness. Christ made it clear in the above verse from Matthew's Gospel that God is aware of everything that takes place within the world, a kind of conscious awareness that is infinitely beyond human abilities. I cannot find my way around a forest, but by listening to the Spirit of God what I can do is 'tune in' so that I can be aware of God's awareness of the life of the forest, and what's more, the life within the forest can become aware of me. We can thus take this further into the more speculative realm. Let us suggest that, although the cedar's awareness of the Forest Church meeting under its boughs, (if such an awareness exists), must be beyond our understanding, in the same Holy Spirit the cedar may become aware of the Holy Spirit's own awareness of what we are doing and be able to respond. Obviously, for this to be the case we need to assign an other-than-human consciousness to the 'Guardian' cedar. Panentheism opens the gateway for us to understand that, in Christ, through the mediation of the Holy Spirit, all things are connected and may be aware of the Spirit's awareness of all things, thereby becoming the medium through which communication takes place. In this way, Trinitarian theology has a vital role to play in nature connection and suggests that the perceptions within Animism, with regards to the seen world, may all take place through the medium of the one that Christians call the Holy Spirit. I can imagine that some of my Pagan Animist friends might be less than enamoured with this interpretation and, likewise, I can imagine that those of a more conservative theological mind would also respond very negatively to this. Of course, there can be no proof either way. This is simply a theology of encounter which makes sense for me of what I have experienced within my own tradition.

I am aware that, from an Animist perspective, I have not considered the issue of unseen spirits here. The reason for that is purely because the three stories of encounter all come from a personal perspective and I have little personal experience to offer of engaging with the unseen world of Animist beliefs at this point in time. What I hope I have achieved is to offer some theory within the Christian tradition of what is for many of us a new set of experiences. I have attempted to follow the model of the Anglican Church which I serve by using scripture, reason and tradition to understand experience, although there is very little tradition here beyond a tradition of suspicion which has a tendency to limit our beliefs rather than giving us the freedom in Christ to explore. I do not expect that this will be the last theological word on these matters and I reserve the right to change my opinion as new information and ideas become available. This, therefore, represents a snapshot of some of what we have experienced and some of my own ideas regarding their interpretation.

Many of us within the Forest Church movement have had to cope with suspicion that we are a syncretistic group who seek to bind Christianity and Paganism into a new religion. Yet what I have found here is, instead, a deep call to prayer, to learning how to be still, how to be silent, and how to listen. Far from being a form of Paganism subtly creeping into our Christianity, I have, instead, been inspired by my Animist friends and their ideas and experiences to look more closely at my own beliefs and encounters and begin to recognise that nature connection is actually a call to prayer. Through a deep and lasting prayerfully-lived life, God's awareness of the natural world, of which we are a part, may become present to us, potentially leading to a joint celebration or working with willing 'other-than-human' persons. 'Nature connection' is ultimately 'God connection', for it seems to me that it is only through the Holy Spirit, who pervades all things, that we can make the connection. Once, however, we do make this connection it challenges us on a very deep level about how we should live.

## Living ethically

Whichever model of understanding Animism we look at, one of its strongest factors is the way in which it can inspire a more ethical treatment of the world and her resources. For most of us, if we see a fellow human being fall over, then we will rush to help. Humans have a natural tendency to help other humans in need. In Great Britain we are characterised as a nation of animal lovers and this tendency to care is extended to anything with fur or feathers, perhaps because we have developed an affinity with other members of the animal family. Consequently, we deal very harshly with anyone convicted of animal cruelty. But for an Animist this will go much further. It is not only animals, (and all animals at that, not just the fluffy ones!), that are treated with respect and care, it is all the plant life too, for any of a myriad of reasons including the possibility that the life in question is inhabited by spirits, or simply because the Animist believes in the right of all life to exist.

Animists will often go further than this, for it may be not just animate creatures but seemingly inanimate objects which could be assigned value as having mind and personhood. In this way, all of creation is treated with respect. For many Christians, this willingness to give way to the needs of animal and plant life over our own human needs, seems to run counter to the command of God in Judeo-Christian culture regarding how the earth and its other inhabitants are to be used:

'Then God said, "Let us make humankind in our image, according to our likeness; and let them have dominion over the fish of the sea, and over the birds of the air, and over the cattle, and over all the wild animals of the earth, and over every creeping thing that creeps upon the earth." So God created humankind in his image, in the image of God he created them; male and female he created them. God blessed them, and God said to them, "Be fruitful and multiply, and fill the earth and subdue it; and have dominion over the fish of the sea and over the birds of the air and over every living thing that moves upon the earth."' Genesis 1:26-8

The interpretation of this challenge to 'fill the earth and subdue it' is a real sticking point in Christian-Pagan relationships. Yet if we move on just one chapter in Genesis, to see how God instructs Adam to look after the Garden of Eden, we find three things that counter the way people use Genesis 1 to excuse all kinds of environmental atrocities. First the name 'Adam' means 'man of dust'. It is a subtle acknowledgement that Adam is made of the same stuff as everything else on the planet. In what could be construed as an early unconscious acknowledgement of panentheism, we can see that Adam is only a living, moving being because God breathes his breath, his Spirit, into him. It is only because God is within him that Adam lives and moves and breathes. Secondly, there are two key words in this phrase from Genesis 2:15:

'The Lord God took the man and put him in the Garden of Eden to till it and keep it.'

'Tilling' means to cultivate – of helping the land to become everything that it is capable of becoming. Farming is certainly a part of this, but it is not the whole of it by any stretch of the imagination. This is, instead, about care. This is further underlined by the use of 'keeping', which comes from a Hebrew word which means to take great care of and guard.

What we find, therefore, is that if we read more of the story, then it emerges that God's plan for humanity is one of nurturing and participating with creation. This is far removed from the wholesale destruction that we are witnessing in our lifetimes, all in the name of human progress. No one who calls themselves 'Christian' should be in any doubt that this runs counter to God's commands and, if we want to use the language of the Christian faith, is surely one of the greatest sins our race has perpetrated. This is highlighted for Anglicans in the fifth of what we call 'The five marks of mission', (which define for us the ways in which the church should be reaching out into the world), which is stated thus:

'To strive to safeguard the integrity of creation and sustain and renew the life of the earth.'

It seems to me that this is entirely consistent with the ethical standards that we find amongst Animists and which could form the basis for deep and useful dialogue. For my part, as I hope has become clear, whilst our understanding of the unseen world may differ, there is much within an Animist understanding of the material world that can make us consider again the depths of God's involvement in the world around us. If nothing more, Animists should inspire Christians to be re-enchanted with the presence of God in the universe and be reminded of our own place as men and women of dust, animate only by the presence of the Spirit of God.

## Notes for Chapter 5

1   Harvey G., *Animism*, London: Hurst and Co., 2005, 4.
2   Harvey G., *Animism*, London: Hurst and Co., 2005, xi
3   Harvey G., *Ibid.*, 103.
4   Yeats W.B., *Fairy & Folktales of Ireland*, Easton Press, 2000.
5   Wenham G.J., *Genesis 1-15*, Texas: Word Books, 1987, 135f
6   Anathaswamy A., 'Roots of Consciousness' in *New Scientist*, Vol. 224, No. 2998, 6 December 2014, 34-7.
7   Restall-Orr E., *The Wakeful World*, Winchester: Moon Books, 2012, 104.
8   Duncan Robert, O., 2012, URL: http://www.scientificameri can.com/article/what-are-the-structural-differences/
9   Bricklin J., 'A Variety of Religious Experience' in Libet B *et al.* (Eds.), *The Volitional Brain*, Imprint Academic, Exeter, 1999, 78.

10  Libet B., 'Do We Have Free Will?' in Libet B *et al.* (Eds.), *The Volitional Brain*, Imprint Academic, Exeter, 1999, 49f.

11  Spinney L., 'Once upon a time', in *New Scientist*, Vol. 225, No. 3003, 10 Jan. 2015, 28-31

12  Midgley M., 'Consciousness, Fatalism and Science', in Gregersen N.H. *et al.* (Eds.), *The Human Person in Science and Theology*, T and T Clark, Edinburgh, 2000, 25.

13  Schwartz J.M., 'A Role for Volition and Attention in the Generation of New Brain Circuitry' in Libet B. *et al.*, *The Volitional Brain*, Imprint Academic, Exeter, 1999, 115-142

14  'A Role for Volition...', 123.

15  'A Role for Volition...', 125.

16  http://phys.org/news/2014-01-elephants-mimosas-memories.html

17  http://onlinelibrary.wiley.com/doi/10.1111/j.1461-0248.2008.01183.x/full

18  URL: http://www.plosone.org/article/info%3Adoi%2F10.1371%2Fjournal.pone.0071365

19  *Ibid.* 91.

20  *Ibid.* 103.

21  Taylor John V., *The Go-Between God*, London: SCM Press, 1975.

## Chapter Six

# Shamanism

## Introduction

'Shaman' is a title which finds its root in the Tunguscan language of a region of Siberia and refers to a person within a village who engages with spirits whilst in an ecstatic trance for the purpose of divination or healing. Given that this book is dealing primarily with western Paganism, one might question what place Shamanism has on these pages. It is not just the origin of the word that might give rise to questions about its place here, because it does indeed mark a departure from the earlier material in this book. Up until this point we have been looking at religious practices but a Shaman is primarily a healer and someone who spiritually enquires on behalf of others. It is almost like including a chapter on western psychotherapeutic practice in a book on the recognised major world religions. I say this because whilst a Druid, a Witch or a Wiccan may follow various spiritual practices as a part of their path, a Shaman is more specifically a healer and someone who will work on behalf of the needs of others. So why include it here rather than as a part of one of the other chapters? It is simply because as well as being a healing practice, Shamanism is also one of the recognised Pagan paths which has its own spiritual world view which is undoubtedly Pagan and Animistic, and which has developed a major role in western Paganism. Shamanic practices are a normal part of traditional Animist cultures and Scottish Shaman, Gordon MacLellan, shared with me his view that Shamanism occupies a priestly function within such cultures. Shamanism also has distinct features all of its own and a focus that, though related, is different in many ways from other Pagan understandings of the spiritual realm. I will describe this focus in due course, but it is also worth pointing out that there are a variety of Shamanic practices and, although their world views are often related, they are far from identical. One of the issues we will engage with is the possible reasons behind this diversity within western practice.

I have placed this chapter after Druidry and Animism because much of western Shamanic practice is related to the understandings of the spirit and material world that are found in both of these paths, and because, as Michael Harner[1] puts it:

> 'Shamans have long assumed that humans are part of the totality of nature, related to all other biological forms, and not superior to them.'

And from our own shores, Philip Shallcrass (Greywolf), the head of the British Druid Order, has often been heard to remark that Druidry is British Shamanism, and although not all British Shamans would agree with this, this perception by some of the similarity between Druidry and Shamanism serves to demonstrate why I have ordered the chapters in this way.

Although I have spoken to a number of British Shamans, you will find that there are fewer narrative examples in this chapter. In part, this is because that, just as doctors don't discuss individual cases, so western Shamans are also less likely to talk about their work in healing or therapy; there is a degree of confidentiality. A key difference, however, is that whilst western doctors make a great deal of use of text books to learn their skills, traditional Shamanism is largely taught by verbal instruction and solitary or accompanied practice. It is only the more western variations that use books from which to teach, and even there the better texts make it clear that a good teacher is needed to guide the student safely.

## What is a Shaman?

The most clear and succinct definition I have found comes from Celtic Shaman, Caitlín Matthews[2], who defines it like this:

> 'A shaman is a person... who can enter alternate states of consciousness at will to travel in spirit between this world and the otherworlds in order to find healing, knowledge, guidance and help for others. A shaman works with power and energy, calling upon the help of many spirits... who choose to help.'

Stuart Harris-Logan[3] develops this further as he ties together the concept of ecstatic techniques for altered states of consciousness with the communal nature of the calling:

> 'The shaman is a specialist in the Sacred, a practitioner of ancient techniques of ecstasy. To the shaman, the spirits are a vital and sustaining presence whose help can be sought in times of spiritual or material crisis. As representatives of and for their communities, shamans must maintain the balance between the two worlds; the corporeal and the spiritual.'

In other words, a Shaman is someone who must be acutely spiritually aware and able to embark on spiritual journeys that allow them to have a foot in this world with a foot in a spiritual realm. This is usually achieved by going into a trance. Harris-Logan[4] goes on to say that:

> 'In trance, the shaman often experiences an ecstasy of spirit, an unbridled joy which finds few comparisons...We can define trance...as a technique which not only brings the practitioner into contact with the spirits, but also with the most free and sacred parts of their essential self.'

This opens up several aspects of the experiential side of

Shamanism that we will explore as this chapter progresses. A strong connection is often made between going into a trance as a vital part of the Shamanic journey, and experiencing a sense of ecstasy, implying that the ecstasy needs to flow from the trance. A word of caution is needed here for those of other spiritual paths for whom ecstasy is not linked to trance; My own experience leads me to want to uncouple these two since, like many others, I have had a number of occasions where a sense of spiritual ecstasy has prevailed, but not from a sense of trance:

*I sat in the chapel, filled almost to capacity with other priests-in-training, settling into our weekly communion together. Yet whilst I was in the group, I felt barely with them. My spirit soared with a sense of joy bubbling up from within, a state of bliss from which I had no desire to leave. And the source of this ecstasy? It had little to do with the service, but instead was tied to a deeper realisation of the creative hands of God stretching across light years of space, continually singing and moulding a universe into being.*

Whilst ecstatic states can certainly be induced through altered states of consciousness, such as a trance, they can also come unbidden as in my own example, and I believe that is because the source may not necessarily come from within. A person may seek a spiritual connection and use whatever techniques are a part of their tradition, be it meditation, singing, praying, drumming, or even hallucinogens, and this puts them in a frame of mind or spirit whereby they can call out for an answer. However, the initiation of the connection may come from an external source, that something which is of spirit may seek us out and we simply respond. For the Christian this may be further complicated by the belief that the Holy Spirit is indwelling us, so the source of ecstasy may be from one who is inside us yet is not us, as opposed to a fully external source.

All of these different possibilities should give us pause for thought because they show how trance and ecstasy may come from numerous different sources, and possibly more than one at a time. They may be spiritual in origin, but some may also be purely induced psychologically, engaging with parts of the self rather than external entities. Unlike those within the more reductionist schools of psychology and neuroscience, I do not believe that one can 'explain away' supposed spiritual states as nothing but a trick of the mind. However, some probably are purely psychological, whatever religious or spiritual tradition we subscribe to, and discerning the difference in one's own experience may not be straightforward.

Whichever view we subscribe to, and whatever spiritual tradition we are a part of, Harris-Logan makes an important point; that an ecstatic state touches on our deepest nature. Anyone who ministers to others needs to be aware that they are not a pure conduit but a filter. In the above experience it was my science background that was the filter through which a spiritual insight came because said insight developed through becoming excited and feeling enlightened by seeing something that I knew in my head through a different, more spiritual perception. Likewise, a Shaman, as with any spiritual practitioner, requires training in order to understand what comes from themselves as well as what comes from somewhere else. This 'somewhere else' is a spiritual cosmology unique to Shamanism which we will explore shortly, although western Shamanic practice has a view of reality that is related to other Pagan beliefs.

## How does a person become a Shaman?

In more traditional cultures the decision to become a Shaman is not a matter of individual choice. Matthews[5] suggests that it is the role of spirits in the universe to decide who is going to be a Shaman. Others, and certainly in the more western practices, would appear to suggest that it is a matter of one's own personal decision. It seems to me that a well-rounded view would probably be somewhat akin to how people come to faith in many religions, including my own; for some there is a great and sudden insight, perhaps a sense of having been called (although, as we will see, in traditional Shamanism the vocational process is often painful and potentially life-threatening), and for others there is a slow realisation that 'This' is the path that they are on. However, there is one common factor to being a Shaman and that is that one can only actually be called a Shaman if one is recognised as such by the community. A person may think themselves to be a Shaman and speak of themselves in those terms, but unless people consistently come to them for spiritual help of their own volition, they are not. This common factor seems to be consistent across cultures. To that end I think it is fair to say that someone may refer to themselves as being on a Shamanic path, that is to engage with the beliefs and practices of Shamanism, but it is the community that recognises that they have become a Shaman. There is a fairly obvious comparison to be made here with how one becomes an ordained priest in the Church of England. A Christian may feel called to that role, but it is formally tested first by their own priest, who observes their spirituality and how others relate to them, then by the diocese of which they are a part and, finally, by representatives of the national church. Without that recognition a person may call themselves a Christian priest, but they have not had the backing of the community and are therefore unlikely to be recognised as such.

I have mentioned that Shamanism requires that the individual communes with the spirits. One might ask how this is different from the work of a medium. I suggest that it is because mediums traditionally believe themselves to be consulting the souls of dead humans. Whilst doing precisely this is, indeed, often a part of the role of a Shaman, many of the spirits they believe they are engaging with are other-than-human, as we will see in due course. However, although a Shaman may be engaging with other spirits, their primary reason for doing so is to aid the person who has come to them for help, and to understand how they might go about doing so we need to understand the dualistic model of what constitutes the person that appears to be common across Shamanic practice. It is to this that we now turn our attention.

## Shamanic Dualism

In order to consider the Shamanic understanding of the nature of what it is to be a human it will be useful to examine the different western understandings in spiritual and material terms. We can then compare that with Shamanic ideas.

Across much of the western world there is a tendency towards dualism, that is that you have a mind, a consciousness, which inhabits the body and which is your essence, that part which defines 'You'. When pressed, westerners will often tend towards equating mind with soul, exactly as I have done previously in this book. This kind of mind-body dualism can be traced back to the philosophy of Plato and is often referred to as Cartesian Dualism after the seventeenth-century philosopher, Rene Descartes, from whom we have the phrase, 'I think therefore I am'. Those who have consciously or otherwise adopted this position and believe in some form of afterlife might imagine the soul to be what we could refer to as an 'escape soul', waiting to be freed from the constraints of the physical body at the point of death in order to depart to a better world, or perhaps to be reborn into this one.

Modern western science, which almost by definition has a materialist agenda in terms of its more recent tendency to be derogatory about the existence of that which cannot be measured or tested, has moved towards a position referred to as 'Monist', that humans are composed of just one substance, the material, and that all of our thoughts, everything that we think of as mind or soul, can be reduced to the biochemical interactions of neurons within our skulls.

However, in Christian theology neither the dualistic nor the materialist model accurately describe orthodox belief. The Judeo-Christian view of the person is not so much that you have a soul, but that you *are* a soul. Each of us is comprised of both spiritual and material aspects that are so closely bound together as to be inseparable and so can be counted as one. Popular western Christianity has also tended towards the idea of having a soul that escapes the body at the point of death, but this may be a sign of being influenced by the Greek philosophical model of Plato in which humans are thought of as having an 'escape soul' which is waiting to leave the body at the point of death. Having said that, even in the Bible there is a sense in the New Testament that there was a movement away from the traditional Hebrew view. Jesus says these words in Matthew 10:28:

'Do not fear those who kill the body but cannot kill the soul; rather fear him who can destroy both soul and body in hell.'

This seems to indicate that a body-soul dualism was becoming adopted in Jewish belief two thousand years ago, perhaps under the influence of Hellenistic (Greek-influenced) Jews. However, the issue becomes further complicated in New Testament thought where body, soul *and* spirit are all mentioned as constituting a person, such as 1 Thessalonians 5:23:

'May the God of peace himself sanctify you entirely; and may your spirit and soul and body be kept sound and blameless at the coming of our Lord Jesus Christ.'

If we are going to try and compare Shamanic belief with Judeo-Christian belief we need a more concrete basis for the discussion. What, then, in the midst of this confusion, is orthodox Christian belief about the constitution of the person? I would suggest that the phrase 'holistic dualism'[6] is probably the best description. By this I mean that the human person consists of the material body and an immaterial essence, commonly called 'the soul'. However, this immaterial essence can be further split to be considered as the innermost part which communes with the Spirit of God, called the human spirit, and the soul, the inner identity. The natural state is for the immaterial and material parts of the person to be bound into one indivisible holistic 'whole'. This, therefore, means that the body and the soul/spirit influence each other; what happens to the body will influence the soul/spirit and vice versa. This is also in keeping with the orthodox Christian belief that the state immediately following death, of one's essence, one's soul, being gathered up into heaven, is merely an intermediate state that precedes resurrection, that ultimately one is to be reconstituted into an immortal body in a new and immortal creation. Embodiment is the natural human state. This event is prefigured by the resurrection of Christ in which his post-resurrection appearances reveal him to be physical; capable of eating and drinking, and yet somehow more than human. To better understand this the reader is directed to the story told by C. S. Lewis, *The Great Divorce*, which in narrative form gives the impression of how in the new creation, reality is somehow more solid and more real than we can comprehend in this world.

This orthodox Christian belief differs from popular western thought which is far more dualistic. Amongst the spiritually minded within our culture the person is still thought of as being constituted of body and soul, but with less of a focus on holistic dualism and more of a tendency towards a belief that the animating soul can be separated from the body. In effect, the soul is what pilots the body. This is also far more in keeping with the world inhabited by the Shaman. I should mention that this can be more complicated in other forms of traditional Shamanism by the belief that a person may have more than one type of soul! I mention this merely for the sake of completion because most western Shamanic practice regards us as having just one soul and this is what we will consider here.

## Shamanic healing of the soul

Western Shamanic practice therefore revolves around the idea that if the soul is a separate part of the person, then just as one can break a limb, it is also possible for the soul to be damaged. MacEowen[7] describes it like this:

'When a person is treated horribly, physically or emotionally assaulted, for instance, a fragment of his or her soul may slink off to a hidden unseen place where it cannot be harmed. In shamanist traditions this phenomenon is called soul loss. The soul knows what is needed for survival and returns again, only when conditions are right or when someone engages in the work of inviting its fullness home.'

It is this concept of soul-loss and soul-retrieval which is the essence of Shamanic practice, particularly in western traditions. At face value many people might dismiss this concept as New Age mumbo-jumbo. However, for those who have suffered a penetrating psycho-spiritual wound it is a concept that makes sense. I find certain resonances within my own experience:

*In the last hours of my eldest sister's life her breathing changed. We all knew that she had lost her battle against the brain tumour that has been gradually stealing her away from us, but that day we knew that the end was imminent, as she went from taking a breath every few seconds to breathing more quickly and with shallower breaths. With the family gathered around, we waited until late that evening my brother-in-law suggested we retired to our beds and he would call us later. We left the two of them to share Helen's final hours, to be woken in the middle of the night by my eldest niece to tell us that it was over. And so the family gathered together around her bed to share the sorrow of loss that families have shared for millennia.*

*The crushing grief and wave of anger and rage that followed in the weeks after her death were difficult to cope with, but I also became aware of something else, something I struggled to put into words. My eldest sister and I were of shared substance, and when she died it felt as if a part of me went with her; a part I can never have back.*

This description of, '...a part of me' was a phrase I used long before I had ever encountered Paganism in any form. Yet when I sat one afternoon and spoke with Mike Stygal of the Pagan Federation, and himself a Shaman, I intuitively made the connection with what he was talking about as he described soul-loss or soul-fracture. Whilst I may have a different understanding of what constitutes a person, what he described resonated with my own experience of losing Helen, moving me to tears. This is a feeling that I still carry around within me, that somehow a part of me died with my sister. It is intriguing that we call this a sense of loss and I find myself wondering whether we only mean that we have lost our loved one to death, or whether there is a deeper sense that somehow we have lost a part of ourselves too.

Whichever way we look at it, the healing of this sense of soul-loss, whether caused by the death of a loved one, a deep sense of personal anguish through suffering and maybe abuse, or even simply of having been cursed, is considered to be the work of the Shaman. It is interesting to note that whilst I subscribe to the Christian notion of holistic dualism, my experience also allows me to identify with what is meant by soul-loss or soul-fracture. This begins to raise the whole question of whether the Shaman is solely accessing something spiritual, or whether there is a strongly psychological element too. I will consider this in due course, but we need a little more background understanding of Shamanism first. To do that we will begin with traditional Shamanism before looking at two derivatives, core Shamanism and Celtic Shamanism.

## Traditional Shamanism

Traditional Shamanism, although not confined to any particular region of the world, often refers to the practices found in North and South America, and in Siberia, perhaps because these are the areas that seem to have been popularised by researchers. As I mentioned earlier, the name 'Shaman' is probably derived from Šamán, a word from the Tunguscan region of Siberia, although what the name actually means will depend on which source one consults. Harris-Logan[8], (citing R. N. Walsh) suggests that it is:

'...thought to denote one who is 'excited, moved, raised', and is also related to a word meaning, 'to know'.'

Unlike those who become priests in some world religions, traditional Shamans tend to have other jobs, earning very little other than gifts from the Shamanic work that they do. It is, nevertheless, a vocational calling, but numerous accounts suggest that in traditional societies it comes after a close encounter with death, perhaps through illness, with the Shaman becoming a wounded healer. Core Shaman, Michael Harner[9], describes it like this:

'If that person suddenly had a miraculous recovery, the local community concluded that a spirit had compassion for the person and interceded to relieve him or her of the illness. In such an event, people in the community would go to the revived and cured patient to see if the healing power could be used to help another individual suffering from a malady, usually a similar one. In other words, the suffering of the ill person could evoke pity by a spirit. In this way a shaman sometimes was created.'

It is worth noting that this concept of the 'wounded healer' is not unique to Shamanism, and, indeed, renowned Roman Catholic

Priest Henri Nouwen wrote a book of the same name. However, in Christian circles this tends to refer to someone who is capable of helping others, *despite* their own troubles or illness, as a sign of God's grace being with them in the midst of their suffering, whereas in Shamanism it tends to be used of those who have been healed and that healing was a sign of the favour of a spirit or spirits. Bear in mind that as elsewhere these are tendencies rather than absolutes, and Core Shaman Mike Stygal has informed me that, at least in Core Shamanic tradition, healers also work on self-healing.

It is also intriguing to note that the belief that one might receive healing from someone who has had a brush with death is not a practice that is exclusive to Shamanism. In Roman Catholic tradition one might occasionally (and unofficially) hear of someone referred to as a 'Victim Soul', that is one who suffers for others after the likeness of Christ. A classic example of this was the case of Audrey Santo who, as a young child, almost died by drowning in a swimming pool accident. Her condition, there-after, was semi-comatose, but her family began to talk of mirac-ulous happenings by her bedside such as statues weeping tears of oil. Regardless of the validity of the claims, it is interesting to note how many people then sought to be in her presence to receive healing even though it was questionable whether she was even aware of them. In some way it appears that, regardless of culture, we seem drawn to those who have survived a close encounter with death and are willing to ascribe healing powers to them.

The process of being called and the requirement for having come close to death is therefore not one that most people would necessarily choose in traditional Shamanic societies. Even once called, the process can be quite unpleasant as many describe a process of spiritual dismemberment where one knows oneself to be taken apart by the spirits before being remade. The numerous visionary accounts of this taking place make it clear that this spiritual dismemberment can be extremely harrowing. One Shaman wrote to me that:

'...you see, feel, are subjected to and also participate in your own ripping apart first. It is often (spiritually) violent in ways I haven't met elsewhere other than in some aspects of Voudoun.'

MacEowen[10] suggests that this process '...abound[s] in various cultures, from the Inuit to the Inca', and therefore seems to be common for the Shaman in traditional societies. This kind of dismemberment would most likely take place when the Shaman undertakes a vision quest, that is that they undergo some kind of ritual, usually in the wilderness and usually including suffering, in which they call upon the spirits for help and for power. Once acquired, it is recognised that the Shaman's power does not come from themselves but from their spirit guides and helpers who can also withdraw the power if they so choose.

It is also interesting to note that, as with so many other parts of Pagan practice, this concept of being remade has resonances within Judeo- Christianity:

'I will give you a new heart and put a new spirit within you; I will remove from you your heart of stone and give you a heart of flesh. And I will put my Spirit in you and move you to follow my decrees and be careful to keep my laws.' Ezekiel 36:26-7

It was also certainly the case that a part of theological training for the Christian priesthood involves a process of leaving behind the old way of life in order to take up a priestly role. My first three months at Ridley Hall, Cambridge, were, at times, quite psychos-piritually difficult because of the need to leave behind old identities in order to make space for something new to emerge. I mention this simply to show that whilst violent spiritual dismemberment in the midst of a vision may have a specifically Shamanic flavour, the concept of being taken apart and remade for a new purpose is not at all uncommon within religious circles. However, the Shamanic model is particularly visceral.

In terms of how a trained Shaman might work, one could envisage a scenario in which the Shaman is approached for help by someone in the community they serve and are recognised by. It may be for healing, or it might be for divinatory purposes, to determine the will of the spirits or of specific deities. (It must also be noted that some traditional Shamans are also Christians[11] and will operate with a spiritual cosmology that is influenced by Christianity.) The Shaman will call to their spirits and, in many traditions, summon them using a drum and/or a rattle. He or she will enter an ecstatic trance to commune with the spirits and, in some traditional Shamanic practice, this may well involve the use of consciousness altering drugs such as ayahuasca (also known as yagé) in Amazonian regions. The Shaman believes that their soul leaves their body to travel with the guiding spirits on a journey to one of the otherworlds (to which we will come in due course) to seek the help that is needed on behalf of the petitioner, but in some cases it may also involve the Shaman being possessed by the spirits which may cause them to physically shake. There is, however, some disagreement about how they work with the spirits: Rivière[12] suggests that this is different from the work of a medium because '...shamans take an active role in their relation with spirits, controlling them rather than being simply possessed by them.' Voicing a different opinion Matthews[13] suggests that:

'Most societies make a distinction between shamans and sorcerers. A shaman *co-operates* with the spiritual worlds and their inhabitants, beseeching their appropriate help; a sorcerer *manipulates* the spiritual worlds and seeks to command their inhabitants without their advice.'

As with many aspects of Paganism, this difference of opinion is likely to be down to experience and tradition. Some Shamans may seek possession and being controlled, others may seek control over the spirits they work with, and others still may seek co-operation. In terms of which spirits they seek, this again will depend on culture. It may be a spirit that presents to the Shaman as a deity, but it is more likely to be the souls of the dead, the spirits of one of the otherworlds or animal spirits, and we will come to these shortly. (Remember that Shamanism originates in Animistic cultures, so the idea of engaging with an animal spirit would be perfectly natural.) In this altered state the Shaman will work as a spiritual mediator in order to seek the answer that is sought, or they will act as healer on the afflicted. As an aside, it is worth mentioning here that not all Pagans are at ease with being possessed by another spirit and some will take steps to protect and care for each other during such experiences.

One final aspect of traditional Shamanism that we should consider, especially since it is a role which also spills over into other forms of Shamanism, is the role of psychopomp. Since a Shaman is able to soul-travel, they can accompany the soul of a dying person as they leave this life, journeying with them and guiding them to the next life, again depending on the spiritual cosmology of the culture in question. Mike Stygal explained to me that there are dangers involved in doing so, suggesting that a Shaman who undertakes this kind of work must have a 'root', something important in this world on to which they can hold to enable them to return.

The concept of the Shamanic journey is central to understanding where the soul of the Shaman goes and so it is important that we have an image of the spiritual cosmology of the traditional Shaman. The difficulty with this is that it is not as fully consistent as some might suggest, with beliefs having some variation across traditions. There are, however, common factors, the most prominent of which seems to be a belief in the existence of a series of layered worlds, usually three: this world, a world above us (an upper world), and a world beneath us (an underworld). The understanding of these varies significantly from one tradition to another and different traditions may add layers to the upper world and the underworld. It is also important that we recognise that they are not to be confused with heaven and hell as derived theologically in the Judeo-Christian world view. That being said, it is interesting that some western Shamans' experiences in the upper world appear to be influenced by western beliefs about heaven. For example, Caitlín Matthews[14] refers to the upper world as a 'paradisal realm of vision' and Harner[15] refers to the presence of a heavenly book that no one could read (both distinctively Christian ideas), and of heavenly choirs and celestial music. If one encounters something deeply spiritual, then we can only imagine that the brain will make use of the experiences and beliefs that it has had in order to try and make sense of what is being experienced. Consequently, if someone is brought up within a Christian metaphysic or culture it should not surprise us if elements of that overlay a spiritual or psychospiritual experience that they go on to have in a different tradition. Yet despite this, it is intriguing to note comments made in a series of interviews with Inuit elders[16] who referred to the upper world in this manner:

'Only after Christianity arrived did we refer to heaven. But before Christianity, Inuit knew there was a place that was very bright that people went to when they died.'

However, they also equated this with going to the moon, explaining that the Inuit went there before the Americans did![17] The influence of the local environment, as with one's own personal history, also informed the Inuit belief of the underworld since they perceived it to be in the depths or beneath the depths of the ocean.

This three-world model also bears similarities to the ancient Hebrew beliefs, that we live on a flat world floating on water. Underneath the flat world was the underworld, Sheol, the place of the dead, and above the world were the heavens, the dwelling place of God. This similarity across traditions leads us to make the observation that, given that Shamanism is usually a religion that develops in primitive societies, the three-tiered understanding of reality is a fairly natural and commonly-held belief which seems to be influenced by local conditions and traditions.

## Core Shamanism

Whilst traditional Shamanic practice is often described as a very early form of religion, being related to an animistic worldview and deeply grounded in the religion of the traditional societies that it serves, Core Shamanism has, perhaps, less of an 'earthy' feel to it. Michael Harner[18] puts it like this:

'By not imitating any specific cultural tradition, core shamanism is especially suited for utilization by Westerners who desire a relatively culture-free system that they can adopt and integrate into their lives.'

Core Shamanism is, in some ways, quite distinct from traditional Shamanism, being developed initially by Michael Harner, the architect of the Foundation for Shamanic Studies, as a result of his own research in traditional Shamanic societies over many years. One of the key differences is that whilst a trance state is still very necessary, the way in which it is induced contrasts with traditional practice. Mind-altering drugs are rarely used, with the trance instead being directed by the Shaman's drum. However, in traditional practice the purpose of the drum is to summon the spirits, and in some cases to 'trap' them in the drum, but in western practice, following a more rationalistic approach, it has been determined that a constant repetitive beat of between

205-220 beats per minute will induce an altered trance state.[19]

The trance state itself has been subject to Harner's research leading him to categorise the different realities that one can access from a trance in this manner[20]:

> '...there are two realities, and... the perception of each depends on one's state of consciousness. Therefore those in the 'ordinary state of consciousness' (OSC) perceive only 'ordinary reality' (OR). Those in the 'shamanic state of consciousness' (SSC) are able to enter into and perceive 'nonordinary reality' (NOR).'

This far more therapeutic approach to Shamanism that Harner has evolved has prompted some to voice their questions to me over whether this is actually genuine Shamanism, or whether it is more akin to Jungian psychotherapy using Shamanic tools. Gordon MacLellan explained to me that:

> 'I think it is profoundly important to appreciate the difference between archetypes and real spirits.'

Going on to add:

> '...we say to people training [as Shamans] that, "You will know. The first time a spirit reaches out and touches you out of an empty room or with the wind through the trees, you will know and then nothing is ever the same again."'

Other British Pagans have voiced similar comments and so I will unpack this a little more in a moment for those unfamiliar with 'archetypes'. However, in addition, I would have to add my own note of caution in that Harner uses the word 'empirical' on many occasions in his writings, referring to the existence of spirits in this way[21]:

'...for the shamanic practitioner, the existence of spirits is not a belief but an empirical fact. In NOR, shamanic practitioners routinely see, touch, smell and hear spirits.'

I think that this falls short of the normal use of the word 'empirical', which usually refers to a theory that has been shown to be verifiably consistent with experimental data. The difficulty with referring to a non-material experience as 'empirical' is that we cannot be sure about what is actually taking place because it is a matter of interpretation. As we will see when we discuss different Shamanic understandings of the spiritual world, whilst there are cross-cultural similarities, that is not the same as saying that there is an 'empirical' consistency. MacLellan's reference above to 'archetypes' suggests that, in at least some of Harner's ideas, we are just as likely to be encountering internal parts of the person (according to Jungian psychological ideas of each of us having subpersonalities to which we may, or may not, give a voice) as we are to be encountering external spiritual entities.

Therefore, without wishing to belittle the huge amount of valuable work carried out by the Foundation for Shamanic Studies, it seems to me that we should at least consider the possibility that some Core Shamanic practices may sit astride a boundary between the spiritual and the psychological. Indeed, I would say that to one degree or another all spiritual experiences are partly psychological because I believe that body, mind/soul and spirit are one interpenetrating whole and because we can only interpret a spiritual experience with the psychological tools forged by our life experience. From the integrity of the Core Shamans I have met I would have to say that some of what takes place is clearly on the level of a spiritual encounter, but it is interesting to note that *some* of the 'spirits' that are engaged with also bear a strong resemblance to the archetypes found in Jung's theories regarding the unconscious. Archetypes can be thought of as characters formed in the unconscious, usually accessible only in a dream or altered state of consciousness, which are common patterns within the human psyche. Classic examples include the *anima*, the female side to a man and its corresponding *animus* for women; the wise old man and wise old woman; the trickster and many, many others. Some are consistent across groups suggesting that they are an embodiment of something innately human, whilst others can be unique in meaning to a given individual. I have my own example of meeting one of these which has distinctly Core Shamanic overtones:

> *I am having a difficult night's sleep, being plagued by thoughts of a problem that seems unsolvable. In my semi-conscious state, and perhaps being influenced by my daytime work on understanding Shamanism and the Shamanic trance, I find myself drifting off to some other 'place' away from the burdensome worry. Eventually, in my semi-lucid dream state, I see a door, slightly ajar, with an inviting light behind it. I walk through the door into somewhere outside. A lady is sitting in a chair looking at me, as if she has been waiting for me. She is not old; instead she somehow appears ageless, yet she bears the wisdom or demeanour of age. "Do you know who I am?", she asks. I find myself responding with, "I want to call you Grandmother." When I awake I know, in my fully conscious state that she was neither of my grandmothers, yet that seemed to be the right name for her. Who was she?*

I confess that at the time of writing I am still unsure how to answer this question. She certainly wasn't either of my late grandmothers, bearing no resemblance to either of them in physical characteristics nor in demeanour. I'm disposed towards the Jungian suggestion that, like any encounter in a dream, she was an archetype of myself who would probably be called the 'wise old woman'. However, a Core Shaman suggested to me that she might have been a spirit who was offering herself as my spirit guide. Whilst exercising caution, it is possible that she could be either or neither of these, and that in itself defines the difficulty with Core Shamanism, that the encounters within one's psyche could actually *be* the different aspects of one's psyche. Shamanic dancing couple, the Darling Khans[22] actually make this point themselves:

'In the shamanic paradigm those guardians are called spirits. In a more western therapeutic paradigm, we might call them archetypes. It doesn't matter.'

It is intriguing to note that in terms of Shamanic journeying, the Darling Khans are not the only western Shamans who make a connection between the Shamanic journey and psychological factors. Caitlín Matthews[23] describes it like this:

'It is not unlike lucid dreaming, wherein the dreamer is enabled to become interactive with the dream rather than a mere passive observer of events.'

Indeed Harner[24] himself suggests that the answers that Shamans receive when they seek knowledge are usually given in a symbolic fashion and this is also a distinctive factor of working with our own archetypes in dream therapy. Many years ago I had a spiritual director who was also a Jungian specialist and who gave me a degree of training in the understanding of my own dreams to the extent that I now have a reasonable comprehension of what the different personal meanings are for my own symbols, (bearing in mind that dream dictionaries are generally a waste of time because the same symbol may have different meanings for different people). For example, if I am troubled about my own journey through life I will often dream of a mode of transport, usually a car but sometimes a train, and the state of the vehicle communicates much to me about how I am coping. During one particularly troubling episode in parish life, I dreamt of a train hitting some buffers at full speed. The message to slow down was very clear!

The cosmology of the Core Shaman is very similar to that found in traditional societies with this world, the middle world, being the material world we are familiar with, together with its own spiritual realm, whilst there is also a lower world and an upper world. To enter these places let us return to Harner's model that we referred to earlier. A Core Shaman may perhaps talk of the trance state required as being a 'Shamanic State of Consciousness' (SSC) and will distinguish between the reality we experience in day-to-day life as 'Ordinary Reality' (OR), and the worlds accessible in Shamanic trance as 'Non-Ordinary Reality' (NOR). Once a Core Shaman has entered a SSC they may access the lower world through visualising something like a tunnel or cave that they perceive themselves travelling into and through. Likewise, entrance to the upper world is accessed by visualising something that goes upwards, such as smoke going up a chimney, or themselves climbing a tree or a mountain. Spirits are present on all three levels, but the lower and upper worlds are purely the domain of spirit. They also have their own characteristics, with the lower world being thought of as a power house, a place from where the roots of the other worlds draw their strength. The upper world is the place of great spiritual knowledge and wisdom, with a distinctly celestial cast to it.

I have quoted a number of people who have made comments regarding Core Shamanism and psychology, so it is perhaps interesting to see how these three worlds seem to be reflected in human psychospirituality. In myself I find that I consciously occupy a world which is both material and deeply spiritual, including the immanent presence of God. Access to the more spiritual side of this world is through quiet contemplation and an open-eyed mindful approach to life. This, then, bears comparison with the middle world. Beneath my everyday experience flows my unconscious mind, a repository of forgotten knowledge and buried experience which I access through my dreams and which I am aware affects everything that is built upon it. This can be compared to the lower world. Then, there is the side of my nature, that which I call my spirit, which engages with God's transcendent nature through prayer, sometimes leading to ecstatic experiences. This has similarities with the idea of an upper world. Whilst I do not wish for a moment to suggest that Core Shamanism is nothing more than visualisation of different aspects of the self based on Jungian psychology, the ready comparisons point towards some influences of this in Core Shamanic experience and one can see why it is beginning to be considered as a tool in some psychotherapeutic practice.

## Celtic Shamanism

The Celtic model of Shamanism is an intriguing special case as it has characteristics of two traditions. It has many traits of traditional Shamanism, but also seems to have much in common with Core Shamanism as well as its own unique attributes. The key difference appears to be that the practice is located in the history, traditions and locality of Celtic Britain. This means that, in common with other forms of Shamanism, the spirits that are encountered may be thought of as deities, the dead or animal spirits. In addition, those who are thought of as 'faerie' may also be engaged with, and hence the cosmology of the Celtic 'Otherworld' is incorporated into the Celtic Shamanic model. Whilst Core Shamanism is distinctly systematic, influenced by western rationalism, Celtic Shamanism is connected closely to the land and its stories.

Initiation into Celtic Shamanism again follows the same path as traditional Shamanic routes, although western influences are seen in the ways in which the encounter with death usually has more in common with Core Shamanic principles, being more to do with a psycho-spiritual experience than an actual life-threatening event. John Matthews[25] puts it like this:

'This is traditionally the moment when the shaman enters the Otherworld stage through illness or a near-death experience. More usually today this comes as a result of realising how futile your life has been until now. Thus you 'die' to your former self and accept the possibility of rebirth and transformation.'

The Celtic Shamanic cosmos is again similar to that which is found in traditional and core models, consisting of three levels, but according to John Matthews[26], the three worlds are linked by a Great Tree, with the otherworld overshadowing this middle world of which we are a part, so that it is possible to venture into this parallel world without having to go either 'up' or 'down'. In his view the centre of the middle world which we inhabit is surrounded by a great wheel with the eight points of the Celtic year that we described earlier in the discussion about Wicca and Witchcraft. Beneath us lies the underworld which is a place of ancestral wisdom, down into which the roots of the Great Tree penetrate, and above us is the upper world, the place of deity.

Whilst the Celtic Shaman's model of working to alleviate soul-loss is held in common with other Shamanic traditions, the soul itself may be understood differently. Frank MacEowen[27] suggests that there are three cauldrons which make up the soul:

'[The] cauldron of warming (life force), located in the belly, the cauldron of vocation (calling), located in the heart or solar plexus, and the cauldron of knowledge (wisdom), located in the head.'

Wholeness in the Celtic model therefore requires spiritual, psychic and physical health and the Shaman will, if asked, become involved in the healing of any of these aspects.

However, there is an intriguing counterpoint, put by Caitlín Matthews[28], to the idea that Celtic Shamanism, or indeed any form of Shamanism, is especially distinct from any other form. She writes:

'There are no terrestrial or cultural boundaries in the other-worlds: the knowledge that you find there is universal in practice.'

This brings us back again to the concept of spiritual perception and the ways in which our own world views colour what is experienced in trance. A Celtic Shaman may have a spiritual encounter that is in many ways identical to one had by a Core Shaman or a Shaman of any other tradition. However, it is the history and one's own culture which shapes the understanding of the encounter. Yet, at the same time, it is necessary to acknowledge the danger inherent in adopting this view in that it would be very easy to slide from this into suggesting that the interpretation of all spiritual encounters is purely a matter of cultural references. Undoubtedly, we cannot easily escape our own histories, but whilst they clearly influence our under-standings, it might be a step too far to imagine that all spiritual experiences are from the same source and coloured only by our cultural influences.

## Who are the guides and why do they help?

Throughout this chapter I have referred to a Shaman's spiritual guides which are often perceived as human ancestors or power animals. It is now time to consider who they are in Shamanic thought, bearing in mind that there will again be different inter-pretations according to culture. It is also worth noting that in Shamanism, perhaps more than anywhere else in modern Paganism, there is a distinct influence from New Age beliefs to the extent that it is quite difficult to find out what is really believed by those who are recognised within their communities as genuine Shamans, as opposed to those who simply call themselves Shamans yet have no community role. To that end, the simple definition of a spirit guide is more or less a being of spirit who comes to the Shaman on one of their journeys and offers to help them. However, there are some guidelines that help us to understand at least some of what a Shaman would expect when they seek help.

In common with many other forms of Paganism, a considerable weight of importance is laid on one's own ancestors. It is not uncommon, particularly in Roman Catholicism, for Christians to imagine their forebears looking down on them from above, and it may even be thought that they lend a helping hand in times of need (although this may also be attributed to angels, and sometimes people will conflate the two, believing that a person can become an angel when the two are actually different orders of being). In Shamanism this can go a stage further to calling on ancestors, when in a trance state, to come and lend their power to helping. 'Ancestors' in this case is often far more distant than 'Aunty Mabel who died two years ago.' Ancestral spirits can refer to the spirits of a people or race rather than just to close or even distant blood relatives.

One might ask why such ancestral spirits would actually want to help, although that question perhaps belies a prevailing western view that all help should be bought and paid for. In more traditional and hospitable societies one offers help because it is simply the correct thing to do and so the argument can be made that an ancestral spirit offers to help the Shaman purely because help is needed, with no ulterior motive. The expectation is then that the Shaman will help another in order to reciprocate the help that they have received from their spirit guide.

At the other end of the spectrum, and probably influenced by more New Age beliefs, another source of help may be those who are sometimes referred to as 'evolved beings' without any explanation as to what is actually meant by this. One might also find references to 'Beings of Light', which is a phrase that sometimes occurs when angels are being discussed. Therefore, in some schools of thought, there appears to be an idea that through successive incarnations a person can steadily evolve away from this mortal plane towards ascending into the heavenly realms in an angelic form, willing to help more primitive beings, such as ourselves, to follow the same path. One might also encounter this order of beings referred to as 'gods'. I hasten to emphasise that this is far more of a western New Age model and unlikely to be found in traditional Shamanic practice.

Following the more Animistic and traditional cultures in which Shamanism was born, the relationship with animal spirits in the west is of great importance. Once again, there has been a strong influence of the New Age movement and the internet abounds with overly-romantic, pretty pictures that bear little resemblance to the experiences of those genuinely recognised as Shamans in their communities. When it comes to animal spirits, the connection is more profound because of the natural relationship between us, given that humans are animals, although the West appears to forget this. What is more, in some traditions the connection is thought of as going the other way too, with animals being a form of human. Traditional stories in all cultures abound with animals talking to each other, including our own, such as in *The Wind in the Willows*. Whilst some would doubtless view this as part of our natural ease at anthropomor-phising, the Shamanic interpretation of this would probably be of a race memory of the time when animals and humans conversed, but this time has passed in the middle world. Harner[29] explains:

'While the mythical paradise of animal-human unity is lost in ordinary reality, it still remains accessible in nonordinary reality to the shaman and vision-seeker.'

A guiding animal spirit is often referred to as a 'Power Animal' and there are numerous published rituals on how one can make contact with a power animal. This is related to the idea of shapeshifting, which should be thought of more in terms of a form of dance in which the Shaman mimics their power animal's movements rather than, for example, actually growing the wings and feathers of a bird. By moving in this way, the Shaman believes that they can align their soul with that of their power animal so that they can dance together in a mystical unity. It also provides them with a different perspective in the same way that, as small children, we often imitate trees and animals in play.

With all of these different spirit guides we should also recognise that whilst there is a belief within western Shamanism that the spirits are helping from a developed form of altruism, we should also acknowledge the dangers inherent in this practice. Despite Harner's comments that there is empirical evidence for what is taking place, the reality is that we cannot know for sure. Some forms of traditional Shamanism speak of being possessed by the guiding spirit and once such a connection has been made, if the spirit proves to be rather less altruistic than first apparent, the Shaman may find themselves in need of help to be freed from a spirit that has taken to enjoy embodiment. In some more conservative Christian circles this will be equated with demonic possession, but, as we will see, once one starts considering some of the more charismatic expressions of Christianity, the lines become rather blurred. Even if we stay purely within the arena of the psychological, some parts of the personality are buried for a reason and we should be cautious about letting them out or following their lead, unless they have first been integrated into the whole.

## Jesus as a Shaman

You may recall the Witch I quoted in Chapter 3 who, when asked about Jesus, immediately responded with, 'He was one of us'. This reflects how some Witches read their own understandings of the Craft into the way in which Jesus appears to manipulate the natural world. Yet, whilst I have not had a similar comment made personally to me from a Shaman, there are numerous references to the Shamanic nature of Jesus across the internet which require us to consider what is meant. We can make a number of observations about the life and ministry of Jesus that permit us to see echoes of what could be considered by some to be Shamanic practice.

The first and most obvious example comes from when Jesus received the Holy Spirit at his baptism in the River Jordan by John the Baptist. This incident was so important that it appears in all three synoptic Gospels and is commented on through the words of John the Baptist in the fourth Gospel. In every case, the same observation is made; that when Jesus was baptised the Holy Spirit descended on him in bodily form like a dove, or, at least, that is how the writers interpreted the eyewitness accounts. However, if one were to cast a Shamanic eye at the proceedings the question that could be asked was, was Jesus receiving the Holy Spirit, or was he receiving his power animal? Of course, one could ask the question, if the manifestation of the Holy Spirit was as a dove in the case of Jesus, are all power animals different manifestations of the Holy Spirit given to different people for different reasons? Many Christians would certainly testify that God meets them in the ways in which they are able to receive him. The imagery of the dove as a power animal would make sense for Jesus because within Jewish culture it was both a symbol of peace and also of sacrifice, and many Christians believe that Christ came as a sacrifice to bring peace between God and humanity, but there is no reason to assume that the Holy Spirit should always manifest as a dove. Indeed, in the Celtic Church a popular symbol is a wild goose.

The second allusion to Shamanism comes in the immediate aftermath of Jesus receiving the Holy Spirit when the Spirit drives him into the wilderness to be tempted by the devil. In some ways this bears comparison with a vision or power quest where the petitioner puts themselves under physical duress in an isolated place in order to obtain help from spirits. Now, in one sense, there is a clear distinction between this and Jesus in that he received the Holy Spirit first and was then led into the wilderness, rather than the other way around as would be expected for a Shaman. On the other hand, there is also a strong similarity in that first he is tested by the devil after a lengthy fast, (which equates to voluntarily undergoing suffering) and then at the end of the testing the Gospel writers Matthew and Mark both record that Jesus was ministered to by angels. From a Shamanic perspective this appears rather similar to the idea of seeking and then receiving spiritual help. Once again, I am not so much suggesting that Jesus' experience was a Shamanic one, but more questioning whether Shamanic experiences may be indicative of receiving help from angels. Remember that we always interpret experiences from within our own culture and so, whilst I may see an angel, another may see an ancestor or a Sidhe. Material human perspectives of spiritual manifestations are profoundly influenced by our understanding, culture and history.

Of course, it is also equally possible to look at Shamanic experiences and refer to them as counterfeit, as imitations of the real thing. This is a rather too easy option, which I have come across many times and to my mind feels rather spiritually lazy and exclusivist. Revealed religions, i.e., those in which the deity 'reveals' themselves such as when God spoke to Moses out of a burning bush, almost habitually describe themselves as the only way to encounter God and will naturally tend towards rejecting any other potential spiritual experience as being fraudulent. This is not an opinion one would be likely to find being expressed by a Pagan. However, as with all spiritual experiences and beliefs, for wisdom's sake one must question and weigh up what takes place to determine its validity. For example, Harner[30] describes a Shamanic encounter of a friend with Jesus in which Jesus gave the petitioner ideas about how to improve the money-making potential of her business choices. This seems rather removed from the man who lived simply and encouraged his followers to do the same thing, which would lead me to ask who it was she actually met. There is always potential to be misled in spiritual experiences and so they should always be considered carefully, whatever the tradition. Christians are no more immune to this than any other faith or belief group.

A third connection between Jesus and Shamanism is in the aims of each which appear to be mutually related to bringing life. In John 10:10b Jesus is quoted as saying,

'I came that they should have life, and have it in all its fullness.'

Caitlín Matthews[31] describes the aims of Shamanism in these terms:

'Shamans believe and work with the power of Spirit, which sustains and flows through all things. The power of Spirit is the vital energy of the universe it is life. Shamans bring life by reconnecting the broken links of power or by removing blockages which impede its flow.'

Clearly the methods are different, but at its best one could argue that Shamanism is trying to accomplish the same healing and restoration of the abundance of life as Christ was intending, and this point alone should be sufficient grounds for an interfaith relationship.

The final comparison I will mention is with regards to suffering, death and resurrection. In the life of Christ this was literal and physical. Following his arrest and mistreatment, he was subjected to a Roman flogging, in itself capable of inflicting wounds from which a survivor would be maimed for life, before his death by crucifixion. Eyewitness testimonies provide the foundation for Christian belief that he was physically raised from the dead on the third day, and that this triumph over death had global and, possibly, universal consequences. Even here, there are elements that could be interpreted from a Shamanic perspective. I doubt that any Shaman would claim a global reach with their ministry, but many would refer to a real suffering followed by a symbolic death, possible spiritual dismemberment, and then a symbolic resurrection, of being returned to life, as being essential elements to their preparation for the beginnings of Shamanic ministry.

> *He showed me the place in his garden where he prepared himself by digging his own grave. His wife took part in the ceremony by back-filling the space in which he lay, an experience that she herself found profoundly moving. There he lay for an hour, with just his face exposed to the air, waiting for her to come back and to dig him out again, returning him to life.*

Let me underline that I am not equating Shamanism and Christianity, merely pointing out elements that appear to be held in common and highlighting how some of the grand themes of different religions seem to be repeated in each other. To that end, it is worth broadening our comparisons beyond the person of Christ to some of the foundations of Jewish and Christian belief.

## Shamanic imagery in Judeo-Christianity

There are a number of stories in the Bible that could be related to a Shamanic world view. In Genesis 28 we read of a vision that Jacob had of angels ascending and descending some kind of ladder into heaven. From a Shamanic perspective, the ladder may be considered to equate to the axis which joins the underworld, middle world and upper world, and given that angels are thought of as dwellers in the upper world, Jacob's vision appears to have elements that could be interpreted as being distinctly Shamanic. Or, there are the numerous occasions throughout the Old Testament where prophets would consult God before going into battle in order to be sure that he was fighting with them, which bears a strong resemblance to the Shuar people's dependence on their guardian spirits and how they would not undertake a risky mission unless the signs indicated that their guardians were stood with them, bringing their protective powers, especially if a battle was being planned.[32] We could also refer to the conversion of St. Paul on the road to Damascus and his subsequent blindness and healing, related in Acts 9, as being similar to a Shamanic calling through being inflicted with ill health after an intense spiritual encounter before being raised up, a type of resurrection, to begin a ministry which had far-reaching consequences.

Harner[33] refers to those who dwell now in the upper world but who were previously alive in this world, as those who watch over us and seek to help us, declaring that in the Christian tradition these are referred to as saints. Whilst there are many disagreements within Christian theology about the roles of the saints, Harner's ideas challenge us to think about the author of the New Testament Letter to the Hebrews who, in 12:1, refers to us as being surrounded by a great cloud of witnesses of heroes in Jewish faith. In the same line of reasoning, St. Paul also refers to someone caught up into heaven:

'I know a person in Christ who fourteen years ago was caught up to the third heaven—whether in the body or out of the body I do not know; God knows. And I know that such a person—whether in the body or out of the body I do not know; God knows— was caught up into Paradise and heard things that are not to be told, that no mortal is permitted to repeat.' 2 Corinthians 12:2-4

Whilst we can easily site this within Jewish and Christian theology, from a Shamanic perspective this has the distinct appearance of a Shamanic journey into the upper world. Although many writers try to make it clear that the upper world should not be equated with the Christian understanding of heaven, within western Core Shamanic practice the experiences are filtered through what is still a Christian-dominated spiritual cosmology. The unanswerable question, therefore, is whether the Shaman is interpreting their journey according to childhood images, or whether the experiences bear comparison because the upper world of Core Shamanism is actually the same place that St. Paul's friend visited.

The action of the Holy Spirit in Christian theology also appears to have parallels within a Shamanic world view. John Matthews[34] writes of the *inner Shaman* and the *Shaman within*:

'The inner shaman is the Otherworldly teacher which you will soon encounter. The shaman within is an inner quality, or aspect of yourself, which is activated once you reach a certain point in your training. Once the shaman *within* is given a voice and consciousness, it is he or she who will begin to dialogue with your *inner* shaman.'

Compare that statement with this from Romans 8:14-16:

'For all who are led by the Spirit of God are children of God. For you did not receive a spirit of slavery to fall back into fear, but you have received a spirit of adoption. When we cry, 'Abba! Father!' it is that very Spirit bearing witness with our spirit that we are children of God...'

Once again, we can see similarities between the two traditions in terms of an inner voice that comes from the One we invited into us speaking to our own inner voice within, that part of us that is awakened by the presence of the one whom Christians refer to as the Holy Spirit. As always, we are on difficult ground here because if a Christian asserts that a Shaman is listening to the Holy Spirit, the Shaman might justifiably feel angry that their beliefs are being subverted by another faith. Likewise, there will be many within the Christian tradition who would consider the Shamanic experience to be demonic and counterfeit. I raise it here simply to ask the questions and promote the debate since there are clear similarities and it will only be through interfaith discussion that we can better understand them. However, once we start pushing at the similarities we can see more emerging. Returning to Harner[35] once more we read about how spirits make their presence known:

'...the room or dwelling may shake as if in an earthquake, a phenomenon known in the North American ethnological literature as the 'shaking tent'. Also many small lights usually appear and move about in the darkness.'

Compare that description with the original story of the coming of the Holy Spirit at Pentecost in Acts 2:1-3 and we find some intriguing similarities:

'When the day of Pentecost had come, they were all together in one place. And suddenly from heaven there came a sound like the rush of a violent wind, and it filled the entire house where they were sitting. Divided tongues, as of fire, appeared among them, and a tongue rested on each of them.'

In both cases there is a disturbance in the local surroundings, and it is not a huge leap to suggest that the shaking of a tent or dwelling could be describing something similar to what seems like the rushing of a mighty wind, and the small lights moving in the darkness bears comparison with the tongues of flame. It is, of course, possible that any intense spiritual interaction with the physical world could produce similar manifestations regardless of the spiritual source. This would suggest that the effects of the coming of the Holy Spirit were the localised physical by-products of the intense and focussed presence of God. Certainly, serious Christians should be far more concerned about whether the presence of the Holy Spirit within them has actually changed them for the better rather than simply providing some good spiritual fireworks! Perhaps rather more controversially, we should ask the question about whether both of the above are descriptions of the same or a related phenomenon. Does the Holy Spirit come by different names? I am not a wholehearted advocate of religious pluralism, but I do believe that the grace and gifts of God stretch far further than many Christians imagine (or wish).

In Chapter 2 I described my own conversion to Christianity and the shaking that accompanied the coming of the Holy Spirit, yet Stuart Harris-Logan[36] writes of how some forms of traditional Shamanism involve being possessed by a spirit:

'In Kimbanguist tradition, to shake is a sign of possession – a sign that one has been chosen by the god.'

We have to ask the question: is this a physical manifestation of an intense spiritual experience, or is it the same spiritual experience that is taking place? I think that the only way we can answer this question is to look at what takes place next in the life of the practitioner. John Hick[37] writes in these terms:

'The central criterion can only be the long-term transformative effect on the experiencer. A momentary experience, or an experience lasting minutes or even hours, is only important if its significance is integrated into one's ongoing life. If, as in the case of the great mystics, their altered states of consciousness have a transforming and energising effect in their lives, leading to a stronger centring in God, the Holy, the Real, and a greater love and compassion for their fellows, this is the evidence accepted within each of the great traditions...'

Here, then, is the foundation for questioning the reality of a spiritual experience; what long-term effect does it have on the person? For me, my encounter with God at the age of fifteen utterly changed the direction my life was taking. The subsequent experiences have gone on to continue reinforcing and furthering that change, (although as my friends and family would testify, there is still an awful lot of work to do!). I find myself in agreement with Hick, though, that a valid encounter with God/Spirit, or whatever term we choose, should move us away from a focus on the self to a focus on the needs of others. Our egos are challenged and we begin to see ourselves in a broader perspective. I would argue that if an experience does not change a person for the better, then it does not bear a full comparison with the life-changing encounters that many have had.

It is interesting therefore to note that it is not just spiritual experiences which have common elements, but also what flows from them. Within the Christian faith there is a tradition of what is referred to as 'Dying to yourself'. This is a strongly biblical theme that reoccurs many times in the New Testament with such verses as:

'Then he [Jesus] said to them all, "If any want to become my followers, let them deny themselves and take up their cross daily and follow me."' Luke 9:23

and

'I have been crucified with Christ; and it is no longer I who live, but it is Christ who lives in me. And the life I now live in the flesh I live by faith in the Son of God, who loved me and gave himself for me.' Galatians 2:19b-20

Indeed, many Pagans have criticised Christianity as being overly focussed on death and suffering. Yet with respect to death to oneself it is also a strongly Shamanic theme, with reference to dying to your old self, as we have already noted. Frank MacEowen[38] goes even further than this, likening the death stage in a Shaman's journey to the Christian concept of the 'Dark night of the soul', indicating his own conclusion that the two experiences are similar and, if genuine, will produce similar psychospiritual outcomes in the person.

Throughout this section I hope I have shown enough evidence that there should be better lines of communication between Christians and Shamans since we seem to have much to discuss in terms of the commonality of some of our experiences, and doubtless the numerous differences too. We need to conclude this section by turning the argument around from aspects of Shamanism that have a similar appearance to Christianity, to aspects of modern Christian practice that appear, actually, to be decidedly Shamanic. Many within the Christian tradition, including myself, have experienced occasions of being overcome by the one Christians call the Holy Spirit. For some this can lead to a sense of ecstasy, or deeply felt peace, for others it can result in tears, laughter or a profound conviction of the need to change one's life, and others find themselves unable to stand, resulting in having to lie prone on the floor, a manifestation known as being 'slain in the Spirit'. All of these have some kind of precursor in the Bible. Yet beyond all of these experiences comes something that few could have predicted, which began in 1994 at a Vineyard Church at Toronto airport and came to be known as the Toronto Blessing. Whilst what was referred to as holy laughter characterised some of the early manifestations, others included people beginning to roar like lions. Religion news blog[39] reported that:

> 'They also made animal noises — braying, barking, howling and roaring. They collapsed to the floor, staggered about as if drunk, shook and jerked; wept, wailed and yelped. Faces contorted with tics. Groans and guffaws hung in the air. Bodies lay prone on the carpet.'

I have witnessed behaviour similar to this at a church in this country where a friend gave her testimony whilst repeatedly bowing over as if being struck in the stomach, yet she felt no pain and appeared to have been deeply moved by the experience. One could argue that repetitive rhythms at the correct tempo, as used by Core Shamans, together with a whipping up of hysteria, is actually inducing an ecstatic trance state similar, if not identical, to that which is used by Shamans. This is not to suggest that Shamanic practice requires a degree of hysterical emotion, far from it, but a frenzied state can be a factor in some traditional Shamanic practices, and so it is enlightening to read the testimony of a number of Inuit elders[40]:

> '...the Pentecostals and the charismatic fundamentalists have often in the past spoken out very harshly against shamanism, at times even branding it as diabolical. Paradoxically, the same Christian movements, which are more recent than the ones that have evangelised the Inuit for about a century, are seen by many Inuit as having practices that remind them of the shamanic practices of past generations.'

Whether the resulting manifestations are the work of the Holy Spirit can only be tested by the long-term effects on how believers go on to live, but many of the manifestations, perhaps most especially the identification with animals which Shamans might consider to be linked to the receiving of a 'power animal', appear to be distinctly Shamanic. Once again, this leads us to ask if this is genuinely a manifestation of the one Christians call the Holy Spirit and is the same member of the Godhead also active within Shamanism? If, instead, we believe much Core Shamanic practice to be more psychological than spiritual, then maybe we should consider drawing the same conclusions about some of what takes place in some charismatic churches. We cannot have it both ways, rejecting one as diabolical whilst calling the other holy if the two are so similar in appearance and the ways in which they are stirred up. I suspect that the truth lies somewhere between these two poles.

## Just a beginning...

Even though this book is very much intended to be an intro-duction to Paganism and its relationship to Christianity, I cannot help but feel that Shamanism, perhaps more than any of the previous chapters, is inordinately difficult to introduce on a simple level. In part, this is because it is a worldwide practice and is likely to have existed so far back into human prehistory, on the assumption that Animism is our first expression of spiritual awareness. Consequently, it has evolved in many different ways across the globe. Western practice is clearly not limited to Core Shamanism and I suspect that a sociological spiritual drive away from western rationalism may see growing numbers engaging with more traditional practices. It is possible that Core Shamanism may, therefore, fall out of favour in time to be replaced by more traditional techniques. I have barely touched on the use of Core Shamanic techniques in therapy, yet this seems to be growing and becoming more acceptable. For a good intro-duction I would direct the reader to the writings of Christa Mackinnon[41] who is a Psychologist, Family Counsellor, Clinical Hypnotherapist and Shamanic Practitioner. However, my impression from the more traditionally minded is that Shamanism risks becoming diluted if it is seen as no more than a therapeutic arm of Jungian psychology.

Pagan readers of this book may be intrigued by the absence of references to the writings of Mircea Eliade. The reasons for this are twofold: first, most of the modern western writers are so influenced by Eliade that whether one is quoting directly from him or not, his influence will have made itself known in what I've said here. Secondly, and perhaps more importantly, the impression I have received is that amongst more learned Pagan scholars there are growing concerns about the accuracy of his research. Much as in the way Ronald Hutton demonstrated the holes in the modern mythology around Druidry and Witchcraft, leading to a deeper and more accurate understanding, so I think a similar process may be taking place around Eliade's work as Shamanism begins to become a more popularised form of Paganism. Certainly, where the edges of Pagan and New Age practice merge, there are large amounts of invention and roman- ticism that are dismissed by serious Shamanic practitioners.

For me, this chapter has proved deeply challenging as the unexpected similarities between some Shamanic and Christian experiences have provoked much food for thought and far more ideas than can be expounded upon in an introductory book such as this. As with each of the chapters, readers are encouraged to delve further to gain a better understanding from the founda- tions I have tried to lay here. For my part, I fully intend to continue to research Shamanism in order to better understand what may be taking place in the place of spiritual encounter.

## Notes for Chapter 6

1   Harner M., *Cave and Cosmos*, Berkley, U.S.A.: North Atlantic Books, 2013, 252

2   Matthews C., *Singing the Soul Back Home*, revised edn., London: Connections, 2002, 21

3   Harris-Logan S. A., *Singing with Blackbirds*, Girvan: Grey

House in the Woods, 2006, xi.

4   *Ibid.*, 44

5   *Ibid.*, 23

6   Chamblin J. K., "Psychology" in Hawthorne G. F., Martin R. P., and Reid D. G. (Eds.), *Dictionary of Paul and His Letters*, Leicester: IVP, 1993, 768.

7   MacEowen F., *The Mist-Filled Path*, Novato California: New World Library, 2002, 4.

8   Harris-Logan S. A., *Singing with Blackbirds*, Girvan: Grey House in the Woods, 2006, xiii.

9   Harner M., *Cave and Cosmos*, Berkley USA: North Atlantic Books, 2013, 11.

10  MacEowan F., *The Mist-Filled Path*, Novato California: New World Library, 2002, 76.

11  For example, in conversation, Pagan author and speaker Liz Williams spoke to me of her experiences with a Siberian Altaic Shaman who was also a Christian and used her gifts to work with the saints, dedicating the three days around a new moon to healing work.

12  Rivière P., "Shamanism and the Unconfined Soul" in Crabbe M. J. C. (Ed.), *From Soul to Self*, London: Routledge, 1999, 71.

13  Matthews C., *Singing the Soul Back Home*, Revised edn., London: Connections, 2002, 27.

14  Matthews C., *Singing the Soul Back Home*, Revised edn., London: Connections, 2002, 169

15  Harner M., *Cave and Cosmos*, Berkley USA: North Atlantic Books, 2013, 208.

16  Aupilaarjuk M. And T., Nutaraaluk L., Iqallijuq R., Ujarak J., Ijituuq I. and Kupaaq M. (Editor D'Anglure B. S.), *Interviewing Inuit Elders Volume 4. Cosmology and Shamanism*, Nunavut: The Language and Culture Programme of Nunavut Arctic College, 2001, 30.

17  *Ibid.* 88.

18  Harner M., *Cave and Cosmos*, Berkley USA: North Atlantic

Books, 2013, 251.

19   Harner M., *The Way of the Shaman*, New York USA.: HarperOne, 1990, 39.

20   Harner M., *Cave and Cosmos*, Berkley USA: North Atlantic Books, 2013, 253.

21   Harner M., *Cave and Cosmos*, Berkley USA: North Atlantic Books, 2013, 253.

22   Darling Khan S. and Y., *Movement Medicine*, London: Hay House, 2009, 35.

23   Matthews C., *Singing the Soul Back Home*, Revised edn., London: Connections, 2002, 77

24   Harner M., *Cave and Cosmos*, Berkley USA: North Atlantic Books, 2013, 144.

25   Matthews J., *The Celtic Shaman – A Practical Guide*, London: Rider, 2001, 91.

26   *Ibid.* 36f.

27   MacEowen F., *The Mist-Filled Path*, Novato California: New World Library, 2002, 26.

28   Matthews C., *Singing the Soul Back Home*, Revised edn., London: Connections, 2002, 14

29   Harner M., *The Way of the Shaman*, New York: HarperOne, 1990, 74.

30   Harner M., *Cave and Cosmos*, Berkley USA: North Atlantic Books, 2013, 146.

31   Matthews C., *Singing the Soul Back Home*, Revised edn., London: Connections, 2002, 39

32   Harner M., *Cave and Cosmos*, Berkley USA: North Atlantic Books, 2013, 9f

33   Harner M., *Cave and Cosmos*, Berkley USA: North Atlantic Books, 2013, 254-6

34   Matthews J., *The Celtic Shaman – a Practical Guide*, London: Rider, 2001, 72.

35   Harner M., *Cave and Cosmos*, Berkley USA: North Atlantic Books, 2013, 201

36  Harris-Logan S. A., *Singing with Blackbirds*, Girvan: Grey House in the Woods, 2006, 46 and 64.

37  Hick J., *The Fifth Dimension*, Oxford: Oneworld, 1999, 163.

38  MacEowan F., *The Mist-Filled Path*, Novato California: New World Library, 2002, 68

39  URL: http://www.religionnewsblog.com/5706/toronto-bless ing-goes-on-10-years

40  Aupilaarjuk M. and T. *et al.* (edited by B. S. D'Anglure), *Interviewing Inuit Elders Volume 4*, Cosmology and Shamanism, Nunavut: The Language and Culture Programme of Nunavut College, 2001, 8.

41  Mackinnon C., *Shamanism and Spirituality in Therapeutic Practice*, London: Singing Dragon, 2012.

# Chapter Seven

# Heathenism

## Another new world

By now I hope it has become clear that although Wicca, Witchcraft, Druidry, Animism and Shamanism are all different from each other, they are also linked. Witchcraft and Shamanism, as well as having distinct beliefs of their own, tend also to be tools that are used in other traditions, whilst beliefs in different deities are easily affirmed in shared rituals and much common ground is held. This, however, is somewhat less the case with the Pagan religion of Heathenism. Whilst there are certainly Heathens who practise the Craft or who are Shamans, the belief system has some distinct differences, including the gods themselves. This is primarily because, whilst the religions we have looked at so far are linked, partly by a common perceived Celtic influence (with the exception of Shamanism which may nevertheless have evolved here separately from elsewhere), and partly because many of those who re-imagined and redeveloped these religions in the West knew each other and fed off each other's ideas. Heathenism, on the other hand, is the religion of the Germanic peoples of Northern Europe. Essentially, therefore, Heathenism is a rather different Pagan religion, and that presents a dilemma. Everything that I have written so far has built on what has gone before, showing the links between the different paths. Heathenism, to a great extent, stands separately and, if I am honest, to do it justice it more or less requires an introductory book all of its own. It is a huge and complex religion with its own folklore, poems and sacred writings, mainly drawn from two collections: the Poetic Edda and the Prose Edda. These are thirteenth-century Icelandic sources, which themselves draw on material dating back to the Viking era. Furthermore, the descriptions and interpretations of the folklore are multifaceted and not always in agreement. In this it is quite distinct from the other Pagan paths covered here which depend on oral tradition, a common imagination, and other people's historical records in order to reconstruct their past.

What this means is that to write an introduction to Heathenism that goes into real depth would require this book to double in length; it is a vast subject. Yet to miss out Heathenism would be to do an injustice to the many followers of this religion and to leave a gaping hole in the discussion. Essentially, therefore, I am left with having to choose to make this a shorter chapter than the previous ones, which will skim over a wider range, but not in the same level of detail.

I have also noticed that, to a greater or lesser degree, there seems to be less integration and communication between Heathens and other Pagans. This is by no means universal, and it is not necessarily that other Pagans reject Heathenism; far from it, although, intriguingly, not all Heathens actually like to be categorised as Pagan. However, because the gods in the Heathen pantheon are so thoroughly different, within the Pagan community understanding what Heathens believe is almost like interfaith work in itself, and indeed some Heathens are fully committed to explaining their beliefs to other Pagans:

*I feel privileged to have been invited to attend this camp, just as an observer. My hosts are a couple, both of whom are Heathens, and are keen to promote interfaith discussion between Pagan and Christian. Suzanne has studied her own religion in some depth as an historian and is keen to help other Pagans understand her beliefs. She has been invited to give a lecture and the number of those present in the marquee indicates that plenty of non-Heathen Pagans are keen to understand her.*

*She wears traditional Heathen dress and describes what each item signifies, before giving us a fairly brief summary of her own beliefs. She then invites any who wish to join her to come to a Heathen drinking ceremony outside. About fifteen take up the offer and I follow as an observer. We leave the confines of the camp and walk into the wooded area where Suzanne locates a suitable clearing and explains how, using the drinking horn, a toast can be given to an ancestor of the participant's choice. Everyone joins in willingly and shows gratitude at the end to Suzanne for allowing them to take part and understand more of her beliefs.*

My own observation is that it is not just the gods and goddesses which are different; there is a contrasting feel to how Heathens tend to work with their deities compared to the other Pagan paths. The British and Celtic paths seem to lean towards honour and love with a desire to serve other people and the planet. They are very eco-aware paths. Heathenism has a tendency more towards respect, and sometimes fear, of their deities. Since their beliefs take in the concept of Ragnarok, the end of the world, there is perhaps slightly less of a focus towards eco-awareness, but this is not to suggest that Heathenism is not an earth-based religion, it is simply a slight shift in emphasis. It is often said of Christianity that the God of the Old Testament contrasts with the God of the New Testament, with the Old Testament God being more battle-hungry and to be feared, whereas Jesus portrays a God of love who sends his Son to rescue people from themselves. To me, a similar distinction seems to present itself between Heathenism and the other Pagan paths, that their deities are feared and more warriorlike. This is not universal – again it is a slight bias rather than an absolute. It is all to do with a shift in emphasis which may be culturally developed more so that some groups of Heathens, especially those dominated by men, tend to be drawn towards the power ethic of Viking folklore. It is also worth noting that, whilst there are monotheists among Druidry and, to a far lesser extent, Wicca, Heathens tend far more towards being polytheists, although even here there is a small percentage which sees the different gods as being attributes of one deity.

We might wonder why it is that British people, with their own Pagan religions, might choose to adopt the Pagan practice of the Germanic peoples. The answer to that will, of course, vary from one person to another. One Heathen told me that she had no choice in the matter because the gods introduced themselves to her and told her she would follow them! I know of plenty of Christians who have the same testimony regarding an experience with Jesus, and, indeed, my favourite is of an ex-occultist friend who told of how she went in search of one deity and was met by Christ who called her to follow him. In the Christian tradition we remember the words of Christ to the disciples, 'You did not choose me, but I chose you,' John 15:16, so perhaps we should not be surprised if other religions have similar traditions.

For others they would say that the Heathen gods are more naturally our gods since they were the gods of the ancient Britons, pointing back to settlement of the Anglo-Saxons in post-Roman Britain in the fifth century onwards. They brought with them the beliefs of the Germanic tribes of which they were a part and their influences have shaped our nation right down to the naming of the days of the week, as we will shortly see. For many, therefore, Heathenism is simply a return to our own roots.

However, for others it is entirely a matter of making a choice because Heathenism offers a quite distinct psychospirituality which is, in some ways, further removed from Christianity than the other Pagan models discussed here. Druidry and Wicca have strong models of service, service to the earth and to the community. Gods and ancestors are honoured and revered. Heathens also have a strong ecocentric, code but also tend more towards a focus on the needs of the self and one's immediate family and dependants. It has an extremely strong honour code in which a key aim of the religion is for the self to grow into the fullness of what it can achieve. This is not to say that Heathenism is an egocentric religion, as I have experienced firsthand just how hospitable some Heathens are, explaining to me that they feel duty bound to be so because of their beliefs. They seem to have a shift in bias so that the growth of the individual, the family and the local community, and the practical meeting of their needs, has a slightly more central role than in other Pagan paths, whilst introspection is not valued quite so highly. I think it would be fair to say that whilst some New Age practices have begun to influence some aspects of the other Pagan beliefs we have looked at, there is little, if any, influence in Heathenism.

Its attitudes to its deities are also different and are at the human-will end of the spectrum of human-deity relationship compared to the monotheistic established religions. What I mean by this is that at one end one finds Islam with its overarching belief in submission to the will of God. Judaism includes this, but also has a history of bartering with God and sometimes even arguing. Christianity includes both of these, but with an intimate parental familiarity through Christ as 'God-with-us', the part of God who took our humanity into himself and so understands what it's like to be human. Once one moves over to the Pagan religions the deities tend to be honoured rather than worshipped, with their greater power and wisdom than humans. By the time we reach Heathenism, humility before the gods is beginning to take more of a back seat:

*She explained to me how a Heathen friend had been taking her to see a sacred place that he had discovered. Unfortunately, finding it again was proving less easy. His frustration grew until he told her to stop the car. He got out and had a real row with his god about why the location of the place was now being hidden from him. Evidently, they struck a bargain since he climbed back into the car, now knowing exactly where they were supposed to be going, and directed her straight there.*

Whilst Jews and Christians might, depending on tradition, argue with God, it is never remotely as equals, but Heathens will hold their heads up high as individuals who have the right to stand before the gods and strike bargains with them. This is quite a psychospiritual departure from most of what is found elsewhere in British and Celtic Paganism. It also gives us an understanding of why Heathenism is popular amongst men. Whilst our society as a whole may be rightly aiming at gender equality, there is still a strong drive amongst men to be the more powerful side of the partnership which can find inspiration amongst the beliefs of Heathenism which are consistent with more of a masculine warrior-code orientation.

This being said, as with other branches of Paganism, the ways in which the gods are understood will vary from one individual to another. Most will believe them to be actual deities but some consider them to be archetypal aspects of the person, and again in common with other Pagan practice, since there is no central dogma, all of these beliefs are acceptable under the one umbrella of Heathenism.

## Modern Heathenism

As with much of what we have covered in this book, modern Heathenism is a re-imagining or reawakening of an ancient belief. The same issues therefore stand, that since there is no continuous unbroken strand, we cannot be sure that what modern Heathens believe and practise is the same as their forebears. Much of the blame for this loss of historical sources is laid at the feet of the rise of Christianity across Northern Europe and the way in which it is said to have laid waste to the histories and writings of the beliefs it supplanted. This destructive influence of Christianity is a popular view in modern culture, with reference often given to Edward Gibbon's account of how political Christianity was responsible for the burning of the Great Library at Alexandria as being a typical example of how

Christians would destroy anything that disagreed with their dogma. However, as with the Alexandrian example, those who make such claims often have their own axes to grind. Just as question marks have arisen over the accuracy and bias of Gibbon's account, so, as we saw earlier in the writings of Hutton, numerous questions have been raised in the last generation regarding the exact reasons for the loss of much Pagan writing and how much the Church was truly to blame. It seems likely that at least some of the loss can indeed be attributed to Christian rulers and a church with too much political power, but the arguments are not as clear-cut as many suppose.

In contrast to most of British Paganism, which relies on oral tradition and numerous re-imaginings, modern Heathens actually have access to a large repository of Nordic texts with special emphasis on the Icelandic thirteenth-century Poetic Eddas and Prose Eddas. These contain numerous poems and stories rooted in Nordic mythology which form much of the core material from which modern Heathenism is being reconstructed. It is helpful if we distil some of this down in order to understand some of the core beliefs of Heathenism.

## Heathen Cosmology

In the last chapter we looked at how across the world there has tended to be a common evolution of a spiritual cosmology based on there being three levels, with this world always as the middle world, with an upper world of more spiritual beings and a lower world which is variously the powerhouse of the universe, or the rich loam into which the Great Tree places its roots, or simply the place of the dead. At first sight a similar kind of cosmology exists within Heathenism, although instead of three levels there are usually thought to be nine, but some also suggest seven. The reason for the confusion is that the source writings and poems do not paint a consistent picture. Generally, though, most Heathens adopt a nine-world model.

With similarities to the Celtic Shamanic model, all the worlds in Heathen cosmology are connected by the Great World Tree known as Yggdrasil. However, in most Shamanic models that we have looked at there is the impression of worlds that lie on the tree according to their place in the cosmos, with the lower or underworlds where the roots are located and the upper worlds connecting to the upper branches. With regards to Yggdrasil, we might question such a linear model. For example, 'Asgard', the highest world, is located at the highest branches by most sources, but I have also seen reference to it being at the roots. The other worlds are often referred to as being located at a point of the compass from each other rather than up or down, which can be confusing for those who have become used to the more Shamanic model. Perhaps the most helpful image of Yggdrasil is of a tree that encircles and links all the worlds rather than a form of ladder that one can ascend or descend.

In terms of the worlds themselves, the world of humans is, again, the middle world, known as 'Midgard'. There are two realms of the gods occupied by the Aesir and the Vanir with Asgard being primarily the home of the Aesir deities and linked to Midgard by the rainbow bridge known as Bifrost. Some of the Vanir deities, who are more associated with nature and fertility, are also resident in Asgard. Their traditional home, however, is Vanaheim. At some point in the distant past there was a war between the two groups of gods and a part of the terms of peace involved some from each group living in the world of the other. As with many religious myths I am aware of speculation that there may be some basis which is located in prehistoric battles and wars across Europe between peoples whose religions were more nature based and those whose religions were more warrior based.

In addition to the three worlds I have mentioned, there are six others, each with their own characteristics and residents. 'Jotunheim' is the world of the giants who are often at war with the gods, although it is important to recognise that a number of the Heathen deities are the offspring of unions between giants and gods. There is also an ice world known as 'Niflheim' which has as its counterpoint a world of fire known as 'Muspelheim' which had a role to play in the creation myths as well as in the end of the world known as 'Ragnarok'. As with much of modern mythology, Heathenism also includes stories of elves and dwarves, both of which have their own worlds, with the beautiful elves living in 'Alfheim', whilst the tunnel-dwelling dwarves live in 'Svartalfheim'. The remaining world bears comparison with the underworld found in many myths and is called 'Hel', the place of the dead who have not died glorious, meaningful deaths, usually in battle. Those who do die well hope to reside in one of the halls of the gods, the most famous and popular being 'Valhalla', the hall of Odin where half of all warriors go. The other half are taken to the goddess Freya's hall, 'Sessrúmnir'.

## Heathen Deities

Once we begin to consider the deities themselves we must recognise an utterly different understanding of godhood from the Judeo-Christian model. The monotheistic model believes that God has revealed God's self to be uncreated, completely perfect and driven by love with all of God's responses to life on earth being anchored to those personality attributes. There is then a recognition that humanity falls far short of this, despite having been created in the image of God, and so the entire focus of the Christian faith is on the lengths that God will go to in order to restore a relationship between the perfect God and an imperfect humanity.

Heathenism, on the other hand, makes no claims whatsoever about the perfection of its deities. Many were conceived through unions between deities, or between deities and other beings, and as a whole they reflect all of human nature, from great love to great cruelty. There is, therefore, no need for a salvation model because Heathen gods are not perfect and do not require humans to be so in order to interact with them. This is an important difference that needs to be grasped as we begin to look at some of the Heathen gods. It must be born in mind that the Heathen pantheon is extensive, so I am merely mentioning just a very few of them here to give an impression of the diversity.

**Odin:** Odin is the chief god and ruler of the Aesir, and is known by a number of names including 'The All-father' (as the father of all the gods). However, those looking for a parallel with the Christian God known as 'Father' would be well advised to look elsewhere. Odin is a war god who is neither necessarily just nor honourable (unlike many of the other Heathen deities), and, instead, will be devious in his pursuit of his own ends including, if he thinks it necessary, starting wars. If we were to think in psychological terms, whilst many religions pursue the subjugation of the ego, Odin is very much the ego personified, with the desire to rule as paramount. This ability to rule by strength is, for many, a part of the warrior ethic and one of the highest desires of a Norse warrior would be to be chosen by Odin to reside in his hall, Valhalla, after death on the battlefield. Yet in contrast with these themes, Odin is also known for his poetry and his wisdom. He has left his mark on British culture by the way in which his alternative name, Woden, has named the middle of the week: Woden's Day or 'Wednesday'.

One thing that has been said to me about Odin from an insider's observation is that it is in his nature to destroy or empower you depending on what suits his purpose. At times, in this book, we have pondered the crossover points between belief and psychology and so one could imagine Odin to represent the egocentric part of our nature, and if we dedicate our lives to serve our egos, then it is quite possible that to do so could destroy us or empower us. I have certainly seen that process take place in the lives of people of different religious persuasions. But this would also do Heathens a disservice since they honour Odin as a deity. I mention it simply because it is sensible for all religions to consider some of the psychological influences that may be present in what they believe.

Before Christians become too judgemental of this attribute of Odin, we should remember that although we believe our God has the best interests of humanity at heart, those who dedicate their lives to him may be required to forfeit them. All but one of the apostles of Christ were martyred, and even today this willingness to do whatever is required is reflected in the Methodist Covenant Prayer in the lines, 'I am no longer my own, but yours. Put me to what you will, rank me with whom you will; put me to doing, put me to suffering; let me be employed for you, or laid aside for you, exalted for you, or brought low for you...' We can argue that the difference would be that the Judeo-Christian God is motivated by love rather than self-interest, but the outcome for the believer may still be a life of hardship. In satirising the American fundamentalist message of, 'Come to Jesus and he will fix your life', I recall the late evangelist Mike Yaconelli saying, 'Well I came to Jesus and he messed my life up!'

**Thor:** If Odin is the ego personified then Thor, one of his sons, is the hero within; the one whose noble character others would aspire to, representing a worthy part of one's own inner being. Whilst Odin was a god for rulers, Thor was a god for the warriors and the ordinary people. He is the God of thunder, and also, of course, where we get our 'Thursday' from. Thor is also known for his famous hammer, known as 'Mjöllnir', which means 'lightning'. It requires little imagination to picture an ancient people marvelling at a storm that they believe reveals the work of Thor engaged in some great battle to preserve order. We can see why warriors would aspire to be like him. Yet for Thor it is not entirely about a warrior lifestyle. He was also called upon to use his hammer to bless, with his blessings being upon the fertility of the land or perhaps of a marriage.

**Loki:** Loki represents the Trickster and is in many ways the polar opposite to Thor. He holds nothing sacred and would willingly mock the other gods. Unsurprisingly, there are few records of him ever being held up as a being for veneration and worship. Indeed I know of a Heathen who will only whisper his name for fear of attracting his attention. Loki perhaps reflects the human rebellious drive to poke fun, or even destroy figures of authority.

It is very tempting, therefore, to imagine Loki to be the Heathen equivalent of the devil in Christianity, but I suggest that this would be a mistake. In the first instance, as I wrote earlier about 'The man in black', modern conservative Christianity has almost evolved into a dualistic religion with the evil devil as the opposition to the perfect God, whilst the story the Bible portrays is a far more evolutionary one. Either way, the devil is ultimately conceived of as a created being that is evil to its core. The same cannot be said about Loki. Whilst certainly capable of malevolent behaviour, his decisions also seem to be about choosing what will be good for him, and so self-centredness rather than outright evil would be a better description of his character.

**Freya:** In some ways Freya (or Freyja) occupies the position of fertility goddess and bears a resemblance in type to the goddess of Wicca, although without the same lunar associations. Linguistically her name, also sometimes simply thought of as 'The Lady', continues to influence modern language with the German 'Frau' stemming from the same root. Although she lives amongst the Aesir in Asgard, she is of the Vanir. As with all the gods she has relationships which seem very human, having a brother, Freyr, a father, Njord, and an unnamed mother. She is married, although sources seem to dispute whether her husband, named Odr, is actually Odin himself. Certainly, the references to his long absences and the tears of red gold that she cries for him would be consistent with Odin, and Odr and Odin clearly have the same root, which carries the meaning of fury, ecstasy and inspiration. Were that the case then this would mean that Freya was identical to Odin's wife, Frigg. Again, there are some suggestions that the many similarities between the personalities of Freya and Frigg could indicate a common mythological character now lost to history.

As mentioned earlier in this chapter, the fallen in battle longed to find themselves in Odin's hall, Valhalla, after death, but Freya receives half of all the battle slain into her hall, Sessrúmnir. What is less well known is that actually it is Freya who has first choice, not Odin, and so, although many outsiders may think that all Heathens yearn for Valhalla, one might argue that having Sessrúmnir as your final destination is a greater honour.

**The Valkyries**: It is appropriate that we move from Freya, who chose for herself the first half of the slain, to the Valkyries, which translates literally as the ones who choose the slain. The mythology surrounding them is rich and varied with some depicted as daughters of kings, and others as more or less extensions of Odin, making their choices of who will die on the battlefield and who will live, thus predetermining the outcome. Whilst Freya chooses warriors for her own hall, the Valkyries choose warriors for Odin's hall, Valhalla, and may appear on the battlefield, flying above in cloaks of swan feathers.

In their earlier appearances, the Valkyries appear almost demonic and fearful with the appearance of Ravens and with all the implications of eating carrion on a battlefield. With time, though, they have come to be pictured as beautiful and powerful maidens who could be much desired by male warriors. They themselves never fought though, but would serve the warriors they had chosen in Valhalla in nights full of feasting after days filled with battle in preparation for Ragnarok.

## Ragnarok

A unique feature of Heathenism, when compared to the other Pagan practices in this country, is that it has an apocalyptic strand in which the end of the world is foretold, although as with the Christian stories found in the book of Revelation, it is not truly an end, but rather the end of the current order and a new beginning. Intriguingly, many of the events of Ragnarok are spelled out in detail in the Poetic and Prose Eddas leading one Heathen to explain to me that all of the gods know exactly who they will fight at the end of the world; who will die and who will survive. Once again, we are reminded of a difference with Heathen gods in that they can indeed die, with Odin, Thor and Loki all being slain in this final battle. The earth itself is to be bathed in fire before being submerged under water. This, though, is not the end. Some of the gods survive and the earth re-emerges with just two human survivors, 'Líf' and 'Lífthrasir', who together re-populate the earth. There is thus, in common with much of nature-influenced Paganism, a cyclical nature even to the whole of creation, with a cycle of death and rebirth.

## Heathenism, Freewill and Determinism

Ragnarok raises an interesting point about the Heathen path with respect to determinism and freewill. This has long been a discussion point in Christianity and I have written about this myself within that context[1]. The debate in Christian circles will usually depend on where one stands on the interface between the interpretation of scripture, philosophy and science. The research that I undertook led me to the conclusion that, within the boundaries of genetic background and upbringing, humans, and indeed the universe itself, do have freewill and that God, as understood in the Judeo-Christian religion, can even be surprised by the choices that we make. As I intend to explore in a future book, I believe that we live in an open universe where our futures are not predetermined. Ultimately, it seems to me that the Christian faith upholds a belief that God has a plan for the future, but not a blueprint, and so God may influence people and events, but they can also make their own choices. Furthermore, the universe appears to have more than just an element of chance built into it.

The biblical book of Revelation is as much a book about what was taking place in the first-century persecuted church as it is a book about the future, and as such its style, Jewish Apocalyptic, leaves much to the interpreter. This is far less the case with the stories and poems surrounding Ragnarok. Some of the information given as to how the battles will unfold is extremely detailed. For example, Thor will fight the serpent Jörmungandr and will be triumphant. Yet during the course of the battle the serpent poisons Thor, so as the serpent dies, Thor manages to take just nine steps before the poison overwhelms him and kills him.

This kind of detail leads us to consider whether Heathenism is, in fact, highly deterministic. This is not something we have needed to ponder before, since such issues rarely surface in the other Pagan paths. Within Wicca and Witchcraft the use of magick, for example, makes it clear that the default position is one of freewill in which a person casting a spell can use their will to impose a change in reality, although that, in itself, poses the ethical question regarding whether the practitioner of magick, in themselves exercising their freewill to change reality, is therefore taking freedom from another.

In Druidry, White and Talboys[2] write:

'...the Celtic metaphysic is based firmly on the principle that we all have free will. We must do as we see fit and we may not coerce others. We can guide when asked, but each must take responsibility for our actions.'

What, then, is the position that the Heathen will take regarding their freewill? To understand this we need to look at a number of different Heathen concepts and how they intertwine. This is a vast subject and so what follows is an overview rather than a detailed treatise.

The first factor is the 'Norns'. These are goddesses of fate who can be either benevolent or malevolent. There are many of them, although there are three in particular who are 'Jotans' or giant-esses. These three tend the World Tree, Yggdrasil with waters from the well of fate. Other lesser Norns make their presence felt at the birth of a child to determine their future, so the child is dependent on whether it is good or evil Norns that will give them a good or a tragic life.

Allied to the Norns is the concept of 'Wyrd', given as the name 'Urd' in Norse for one of the three Norns at the World Tree. Wyrd essentially translates as 'fate' and is related to the word 'weird' in its original Old English meaning. The Norns weave Wyrd to create the future, and so we can see again what appears to be a strong strand of determinism emerging here. The actions of the Norns, however, are not the whole of the story.

What I hope became apparent at the beginning of this chapter is that Heathens usually have a strong belief in self-determi-nation, of using one's energies for personal growth and the growth of family and community. On the face of it, this seems to suggest there should, therefore, be a cognitive dissonance between their beliefs and practice. I suspect that this is resolved in a number of ways. Within Christianity, especially in its more conservative or fundamentalist forms, one will often hear the phrase 'God is in control'. This, too, is distinctly fatalistic, yet in reality even Christians who believe this act as if they have freewill and self-determine their lives. It seems that exactly the same unconscious, mental gymnastics take place within Heathenism. In both strands we may find people who are theological fatalists but functional indeterminists. Beyond this, however, there are many within Heathenism who suggest that at least a part of the issue is that the Eddas were written against a Christian backdrop and may, therefore, have been tainted with Christian views at that time regarding the absolute power of God to determine the fate of an individual. Given the strong archetype of the hero, one can see how such a person would be regarded as heroic if they were able to rise above their fate and fight back in order to wrest control from the Norns. The hero motif is of one who does not succumb to the will of a malignant Norn, but who does what is right. If it is their fate to die, then they will die gloriously, taking as many of their enemies with them as they are able. The general belief seems, therefore, to be that the ending of one's life may have been predetermined, but one has control over the manner in which it takes place and the way it is faced with either courage or cowardice. Once again, the strong honour code within Heathenism makes its presence felt even though this seems to be in opposition to some of the high degree of detail surrounding Raganok in the Eddas.

We can see that there are difficulties with this model of freewill though, much as there are difficulties with many Christian understandings of it, which perhaps merely serves to show the difficulties in comprehending the interplay of Wyrd, chance and human choice. We have made a case that a warrior fated to die in battle has the choice of whether to willingly put up the sword and die or to fight back to take as many of his enemies with him as possible; but what then of his enemies? A logical hole exists in this model in that there is little regard for the enemies being fought. How were they fated to die? Was it at the hand of a hero who must die, or by the final swing of a coward about to give up? This is always the problem with arguments concerning determinism and freewill, such are the complexities involved, and it leads us rapidly in circles as we contemplate the nonsense question of whether we were predestined to demonstrate freewill! As with Christianity, there is clearly a broad spectrum of views about this within Heathenism and we need simply to acknowledge this whilst recognising that this is an aspect of Heathenism that is not present in other Pagan beliefs.

We might also want to contemplate whether this has arisen because of the written word. Since the other Pagan paths are largely oral in tradition, with plenty of books written but no 'Holy Writ', they are, therefore, more fluid and non-dogmatic. Heathenism, however, has a significant body of writing which has the metaphorical effect of casting some beliefs in stone. This can lead to some quite vociferous debates of the meanings of their writings between those who take a more dogmatic approach to what is written, compared to those who do not. From a Christian perspective, this makes for an interesting comparison with our own experiences of a range of views on scripture ranging from fundamentalist to liberal.

## The different traditions

This array of approaches is illustrated by the different traditions that have arisen within Heathenism and, once again, the comparison with Christianity holds, that religions tend to divide into denominations with time, and the written word will add fuel to that fire. One example is Asatru, a branch of Heathenism that was granted status as a legitimate religion in Iceland in 1972. Asatru is very much at the reconstructionist end of Heathenism, using the traditional writings to try and be as close as possible to Heathen beliefs as laid out there. This is quite distinct from many of the other Pagan paths which, as we have seen, have a far more postmodern understanding of knowledge, that it is personal to the one who experiences it, and that it is the experience which teaches, not the written word. Asatru also tends to work more with the Aesir deities. This has led to the rise of another group within Heathenism, the Vanatru who work more with the Vanir deities, who are more closely linked to nature, giving this group a more earthy focus.

Likewise, and as its name suggests, Odinists tend to be those who work more with Odin, yet there is a degree of confusion that arises because of the ambiguous way in which Heathenism and Odinism tend to be used interchangeably by some. It seems likely that this confusion has arisen because of the Christian background in many of the countries in which Heathenism is being reconstructed. The inherited Christian context means that people are used to the term 'Father' as applied to the Christian understanding of God, so when Heathens refer to Odin as the 'All-Father' it is, therefore, assumed by outsiders that all Heathens worship Odin primarily and can, therefore, be referred to as Odinists. I hope that by this point it is clear that the picture is far more complex, and that different Heathens will work with different deities dependent on where they feel drawn or called. It therefore seems sensible to remain with the overarching term of 'Heathen' and allow the individual to place themselves within this spectrum.

## Heathen distinctiveness

In this somewhat 'whistle-stop' tour of Heathenism, we have merely touched on what I am discovering to be a rich and varied tradition, worthy of deeper study. Without wishing to disparage any of the other paths we have examined, I can understand why it is that some in the Heathen movement do not wish to be considered as simply another Pagan religion, since there are distinct differences, as I hope have been illustrated. Having a body of writing, which is treated by many as having authority, makes a significant difference for those who wish to take a serious reconstructionist path since they have something more solid to build on than oral tradition, despite the inherent diffi-culties that can arise alongside this.

# Notes for Chapter 7

1   Cudby P. E. F., 'Openness Theology – A New Evangelical Approach to the Epicurean Paradox', *Modern Believing*, Vol 46:2 (2005), 13-21, and Cudby P. E. F., 'Openness Theology Part Two – Dealing with the Shortcomings', *Modern Believing*, Vol 46:3 (2005), 15-22.

2   White J. and Talboys G. K., *The Path through the Forest*, Girvan: Grey House in the Woods, 2005, 99.

# Chapter Eight

# Becoming What We Were Created to Be and the Role of Forest Church

The last three or four years have seen new horizons opening up for me in my own journey as a Christian and as an Anglican priest. I have more questions now than I had when I opened my first book by a Pagan author because each new page opens up new ideas to be explored. I cannot pretend that this has been easy, and perhaps that's why the name 'The Shaken Path' came in a dream. Yet, in the drive to understand Paganism in this country, and then to try and explain it to others in order to take away their fear of it, and to facilitate interfaith discussions, it would be remiss not to reflect on how this has changed me. The truth is, if you seek to engage properly with Paganism, it will probably change you too, and that's what I mean about being on a 'Shaken Path'. What you do with that change will be for each person to decide. I know of several Christians who felt the draw of Paganism was so strong, and that a particular Pagan path held more answers than the Christian faith which they had, that they changed their path and became Pagan. That has not been the route that I have taken, and the effect of this journey has been to take me deeper into Christ. But what I have discovered is that the richness of the Pagan appreciation of the natural world brings new dimensions to my own Christ-centred path that I would not have expected, as my eyes have been opened to how God speaks through his other people.

## Listening to the lessons of nature

*I sit, completely and utterly motionless, staring at the tree.*
*And at first... nothing.*
*It takes a while for my senses to tune in. And so I wait. Slowly,*

235

*gradually, my human-focussed concerns recede quietly into the background and I become aware of motion, the movement of two squirrels. Perhaps their visibility emerges from my stillness, just as my increasing stillness makes me vanish before them.*

*Busily, yet unhurriedly, they go about their squirrel business. One gradually spirals down the trunk and then up again, stopping occasionally to engage with a tasty morsel crawling through the bark. The other sits on a branch, making his morning ablutions, combing through fur with teeth, tongue and claw, preening in the low light of the early sun.*

*And all the while, as I sit motionless, watching, they remain oblivious of me.*
*They know nothing of the simple joy I feel in watching them.*
*They know nothing of my intent to be here this morning, in this place.*
*They do not comprehend my appreciation of their simple beauty.*

So what? Well, once we start to listen to the voice of God through nature, so the Spirit speaks to us. As I reflected on this the question arose, if the Spirit were the observer, am I like the squirrel? Does God sit, as I did, silently observing, utterly motionless and overflowing in love and appreciation as he observes us going about our ways? And, perhaps more importantly, as the squirrels were oblivious of my presence, so wrapped up were they in their daily activities, am I also so tied up in my own busy-ness that I never become as still as he and see God emerging from the silence?

David Abram[1], though not writing as a practising Pagan, makes an interesting observation:

'...we are human only in contact, and conviviality, with what is not human.'

His point is that we have become so isolated from the natural world, and so enmeshed in a technological society, that the only contact most humans have with other life is purely with other humans. City dwellers in particular will find this. We seek more and more control and can find it only by divorcing ourselves more and more from the world of which we are a part.

Applying this to a faith perspective means that in order to be fully what God created us to be, we must interact with and be shaped by the other inhabitants of our planet, and the planet itself. The stories from the beginning of Genesis cite humanity in the midst of creation, naming the creatures and interacting with them, tilling the soil and caring for it. This is our natural environment and yet we have moved away from it at a far greater speed than evolution can (or should) cope with. It therefore begs the question, how can we grow into the image of God who fills all the world if we spend time only with humans? How can we learn about God and ourselves if we ignore our relatives? We evolved with them to be part of one ecosystem, so if we turn away from them we turn away from that which shapes us to be human. Mother Earth has worked hand in hand with God to make us. Indeed, if you look at the image of Genesis 2, where God creates Adam from the dust of the earth, (Adam means 'man of dust'), the unspoken imagery is of a partnership between God and earth in which God takes that which is of the planet and makes it human by breathing his Spirit into Adam. We humans are the product of a partnership between our ecosystem and its creator. We cannot, therefore, look only at ourselves and our creator and expect to become fully human.This is what I mean by learning from nature, and this is one of the more important lessons that studying Paganism is teaching me. My concern is the hesitation which the church shows in allowing God to speak through God's world. Yet Jesus did this so naturally: 'Consider the lilies of the field...' he said, to show us our place in the world and its, and our, importance to

God.

I know that some reading this will fear that this is about following a path that is more Pagan than Christian and will want to remind me of John 14:6 where we find Jesus saying, "I am the way, and the truth, and the life. No one comes to the Father except through me." So it is helpful to remember that St. Paul wrote these words about Christ in Colossians 1:16-17:

> '...for in him all things in heaven and on earth were created, things visible and invisible, whether thrones or dominions or rulers or powers—all things have been created through him and for him. He himself is before all things, and in him all things hold together.'

It should therefore be no surprise that, when we draw our attention to the natural world, it is Christ who we encounter. This naturally leads us into the work that has emerged from this study in terms of Forest Church.

## Forest Church: Christian or Pagan?

Why write about Forest Church in a book on Paganism? It is partly to correct some impressions about who or what Forest Church is, and partly to offer this as a way forward for those who find themselves caught between two places: desiring a Christ-centred path and the joy of spiritual engagement in the natural world, whilst finding church to be spiritually dry, cold and/or dogmatic. I hasten to add that not all churches, by any stretch, can be described in this way, but for serious spiritual seekers with deep and difficult questions and an inherent sense of nature connection, some churches may not always be helpful, and may sometimes leave a person feeling unsafe and open to criticism. Forest Church could, therefore, offer an alternative to the more regular forms of worship.

What then is Forest Church? It began for me with a light bulb moment in a debate. I am sometimes asked to be a small group discussion leader at diocesan lay education days, and in one such small group of about twelve people, one of the topics under discussion was, 'Where do you feel closest to God?'Of that entire group just one person said, 'In the church I attend'. For the rest of us we all came out with places in the natural world; next to a river or lake, watching the ocean, sitting in a field, leaning up against a tree, walking through a *Forest*.

Having chaired the group, the question that it left me with was, why, if so many of us feel much closer to God outside, do we insist that church takes place in a building? In fact, if you stand in many traditional Anglican church buildings and look around, what you see are stone pillars like tree trunks, reaching up and over with arches like branches. Suddenly, I found myself wondering if what we had done with our architecture was create stone groves. So, why not worship in the real ones? In this way Forest Church was born in my imagination. Curiously though, I discovered that I was not the only one thinking like this, and my experience of the way in which the Holy Spirit moves is to confirm her ideas by giving them to more than one person.

So it was that in April 2012, just two months before leaving to start my sabbatical study leave, I attended a conference for Christians working alongside people in alternative spiritual movements. On the first evening I found myself deep in conversation with a man by the name of Bruce Stanley. As we discussed our visions for the future, so it emerged that Bruce was also thinking along the same lines about the need for a Christ-centred place of worship that met outside in the natural world. Together we decided to work under the name of Forest Church, although our understanding of what that would entail would be very broad. In essence, the only box that needs to be ticked for something to qualify as a Forest Church is that it is a Christ-centred group that seeks to connect with God through the natural world. However, this is not simply taking a Sunday service outside. I have witnessed this happen on a number of occasions where the congregation simply takes chairs outside and sits in rows, just as they do inside, with the minister leading from the front, just as they do inside. There is nothing wrong with this and it can be a perfectly beautiful experience. But it is not Forest Church because it is not aiming to encounter God through the natural world; it is simply doing normal church outside.

Forest Church, however, begins from a different place. We recognise that we humans are just as much a part of the natural world as the plants and wildlife surrounding us. They then become 'sisters' and 'brothers' in sharing with us in the experience of the presence of the Holy Spirit, suffusing all creation with the divine presence. A basic rule that we have is that we never take anything more into our place of worship than we can carry with us, and we leave it as we found it. We do not use PA systems, merely our voices, and we do not sit in rows but gather in a circle when we engage in the ritual we have devised or simply walk informally if we are going to a place to meditate. Hopefully, it goes without saying that Forest Church does not have to take place in an actual forest; it is simply a name that signifies that we meet outside, always, whatever the weather.

Different Forest Churches meet in different ways with different emphases. Bruce has written extensively about his practice elsewhere[2] and so I will not focus here on his model which tends to be less ritual based. My wife and I are part of a core group of five that leads Ancient Arden Forest Church. The core group meets regularly for our own private prayer rituals and then leads a ritual for the wider group eight times a year, following the eight-fold year detailed earlier. The reason we have done that is because of our connections to the Pagan community. Our Druid and Wiccan friends are well versed in how to follow the changing seasons and how they affect the natural world, and so why reinvent 'The Wheel'? The lovely part of this for us is that some of those to whom we have gone to gain understanding in their own moots have now come to join us occasionally at Ancient Arden Forest Church, and we are not alone in this experience. This has led some to criticise Forest Church as being a syncretistic movement, but those who come know that we are Christ-centred; we have never made any secret of that. However, our use of forms that are familiar to Pagans, the careful use of non-dogmatic open language and the choice of meeting in a circle has, hopefully, made our Forest Church a safe place for people of different paths to meet. In terms of why we have adopted these models I would direct you to my wife's description of the appropriateness of meeting in circle in *Earthed*.[3] Here I wish to centre on how it is that Pagans and Christians can engage in rituals together.

## Like Water and Oil?

A sense of horror or disbelief is typically characterised amongst branches of both Pagans and Christians at the idea of sharing in ritual together. Our research has demonstrated that many Pagans, particularly amongst those who are middle-aged and older, were brought up with a conservative 'Thou shalt not!' approach to Christianity. I have described earlier the numerous stories we have heard of spiritually dry services which left them cold, and church leaders who had no comprehension of the joy that they found in engaging with the spirituality of nature. We have heard comments about ministers who forbade them from asking the kind of deep questions that undermined a monochrome faith, and so for such people the thought of mixing with Christians in some kind of ceremony may be met with bemusement at best, and at worst, bitter condemnation.

From the Christian perspective, therefore, I believe the onus is on us. The Pagan perspective tends to be more experiential, so Christians need to be cautious that they don't react against this by becoming dogmatic. It would be too easy, when we don't understand something, to react in a more fearful manner, picking and choosing passages from scripture that reinforce a particular viewpoint. We might reflect on the emphasis Jesus had on hospitality and inclusion and the way in which he went out of his way to spend time with those whom polite religious society had rejected. Centuries of Christian theology have shown that for every 'proof-text' in the Bible in favour of one argument, another can often be found to make a counter-argument. My sense is that this is a movement of the Holy Spirit and, whilst we may not necessarily understand this, we should follow the leading and be prepared to make mistakes along the way.

Within some 'branches' of Forest Church there has emerged quite naturally an understanding that shared ritual is not only permissible, it is, actually, of potentially great value to all those who share in this way. However, we must recognise that Christianity is a doctrinal religion that places great emphasis on scripture, reason, tradition and experience. Therefore, if we are to create a new tradition and justify our experiences of shared ritual, we need first to lay a foundation of scripture and reason in order to show that the conservative interpretations that are used to justify a policy of condemnation of other religions are flawed and incomplete, drawing more on fear than love.

## Inclusive Love as a Sign of Divine Presence

Pagans are generally non-proselytising. That is not to say that none of them appreciate someone learning something new from them, as indeed we have done with some aspects of Forest Church. But within Paganism, there is no analogue to the command of Christ to go into the world and make disciples. For those of us who are Christians, this means that there is a reassurance in the purity of motive behind the sense of warm invitation and loving embrace that so many of us have experienced from our Pagan friends. It is unfortunate that the converse is not always true. Whilst many of us have experienced genuine love from fellow Christians, we have also observed those who offer a welcome with strings attached, that it is on the unspoken grounds that it might mean someone will stay and 'join-up'. Indeed, I have attended a leadership seminar led by a director of a successful retail company who encouraged church leaders to make their churches more welcoming to ensure people go there on a Sunday morning rather than some other secular establishment. Whilst we could argue that whilst this may make sound common sense, it also presents as having far more to do with marketing than love, and so its value in spiritual terms ought to be questioned in order to determine whether it is grounded in a genuine Christ-centred welcome or whether it is tarnished by the need to support an institution. At its worst, the so-called 'love' can be little more than just a tool to entice unsuspecting visitors. One can then make a reasonable argument that actually the loving acceptance in some Pagan circles may potentially be more indicative of divine presence since it comes with no strings attached.

So if love should be the indicator, what then do we find in scripture to justify Christians working alongside Pagans, or indeed people of any religion? Brian McLaren[4], in discussing his own interfaith work, suggested that we should move away from a concentration on John 14:6, which quotes Jesus as saying, "I am the way, the truth and the life, no one comes to the Father except through me", towards verses from 1 John 4.Verse 7 of this letter includes, '...everyone who loves is born of God and knows God' and verse 16 explains, 'God is love and those who live in love live in God, and God lives in them.' For many of us who are on a Christ-centred path, we believe that we have experienced genuine undemanding love from our Pagan friends. We may well differ from them in our beliefs as to its source but, from a Christ-centred perspective, we would direct our gaze towards God as its author and so, when we share in ritual with those who mutually desire to do so, we acknowledge the presence of God amongst us. This, however, can cause difficulties because the name 'God' has so much history attached to it for many Pagans. We have therefore sought to find alternative names with which we can feel mutually at ease.

## The Names of God

In modern Christianity, perhaps under the influence of the rationalism that has arisen in the Christian faith under the enlightenment, the names which are permissible for God seem to have diminished in number. Essentially, mainstream Christianity calls God simply God, Father, Son and Holy Spirit, usually all with the masculine pronoun. Each of these names, but especially 'God' and 'Father', carry a burden of bad memories for many ex-Christian Pagans and indeed for many Christians. This is generally because their experience of church has been of simply not fitting in to a narrow definition of what a Christian should look like and what questions they should or shouldn't ask, and hence they may associate those names with the pain of rejection. Yet history is replete with other divine names. In the Old Testament the names given to God are rich in diversity and it is possible to see how some of them appear to have their origins in the Canaanite Pagan religions that the Hebrews supplanted when they invaded the region. Foremost amongst them is the name 'God most High', or 'El Elyon', a name which is found in both Canaanite religion and in the Old Testament, with the intriguing verse, Deuteronomy 32:8 apparently suggesting how monotheism was a later revelation in scripture:

'When the Most High (*El Elyon*) apportioned the nations, when he divided humankind, he fixed the boundaries of the peoples according to the number of the gods;'

The name 'El' comes up repeatedly as a prefix throughout the Old Testament, with El Shaddai being used thirty-eight times, translated by most as meaning God Almighty. Yet this interpretation has been questioned with the recognition that the root word for Shaddai may be a number of possible words. It could be Shadad, meaning 'Destroyer', or it could be Shadu, meaning 'Mountain'. But, in more recent times, Lutzky[5] has suggested that it is derived from the word Šad meaning 'Breast', having feminine connotations of 'God the breast'. Rapidly, we find that once we start to mine the Old Testament, the names given for God are far more rich and diverse in meaning, and specifically more open to interpretation, than the ones usually permitted by the Church. Using this as our starting point, and following the lead given by Tess Ward[6] we have looked for other names that we can use for God that are more descriptive and which are, therefore, far more open in their use. This permits all participants to attach their own meaning to shared words and labels. Our practice at Ancient Arden Forest Church is to use open language this way in order to welcome in our friends, giving them space to use the names to mean what they wish. In so doing, in our rituals we have tried to offer the hand of friendship through inclusion despite the differences in belief.

Some Christians might not understand this approach, yet what we are finding is simply that some Pagans do within Forest Church exactly what some Christians do when we attend a Pagan ritual: we spiritually translate what is being said into an internal liturgy that honours the path that we are on. My own experience of this has been at a Pagan drumming circle, or in a Druid ritual; parts of what takes place are outside my own beliefs and so I silently do not take part in a manner which would draw attention to myself and detract from the experience of the other participants. Often other parts do echo my own beliefs, but with a different language and different names, so I take part whilst internally translating. This, I imagine, is exactly what Pagans do at Forest Church, and I know that it is also what takes place amongst Pagans within their own open rituals.

Remember that in terms of Pagan orthopraxy, many people can participate in the same ritual but it will mean something different for each person and how they engage with it.

## Interfaith?

Let me underline once more that Forest Church is a Christ-centred group. We are not an interfaith movement. However, we are determined to be genuinely welcoming to all who wish to take part and for it to be a non-judgemental place of friendship. I feel deeply honoured that some Pagans have chosen to join with us, because in so doing they are affirming that a genuine connection with the natural world is taking place. As I wrote in the chapter on Animism, I believe that all such connections take place through the awareness of God in the indwelling of the Holy Spirit. The fact that my Pagan friends may believe something different about what is taking place does not actually concern me. If we are to be genuinely welcoming, then that welcome must have no strings attached. They are welcome because Christ welcomes them, as he welcomes all of us. We have not tried to make Forest Church look a bit Pagan in the hope that some will be enticed in and become Christians and then start coming to 'real' church, but we have adopted some Pagan 'shapes' to what we do at Ancient Arden Forest Church simply because we have found those shapes to be helpful in terms of connecting to nature since that is what they were designed to do.

Forest Church is not a denomination and has no intention of becoming one. There are no bishops, and no vicars. I am not sure I would even want to define it as a movement. It is, instead, a network of like-minded people who have a broad range of practices that are intended to allow us to engage with Christ as expressed through the natural world that he has created. Those of us who coined the name merely hope that others will honour it and what it stands for. In partnership with our Creator and the planet of which we are a part, Forest Church is offering a way into becoming that which we were created to be: fully human and centred on Christ, walking a path of re-enchantment with all that God has created.

# Notes for Chapter 8

1    Abram D., *The Spell of the Sensuous*, New York: Vintage, 1997, ix

2    Stanley B., *Forest Church*, Llangurig: Mystic Christ Press, 2013

3    Eve A., 'The Sacred Circle: Elements of Ritual' in Stanley B. and Hollinghurst S. (Eds.), *Earthed*, Llangurig: Mystic Christ Press, 2014, 244-271

4    McLaren B. D., Speaking at the Greenbelt Festival, 2014.

5    Lutzky H., *Shadday as a Goddess Epithet* , Vetus Testamentum, Volume 48, Issue 1, p15–36, 1998.

6    Ward T., *The Celtic Wheel of the Year: Celtic and Christian Seasonal Prayers*, Winchester: O Books, 2007.

# Postscript: Silent Burning

Have you ever sat outside and simply watched the light change as the night recedes and dawn begins to infuse colour back into the world? I did this not so long ago on a misty October morning. My daily prayer ritual often revolves around getting up early, putting on a heavy warm coat, picking up a blanket and my prayer book, finding a folding chair and then sitting outside.

The first few minutes are spent just trying to find a sense of calm. The ease with which that will happen usually depends on how good the night's sleep was, what's on my mind, and how intrusive the sounds of humanity waking up are, as cars drive past and the motorway network feeds people into the routes they must take to get to work.

But if I am persistent, usually, eventually, the oft-felt sense of inner turmoil will begin to calm down and my mind will start to still its frantic ramblings. And so it was on this misty October morning. When I had first sat outside I had taken a torch with me because the light was so dim that I suspected I would be unable to read my prayers, but on that particular morning I simply sat and found myself drawn into nature's rather noisy under-standing of silence.

Those who live in cities and yearn for the peace of the countryside are sometimes surprised at the volume of the natural world going about its daily business, but it is a different kind of noise. It is a natural noise rather than a technological one and, when we begin to still ourselves, we find that our own natural rhythms can lock into the sounds inherent in nature. That happens simply because we are a part of it, even though our lives are usually too busy to recognise this.

Thus, on that morning I found myself merely sitting, listening and watching. The only glimpse I had taken of my prayer book at that point was to notice that the title for the day's prayers was

'Silence'. 'How apt', I'd thought to myself.

And so I sat and watched, and listened. I heard the bird song, not just as a general melee, but as individual birds in separate trees. I listened as new songs began to fill the spaces between my breaths, as the wind lightly flicked the leaves in the trees, and I watched as light began to seep into the sky.

The curious way about the early light on a misty autumnal morning is the way it works its way through the spectrum and so slowly, almost imperceptibly, I noticed a redness creeping into the world, but it was suffused with a sufficient breadth of colour that I could also see the greens escaping from the monochrome of night. But the reason the red light was so important was because the tree in front of me, a copper beech, had reddish-purple leaves. Gradually, I became aware that this tree was shining. It is difficult to describe unless you have seen it for yourself, but all I can say is that it was with a light that seemed to make the tree almost glow, as if it was shedding haloes of light abroad. And with that thought came to mind the story of Moses and the burning bush.

For those who are unfamiliar with the story, this is Moses' first encounter with God, as God speaks out to him from a bush that seems to be ablaze, yet is not burnt up. But the question that a number of commentators have asked is, was the bush really any different from normal, or was it that on this occasion the eyes of Moses were opened to see that this bush, like every bush, was on fire with the glory of God, the power of God that sustains it and all life in its existence?

Then God tells Moses to take off his shoes for he stands on holy ground. But is that truly what God meant? Was the ground really holy or was it that Moses' eyes had been opened by the presence of God to comprehend that all ground is holy for all ground is the Lord's? Was this a miracle of God's presence dwelling within a burning bush, or a miracle of Moses' eyes being opened to how every common bush is ablaze with the glory of God? I cannot provide the answer to that, but all I can really say is that on that morning when I was watching the vibrant colours of the tree it felt to me like I was seeing the glory of God, not burning but softly glowing.

And it made me realise, once again, that many Christians are simply walking around with their eyes in their prayer books and their song sheets and even in their Bibles, and not enough time is being spent also looking at the world, taking the time to watch the light change as the glory of God makes itself so clearly apparent in the world around.

However, this approach demands questions of us because it would be very easy to romanticise the presence of God into only being in pretty things. How can an earthquake, or a hairy house spider, or a pouncing lion be ablaze with God's glory? Those are questions we each need to answer for ourselves and, as I mentioned earlier, this is the direction I intend to take with the next book, but this is the thing that I have learnt most deeply from engaging with Paganism: that we need to look, to gaze, to stay and listen and to engage with the world around us.

I began this book by saying that I wanted to justify my belief that the Church should be engaging in interfaith relations with the Pagan spiritual paths, and yet also, when it comes down to it, one of my deepest reasons is for my own spiritual journey. Interfaith is different from evangelism, although I am sure there will be some who will think that converting Pagans is ample justification for meeting with them. No, one of my most important reasons is because what I have learned from them is to open my eyes to the glory of God around me and I would like other Christians to engage with this too. If it is to be true interfaith work, then we must be prepared to learn too, and not just see ourselves as the educators.

Who knows, (and it seems highly unlikely to me), but perhaps there was a secret desire amongst one or two of the people that I met that I would choose to abandon Christianity. There was certainly some concern amongst some of my fellow Christians that I might turn away from Christ and worship at the altar of a Pagan deity, but quite the reverse has happened. In seeking to understand their beliefs and their experiences, I have found a far deeper and richer relationship with God as I have discovered for myself the gentle, breathy voice of the divine feminine, the stillness and silence at the heart of the Father and the leading, gently challenging voice of the Son, saying,

'Come this way, along this Shaken Path and see that every bush is burning.'

CHRISTIAN
ALTERNATIVE
# THE NEW OPEN SPACES

Throughout the two thousand years of Christian tradition there have been, and still are, groups and individuals that exist in the margins and upon the edge of faith. But in Christianity's contrapuntal history it has often been these outcasts and pioneers that have forged contemporary orthodoxy out of former radicalism as belief evolves to engage with and encompass the ever-changing social and scientific realities. Real faith lies not in the comfortable certainties of the Orthodox, but somewhere in a half-glimpsed hinterland on the dirt track to Emmaus, where the Death of God meets the Resurrection, where the supernatural Christ meets the historical Jesus, and where the revolution liberates both the oppressed and the oppressors.

Welcome to Christian Alternative... a space at the edge where the light shines through.
If you have enjoyed this book, why not tell other readers by posting a review on your preferred book site. Recent bestsellers from Christian Alternative are:

**Bread Not Stones**
The Autobiography of An Eventful Life
Una Kroll
The spiritual autobiography of a truly remarkable woman and a history of the struggle for ordination in the Church of England.
Paperback: 978-1-78279-804-0 ebook: 978-1-78279-805-7